Copyright K. M. Ashman – January 2025

All rights are reserved. No part of this publication may be reproduced, stored, or transmitted in any form or by any means without prior written permission of the copyright owner. All characters depicted within this publication are fictitious, and any resemblance to any real person, living or dead, is entirely coincidental.

Also by K. M. Ashman

Seeds of Empire
Seeds of Empire
Rise of the Eagle

The Exploratores
Dark Eagle
The Hidden
Veteranus
Scarab
The Wraith

The Brotherhood
Templar Steel
Templar Stone
Templar Blood
Templar Fury
Templar Glory
Templar Legacy
Templar Loyalty

The India Summers Mysteries
The Vestal Conspiracies
The Treasures of Suleiman
The Mummies of the Reich
The Tomb Builders

The Roman Chronicles
The Fall of Britannia
The Rise of Caratacus
The Wrath of Boudicca

The Medieval Sagas
Blood of the Cross
In Shadows of Kings
Sword of Liberty
Ring of Steel

The Blood of Kings
A Land Divided
A Wounded Realm
Rebellion's Forge
The Warrior Princess
The Blade Bearer

The Road to Hastings
The Challenges of a King
The Promises of a King
The Fate of a King

The Otherworld Series
The Legacy Protocol
The Seventh God
The Last Citadel
Savage Eden
Vampire

Character Names

Main Characters:

- Gaius Julius Caesar - Young Roman aristocrat, military commander, future political leader
- Marcus Antonius Gracchus - Caesar's childhood friend, soldier
- Cornelia Cinna - Caesar's wife, daughter of Lucius Cornelius Cinna
- Aurelia Cotta - Caesar's mother, strategic and politically astute

Family and Early Connections:

- Gaius Julius Caesar (elder) - Caesar's deceased father, former praetor
- Lucius Cornelius Cinna - Cornelia's father, former consul
- Gaius Marius - Caesar's uncle by marriage, famous military general

Military and Political Figures:

- Lucius Cornelius Sulla Felix - Dictator of Rome
- Marcus Minucius Thermus - Roman general in Asia
- Publius Servilius Vatia - Roman provincial legate
- Marcus Junius - Governor of Pergamon
- Quintus Lutatius Catulus - Senior Roman senator
- Lucius Cornelius Lucullus - Naval commander

Companions and Allies:

- Quintus Aquillius - Fellow student and traveller
- Heracleo - Cilician pirate captain
- Anticrates - Military commander in Miletus
- Titus Varro - Family friend who helps Caesar during exile
- Rufio - Veteran Centurion who trains Caesar

Other Notable Characters:

- Apollonius Molon - Renowned rhetoric teacher in Rhodes
- Aulus Crispus - Philosopher encountered during sea voyage
- Nikias - Ship captain who transports Caesar
- The Virgo Maxima (Vestal Virgin) - Influential religious figure

Minor Military Characters:

- Balbus - Military officer
- Hostilius - Veteran Centurion
- Syrax - Pirate training master

Naming Conventions in This Novel

In ancient Rome, names carried great significance, reflecting status, formality, and personal connection. Caesar's full name, *Gaius Julius Caesar*, identified his personal name (praenomen), family name (nomen), and clan (cognomen). How he was addressed depended on who was speaking and in what context:

Example

- 'Gaius' was probably used by close family and intimate friends, such as his mother Aurelia and his wife Cornelia.

- 'Julius' was his family name, often used by peers or in less formal settings.

- 'Caesar' was used by strangers, soldiers, and political figures, often in formal or authoritative settings.

For the sake of clarity and consistency, he is mostly referred to as Julius throughout this novel, both in narrative and dialogue. This balances historical accuracy with readability, ensuring a smooth and immersive experience.

Map

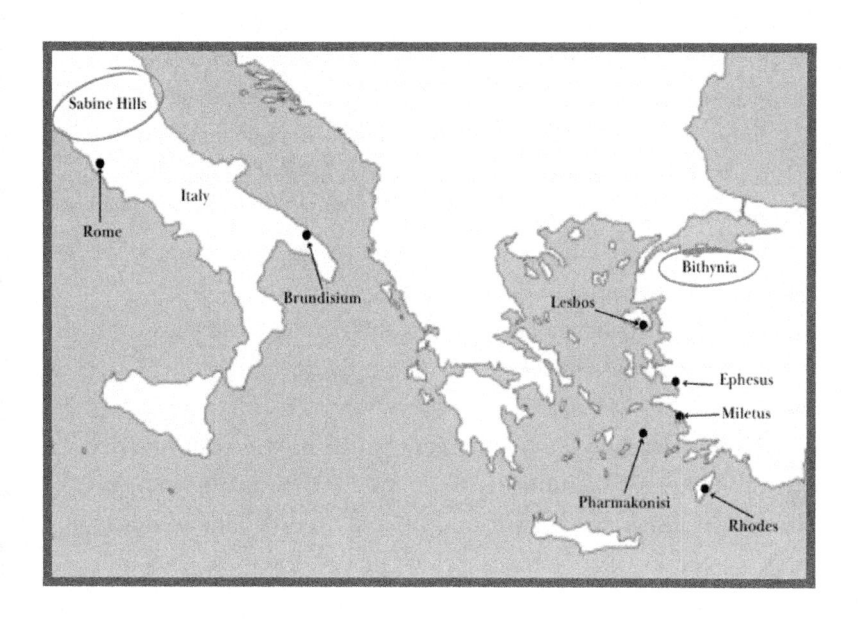

Prologue

Rome, 100 BCE. A city of marble and clay, grandeur and grime. The mighty Tiber snaked lazily through its heart, a lifeblood as ancient as the hills of the Palatine. This was a city on the cusp of change, an empire unborn but already restless, where senators and generals plotted their legacies, and the masses clung to bread and spectacle to survive.

Amidst this turbulent backdrop, a child was born into the modest yet ancient Julian family, claiming lineage from Venus herself. Gaius Julius Caesar. The name would one day carry the weight of greatness, though the infant bore only the cries of the ordinary.

His mother, Aurelia, cradled him with a mixture of pride and determination, her eyes glinting with the resolve that would shape his early years. His father, also Gaius Julius Caesar, stood tall and stern, a praetor, a man of standing but not quite power. Yet even he could not have foreseen the shadow his son would one day cast over Rome and the world.

As the boy's earliest years unfolded in the Subura, a district where patrician dignity met plebeian struggle, Julius learned the art of survival. The streets were loud with the cries of merchants and the clash of cart wheels, but they were also the proving grounds of ambition.

His father's political ties ensured he would know the privilege of education, Greek tutors who instilled in him the epics of Homer, the strategies of Alexander, and the eloquence of Cicero. Yet it was Aurelia who became his true guide, a woman who taught him not only the virtues of discipline but the subtle art of influence.

But Rome was no nursery for the weak. Julius's childhood was shadowed by the rise and fall of men who dared to seek dominion. Sulla, the iron-fisted dictator, loomed large in these years, a reminder that even the greatest were vulnerable to fate's cruel hand.

And then, there were the whispers, talk of alliances, betrayals, and blood spilled in the Senate chambers. All of it fed a growing fire within the boy, a hunger to rise above the chaos and carve his own path.

Yet life is fickle and when Julius was just sixteen, the world he knew tilted. His father, the man whose name he bore, whose stature had offered a measure of stability, was struck down by sudden death. The loss left a void that neither family lineage nor education could fill. It was a cruel reminder of mortality, and the young Caesar faced the stark reality of Rome's unforgiving stage.

Yet even in grief, there was resolve and with his father's death, the boy became a man, his path no longer shaped by another's ambition but by his own.

In the shadow of his family's modest home, beneath the weight of Rome's unyielding expectations, a legend began to stir. For in the heart of this young Roman beat not just ambition, but destiny. And Rome, the eternal city, would never be the same again.

Chapter One

Rome – 85 BC

The streets of Rome were silent save for the mournful wail of flutes. Smoke from incense coiled through the cold morning air, rising in delicate spirals before vanishing into the sky. At the head of the procession, a bier draped in dark purple cloth carried the body of Gaius Julius Caesar, Praetor of Rome. His death had stirred only a whisper of attention in the Senate, just one of many, a name in a long line of fading patricians but to his son, he was the fulcrum of a world now tilting dangerously out of balance.

Sixteen-year-old Julius walked near the bier, his head held high despite the knot of grief tightening in his chest. Beside him stood Aurelia, his mother, her face carved in calm restraint. She held her daughters close, her gaze fixed ahead as if willing the day to pass more quickly.

Julius adjusted his toga, the black wool heavier than it had ever felt before. His eyes flickered to the statues in the Forum, each a silent reminder of Rome's history. He saw Romulus with his wolf, the towering figure of Hercules, and, further on, the noble visage of Aeneas. He swallowed hard. His family claimed descent from Venus through Aeneas, but what did that mean now? Prestige did not pay debts.

The bier came to a stop in the Forum, where a modest crowd had gathered. Friends, distant family, and clients stood scattered in the square, murmuring to one another. There was no sea of mourners, no overwhelming grief. His father had been respected but not revered.

'Do you think they'll stay through the whole eulogy?' a voice muttered beside him.

Julius turned to Marcus, his closest friend. Marcus was also dressed in mourning black, his hair dishevelled in a way that suggested he cared little for how the world perceived him. He was the same age, but stockier, with a certain rough charm that had endeared him to Julius since they had met in the Subura years before.

'You should keep your voice down,' Julius murmured, 'they'll hear you.'

'They're too busy pretending to be sad to notice. Look at Lucius over there, he's already scanning for his next appointment. Your father deserved better.'

Julius glanced in the direction Marcus indicated and saw Lucius Domitius, a wealthy eques, glancing impatiently at the sun's position. His stomach churned, but his face betrayed nothing.

'He did deserve better,' he said softly, 'but this is Rome. Even the gods grow bored of men once they've had their turn.'

The priest stepped forward, a solemn figure in white robes. He raised his arms, signalling the beginning of the rites. The murmurs faded, replaced by the crackling of the incense brazier. Aurelia adjusted her veil, her fingers trembling slightly and Julius reached out, brushing his hand against hers in an unspoken promise.

When the priest finished the invocation to the gods, a herald called for the eulogists to step forward and Julius's uncle, Sextus, took the first turn. His words were respectful but perfunctory, listing his brother's modest achievements, his time as a praetor, his victories in minor disputes, his adherence to Roman tradition, but there was no fire in his speech, no conviction. Marcus leaned closer.

'If he drones on any longer, half of these people will be asleep.'

Julius almost smiled.

'Then let's hope I can wake them up.'

When Sextus stepped down, Julius felt his mother's hand on his arm. He turned to her and saw a faint glimmer of pride in her eyes.

'Go,' said Aurelia quietly. 'Let them see what a Julius truly is.'

He nodded and stepped forward, his heart pounding in his chest. As he ascended the small platform, the murmurs of the crowd quieted. He stood for a moment, his eyes scanning their faces.

'I will speak of my father,' he began, 'not because of what Rome already knows, but because of what she has forgotten.' A ripple of curiosity passed through the crowd and Julius paused, letting the silence grow heavy. 'He was a man,' he continued, 'who, though not the most powerful in Rome, was among the greatest. Not because of the titles he held or the wealth he amassed, but because of the values he lived by and the example he set for all who knew him.'

Julius paused, letting his words hang in the air. His eyes flicked to a group of senators clustered near the front, men who had barely acknowledged his father in life.

'Rome,' he continued, his voice growing stronger, 'is a city built by men like my father. Not all of them are named in the annals of history, and not all of them stand immortalised in marble. My father was no dictator, no consul, no conqueror, but he was a Roman in the truest sense of the word and understood that greatness is not always measured in victories or monuments, but in duty, loyalty, and the quiet strength to persevere.'

A murmur rippled through the crowd, some nodding in agreement, others shifting uneasily. Julius stepped closer to the edge of the platform, his hand gesturing toward the bier where his father's body now waited to be taken to his pyre on the Fields of Mars outside the city walls.

'He served this Republic faithfully as praetor,' he continued, 'carrying out the law with fairness and integrity. He upheld the traditions of our ancestors, not out of obligation, but because he believed in them. My father knew that Rome's greatness lies not in the wealth of its elite, but in the strength of its values. He was a man of modest means, yet he gave generously to those in need. He asked for no reward, no praise, no glory. His only ambition was to see his family honour the gods and live with dignity.'

Julius's voice faltered slightly, the weight of his grief slipping through for a brief moment. He steadied himself, drawing in a deep breath.

'To me, he was more than a father. He was a guide, a

protector, and a man whose shadow I will never escape. He taught me that our family's name is not something to be worn like a badge of privilege, it is a burden, but one that must be carried with pride and responsibility. He taught me that to be a Julius is to live not for oneself, but for something greater… for family, for honour, for Rome.'

He turned to the statues that lined the Forum, their marble faces gazing impassively down at the crowd.

'My father also knew the meaning of sacrifice. He sacrificed his comforts, his ambitions, and his life to serve his family and his Republic. And though his name will not be carved on the Capitoline Hill, it will live on in the hearts of those who knew him, and in the lives of those who follow in his example.'

Julius's gaze swept across the crowd, his voice now a touch quieter but no less resolute.

'I stand here today as his son. I am young, and I have much to learn. But I vow to honour his legacy, not only with words, but with deeds. My father believed in the greatness of Rome, and I will not let that belief die with him. He may have been humble in life, but the lessons he left behind are far from small. They are the foundation of all that I will become.'

He stepped back and turned to face his father's wrapped body to deliver his final words.

'Gaius Julius Caesar, father. You lived as a true Roman: steadfast, dutiful, and loyal. May the gods welcome you as such. May your spirit find rest among the stars, and may your example remind us all that greatness does not lie in power, but in honour.'

Julius bowed his head, his hand resting briefly on the edge of the rostra to steady his shaking. The Forum remained silent for a moment, the weight of his words pressing on the gathered crowd. Then, slowly, the applause began, not thunderous, but respectful, the sound rippling outward as the citizens of Rome acknowledged the eulogy of a son for his father.

The crowd began to shift as the eulogies ended, the mourners falling into their own quiet clusters, their conversations muted. Julius stood to the side, his posture rigid, his dark eyes scanning the movements of senators, military officers, and prominent citizens who had gathered to pay their respects, or, more accurately, to make an appearance.

'Do you see that?' Marcus murmured, leaning slightly towards him.

'See what?' Julius asked, not looking away from the group of men gathered near the rostra.

'The way old Crassus just nodded to Lucius over there. Barely a tilt of the head, but Lucius is already stepping back, looking like a scolded dog. If you blinked, you'd miss it.'

Julius's gaze sharpened, fixing on Marcus Licinius Crassus, the wealthiest man in Rome, his lined face impassive as he stood surrounded by senators. Crassus tilted his head again, this time towards a junior Tribune, who hurried off into the crowd.

'I see it,' Julius murmured. 'A man like Crassus commands armies without raising his voice. He doesn't need to.'

Marcus stared as he leaned casually against a column.

'I suppose I'll just need to amass a fortune to learn his secrets, then.'

Julius allowed himself a faint smile but said nothing. His attention had already moved on. He noted the way that senator Lucius Domitius Ahenobarbus gestured expansively while speaking, his hands slicing through the air as if to carve out dominance in the conversation.

'I wonder what he's saying,' said Marcus.

'It doesn't matter what he's saying,' Julius replied. 'It matters how he says it and who he's saying it to.'

Marcus straightened, following Julius's gaze.

'You'll be one of them one day,' he said after a pause.

Julius turned to him, one eyebrow raised.

'One of who?'

'Them,' said Marcus, motioning to the senators and generals who moved through the Forum like actors on a stage. 'The ones who can make or unmake a man with a single word.'

'No,' said Julius, eventually. 'I'll be better.'

Marcus turned to him, his brow furrowed.

'Better?'

'Better than all of them,' said Julius. 'They think power is inherited, or bought, or seized with violence. But they don't understand that power is only as strong as the people who believe in it.'

Marcus laughed softly.

'Spoken like a true philosopher. Maybe I should introduce you to one of the stoics I know. They love talking about belief.'

The two boys stood in silence for a moment, watching as the men of power talked quietly amongst themselves. For a brief moment, one of them looked over, his gaze meeting that of Julius, pausing for a few moments as if assessing the boy.

'I think he noticed you,' said Marcus.

'A man in his position notices everything,' said Julius. 'He has to.'

'Well. If he notices everything, maybe he'll remember you when you're a senator.'

'I don't plan to wait that long,' replied Julius.

Marcus tilted his head, studying him.

'You mean that, don't you?'

Julius nodded.

'Of course. Rome isn't kind to those who wait.'

The two boys lingered in the Forum as the crowd began to thin, their words trailing off into the growing hum of the city. Though the day belonged to the past, Julius's thoughts were already on the future.

Several hours later, outside the city walls, the crowd began to disperse, leaving only the faint scent of incense and the dying embers of the funeral pyre in the air. Julius stood alone, staring at the last flickers of flame that had sent his father into the afterlife.

'Gaius,' came his mother's voice.

He turned to find Aurelia standing a few paces away, her expression composed, though her eyes betrayed a trace of weariness. Her black veil was pulled back, revealing the lines of a woman who had spent her life balancing the demands of nobility and the realities of decline.

'Come,' she said softly, gesturing for him to follow.

Julius hesitated, glancing over his shoulder at Marcus, who gave him a subtle nod. Julius straightened his shoulders and walked after his mother, his sandals clicking softly against the stone as they stepped away from the remnants of the gathering.

They stopped beneath the shade of a tall cypress tree near the gates to the city and Aurelia turned to face her son, her hands clasped tightly in front of her. For a moment, she said nothing, simply studying him.

'You stood well today,' she said at last. 'Your words were measured, and your bearing was strong. Your father would have been proud.'

Julius inclined his head, unsure how to respond. Aurelia's approval meant more to him than any applause from the crowd, but he sensed that her praise was merely the preamble.

'I am proud too,' she continued, her tone growing firmer, 'but pride is not enough. Not in Rome.'

Julius nodded slowly, his gaze steady.

'I understand, Mother.'

'Do you Gaius? You're just sixteen years old, and now the head of this family. That is not a title, it is a burden. One that will crush you if you do not learn to carry it.'

'I will carry it,' said. 'And I swear that one day I will make you proud.'

Aurelia stepped closer, placing a hand on his shoulder.

'You must be more than willing, my son. You must be clever.

Disciplined. Even ruthless when the time calls for it.'

Julius stiffened slightly at her words, but she pressed on, her voice steady and unwavering.

'Look at this city,' she said, gesturing to the walls above them. 'It is built on alliances between men, between families, between factions. The wrong alliance will destroy you, and the right one will raise you higher than you can imagine. You must choose carefully, even your friends.'

Julius thought of Marcus and felt a flicker of doubt.

'Are you talking about Marcus?' he asked cautiously.

Aurelia's lips twitched in a faint smile.

'Marcus is loyal enough, for now. But men's hearts are fickle, especially in Rome. Always remember that even the closest friend can one day become an enemy. Keep him close but never blind yourself to what he might become.'

Her words settled uneasily in his chest, but he said nothing.

'Discipline is your foundation,' she continued. 'Without it, ambition becomes recklessness. You must think three steps ahead of everyone around you and never let them see what you truly want until it is too late for them to stop you.'

Julius felt the weight of her words pressing against him, but he also felt something else stirring, a quiet determination, a sense of purpose taking root.

'And cunning,' Aurelia said, her voice softening slightly. 'There will be moments when strength and discipline alone will not be enough. You must see what others do not. You must know when to strike and when to wait.' She paused, studying him for a long moment. Then she reached up, brushing a stray lock of hair from his forehead, the gesture startling in its tenderness. 'I see so much of him in you,' she murmured. 'But you must go further than he ever did.

The gods have given you something rare, Gaius, a mind that can move mountains if you let it. Don't waste it. Let today be the end of one life and the beginning of another. You're not a boy anymore, you are the man this family will depend on.'

The moment passed, and Aurelia gave a deep sigh before stepping back, her composure firmly in place once more.

'Come,' she said, glancing toward the road leading in through the gates. 'There's much to do, and little time to waste.'

As they walked back toward their home, Julius felt the weight of her words settle over him like a cloak. It was heavy, but it did not crush him. Instead, it gave him clarity, sharpening his thoughts and solidifying his resolve. If the gods had given him a mind to move mountains, he had to decide where to begin.

Later that evening, Julius stood before the shrine of his ancestors, tucked into a small alcove of their domus. It was a modest shrine for a patrician family, though its simplicity only emphasised the weight it bore. The bronze bust of Venus, their divine forebear, sat atop the altar, her serene features gleaming in the flickering light of the oil lamps. Below her, smaller busts of the Julii ancestors lined the shelves: men who had served as consuls, praetors, and senators in the Republic's early days.

Julius knelt, his black toga still heavy around his shoulders. He placed his hands on the cold stone, his head bowed. The events of the day replayed in his mind, the funeral procession, his mother's stern guidance, and, beneath it all, the absence of his father, a gap that felt as though it would never be filled. The silence pressed down on him, forcing him to confront the expectations etched into every bust before him. They stared down at him, unyielding, his family's name carrying the weight of centuries. He spoke softly, his voice barely above a whisper.

'You built this name into something great,' he said, 'but what am I to do with it now?'

He exhaled sharply and leaned back on his heels, his gaze drifting to the largest bust, a depiction of his father. The sculptor had caught his stern eyes and high cheekbones well. Julius remembered sitting in this very spot with him years ago, watching as his father poured a libation to Venus, his voice steady as he prayed for the family's prosperity.

'Do you hear me, Father?' Julius asked, his voice cracking slightly. 'If you were here, what would you tell me? What am I supposed to do now?'

The room gave him no answer, but the silence made the question weigh heavier. He could feel the frustration welling up inside him, the anger at the factions that had long mocked his family's standing, the men who had laughed while others cried at the funerary service, at the world that seemed to have little room for mourning.

'They think we're finished,' he muttered. 'They see our name as nothing more than a shadow and will walk over us unless I stop them.'

He stood suddenly, his knees stiff from kneeling. His gaze swept over the shrine again, pausing on Venus, her serene gaze unbroken by the turmoil in his chest.

'You brought Aeneas out of Troy,' he said, his voice growing steadier. 'You gave him a path through fire and ruin to build something greater. If I truly come from your line, then show me the same path. Help me bring us back to what we should be.'

He poured a small libation of wine into the shallow dish before the shrine, the liquid pooling like blood in the soft glow of the lamps. For a moment, he stood in silence, his chest rising and falling with measured breaths. Then, with a final glance at his father's bust, he turned on his heel and strode toward the door.

Marcus waited outside, lounging casually against the wall.

'Done making promises to the gods?' he asked, the faintest hint of a smile tugging at his lips.

Julius met his gaze, his expression sharper now, as though a new resolve had been etched into his features.

'No more promises,' he said firmly. 'Now it's time for action.'

Marcus raised an eyebrow, standing straighter.

'Should I be worried? That sounds like the kind of thing someone says before doing something reckless.'

'Not reckless,' Julius corrected, 'deliberate. There's a difference.'

Marcus studied him for a moment, then shrugged.

'Fair enough. I'm not sure what you've decided, but whatever it is, I'll be there. Someone has to make sure you don't get yourself killed.'

Julius allowed himself the faintest smile.

'You'll see soon enough. But I won't fail, Marcus. Not now, not ever.'

The two walked together toward the atrium, their footsteps echoing softly against the stone. The faint hum of Rome outside the walls seemed louder now, as if the city itself were calling to him. Julius lifted his chin slightly, his dark eyes glinting with a mixture of ambition and purpose. For him, this wasn't just a vow, it was a destiny, one he could already feel stirring on the horizon, waiting for him to seize it.

Chapter Two

Rome

The morning filtered through the open atrium, glinting off the mosaic tiles and illuminating the small household shrine. The house was quiet, too quiet. The absence of his father's measured voice, of his quiet footsteps pacing the halls, made the silence feel… unnatural.

Julius, now the *pater familias* at just sixteen, sat at the central table, running his fingers over the edge of a wax tablet. He had spent the morning reviewing the household accounts, grain expenses, debts owed, the limited income from their properties. His father had always managed these matters, balancing the books with careful precision. Now, it was his burden. He glanced up as Aurelia entered, moving with the same grace and quiet authority that had always marked her presence. She carried herself like a woman accustomed to command, though she rarely spoke of it.

'Have you eaten?' she asked, softly.

Julius shook his head.

'Not yet.'

Aurelia sighed but said nothing, pouring a cup of watered wine and setting it before him. She studied the accounts over his shoulder, her keen eyes scanning the numbers.

'And?' she asked.

Julius exhaled, rubbing his temple.

'We're stable, for now. But if we're not careful, we'll be relying on favours before the year is out.'

Aurelia nodded, unfazed.

'Then we will be careful. We have enough to maintain appearances, and that is all that matters.'

Julius met her gaze.

'For how long?'

Aurelia looked down at his upturned face.

'Long enough for you to secure our future.'

Julius said nothing. She had told him as much after the funeral, that his path would not be one of mere survival, he was to restore the Julii name, to elevate it. But ambition required patience, and patience required discipline. A knock at the doorway interrupted his thoughts.

'Are you going to sit in here all day, Julius?' came a familiar voice. 'The Forum doesn't govern itself, you know.'

Julius looked up to see Marcus, dressed in a simple but well-cut tunic.

Julius smiled faintly.

'And I suppose you think it needs your help?'

'Someone has to keep the streets interesting,' said Marcus stepping inside and grabbing a fig from the table. He popped the fruit into his mouth, chewing thoughtfully.

'Come on. I hear Varius is meeting with some of the veterans today. Might be worth listening in.'

At the name Varius, Aurelia's eyes flickered with something unreadable. Julius caught it, but before he could speak, she turned to him.

'You should go,' she said. 'Listen, but do not involve yourself. Varius is still powerful, but power fades quickly in Rome and if you are wise, you will not tie yourself to a sinking ship.'

Julius nodded. Varius had once served alongside the most powerful man in Rome, Gaius Marius, the great general who had reformed the legions and defeated the barbarian hordes. But Marius was dead now with only the memories of the older soldiers like Varius to pass on the tales of his greatness. Still, Varius was a man of immense knowledge and garnered huge respect… and Julius wanted to see him. He stood up and handed the accounts to his mother.

'I will pick up on this tomorrow,' he said and after receiving a warm smile in return, joined Marcus and walked outside, heading towards the heart of the city.

The Forum Romanum was quieter than usual, the air thick with the growing heat of the day and the scent of baked stone and distant incense mingling as merchants sat in the shade of their stalls. In the shadow of the Basilica Aemilia, a group of old men sat on a worn marble bench, their voices carrying the weight of years. They were veterans, men who had once marched under the eagles, who had felt the weight of shield and spear, who had watched comrades fall and seen the banners of Rome raised high in victory. Now, their only battles were fought with memory, their stories the only weapons left to wield.

At the centre of them sat Quintus Varius Paetus, a man whose body had grown old, but whose voice still carried the fire of his youth. His tunic was faded, his hair white, but his back was straight as he leaned on his staff. His hands, though gnarled with time, still bore the scars of war.

'By the gods, I tell you, there was no greater sight than the day we stood at Vercellae!' Varius thumped his staff against the ground, his voice rising with excitement. 'The dust was thick as storm clouds, the sun burning down on our helmets, and there, there, was Marius, standing tall before the legions, his scarlet cloak catching the wind.'

One of the other veterans, Servius Laenas, grinned through broken teeth.

'And what did he say, Varius?'

Varius chuckled, shaking his head.

'What did he say? He said, *'There is no road back, only forward, only victory,'* and by the gods, he was right. We didn't just fight that day, we tore the Cimbri apart. They called us cowards before, said Rome was finished, but Marius... Marius taught them *fear.*'

The veterans laughed, nodding, some lost in the memories of that great battle, others murmuring quiet prayers to those who had not lived to see this day.

23

Standing at a distance, Julius watched in silence, listening as the old soldiers recalled the days when Rome had needed men like Marius, when it had begged for his strength, only to cast him aside when the danger had passed.

Varius paused and looked across, seeing Julius standing near a pillar.

'You there!' he called, 'don't skulk in the shadows like a thief. Step forward, like a Roman.'

Julius met his gaze for a moment, then stepped toward them.

'Ahh,' Varius muttered, studying him, a small smile curling at the corner of his lips. 'The young Caesar. You've your father's face, boy, but you carry yourself differently. More like... someone else.'

'Did you know my father?' asked Julius.

Paetus nodded, resting his hands on his staff.

'Aye. A good man. Steady, honourable, a true Roman.' His eyes flickered with something deeper, something unreadable. 'But you... I see something more in your eyes. You're not just steady, you seem to be watching, thinking, waiting. Tell me, young Caesar, do you dream of power?'

Julius met his gaze equally.

'I dream only of Rome.'

Varius barked a laugh.

'Spoken like a politician already.' He leaned forward slightly. 'Listen to me, boy. Rome does not belong to those who wait. It belongs to those who take. Your father served the Republic, but Marius saved it. And you...?' He tilted his head, watching Julius carefully. 'What will you do?'

Julius could feel the weight of their stares, the expectation, the challenge.

'I will not waste my name,' he said at last.

Paetus nodded approvingly.

'Good answer,' said Varius. 'I have lived long enough to see great men rise and greater men fall, men like Gaius Marius. Perhaps one day, there will be another man, one who will not be content to sit in the Senate and murmur like an old woman, but one who will carve his name into the bones of this city.' His eyes narrowed slightly. 'Perhaps that man is you, Julius.'

The air between them grew heavy, the murmurs of the other veterans dying away.

Julius straightened his back, nodding once.

'I know not what the fate has in store for me,' he said eventually, 'but I know this. One day, I will make my mother proud, and the name Gaius Julius Caesar will be known across Rome. Whether that is for good or ill, only the gods know.'

Varius smiled again

'Good. Then go, boy, and do just that, make Rome remember your name.'

Julius turned and walked away, his thoughts racing, his heart pounding. He had always known what he wanted. Responsibility, legacy, power, but now, for the first time, he felt something else. The weight of expectation, the whisper of destiny, the call to be more than just another name in history, and one day, somehow, he knew he would answer it. But for now, he just did not know where to begin.

Several weeks later the streets of Rome were once again alive with movement as Julius made his way through the Forum, the scent of fresh bread mingling with the sweat of merchants haggling over goods. It was a city of constant noise, a city of ambition, where every man's future was dictated by the alliances he forged. And today, Julius knew, he was about to forge his most important one yet.

It had started as a chance meeting, as most important moments often did. He had first seen Cornelia Cinna during a private gathering of the Populares faction at her father's villa. She had been standing to the side, watching with quiet amusement as men twice her age debated politics with fire in their voices.

Julius had watched her too, though at first, not for the reasons a young man might. She was the daughter of Lucius Cornelius Cinna, a former consul and one of the most powerful figures in the Populares. Her family name carried weight, and in Rome, marriage was as much about strategy as affection.

But Cornelia intrigued him. She was not the type to seek attention, nor did she shrink from it. Her dark hair framed a face that was intelligent rather than delicate, her eyes filled with something that Julius found rare among the daughters of Rome's elite, conviction.

'You listen well for a soldier's son,' she had remarked that evening, her tone teasing but not unkind.

'And you listen well for a senator's daughter,' he had responded.

Cornelia had tilted her head.

'I listen because I want to understand.'

'And what have you understood so far?'

She had studied him for a moment before replying. '

'That Rome is more than the men who claim to govern it. And that some voices are worth more than others.'

He had known, then… that she was different.

Julius's admiration for Cornelia had continued since that fateful night and it was no surprise to anyone when whispers of a potential betrothal reached his ears. It was a perfect match in the eyes of the Populares, Cinna's daughter and a rising young man from the Julii.

But for Julius, it was more than just politics. Cornelia challenged him, sharpened him. She understood what it meant to be born into expectation and yet still want more. The two grew closer until one day, a few months after the death of his father, the formal announcement came at a private gathering in Cinna's villa. Julius stood beside his mother while Cinna addressed the assembled guests.

'Today, we strengthen an alliance that will shape Rome's future,' Cinna declared, raising his cup. 'My daughter, Cornelia, will be wed to Gaius Julius Caesar.'

The room erupted in murmurs of approval as Julius turned to Cornelia, whose eyes met his with quiet confidence. There was no hesitation, no forced obedience in her gaze, only certainty, and as he took her hand in his, he felt the shift in his path. This was not just marriage, this was the first step toward something greater. Marcus, standing at his side, leaned in and muttered,

'So, this is it, you're truly committing to the Populares. I hope you're ready for a fight.'

Julius smiled.

'I was never meant to stand with the Optimates, my friend, as well you know.' His grip tightened around Cornelia's fingers. 'And as for being ready for a fight… I always have been.'

Chapter Three

Rome – 83 BC

The scent of crushed myrtle and fresh garlands hung heavy in the air, mingling with the sweet aroma of honey cakes and spiced wine. The Julii domus was alive with the hum of conversation, the murmur of prayers, and the occasional bursts of laughter from the gathered guests. For a moment, just a moment, Rome's chaos felt distant, as though the city itself had paused to honour the union of two of its most prominent families. Yet beneath the surface of celebration, there was an undercurrent of tension, a quiet unease that even the most lavish feast could not entirely dispel.

Julius stood at the edge of the atrium, dressed in his white tunic with a crimson-bordered toga, the fabric draped carefully over one shoulder. A thin gold circlet rested in his hair, a symbol of his lineage and the weight of his name. He had endured the rituals of preparation, the purification rites, the offerings to Jupiter, the blessings from the household gods, but his mind was elsewhere, racing ahead to the implications of this day.

Across the room, Cornelia stood with her mother, her flammeum, the traditional orange veil of a Roman bride, casting a soft glow over her face. She was composed, dignified, but even from a distance, Julius saw the tension in her posture. She knew, as he did, that this was more than a wedding. This was a declaration of allegiance, a binding of fates that would echo far beyond the walls of this house.

Their union would bind him to the Populares, to Cinna's cause, to the faction that still resisted Sulla's inevitable return. It was a step that could not be undone, a choice that would define his path for years to come. Julius felt the weight of it pressing down on him, but he also felt a strange sense of resolve. This was not just a marriage of convenience; it was a partnership, one that could shape the future of Rome itself.

'You're supposed to look happy,' came Marcus's voice at his side, breaking through his thoughts.

Julius smirked but didn't take his eyes off Cornelia.

'I am happy.'

'Then try not to look like you're marching into battle.'

'In many ways, I am,' replied Julius.

Marcus chuckled.

'That's the spirit. A wedding should feel like war. Gods know most marriages end up that way.'

Julius let out a dry laugh, but his mind was already moving ahead. Cinna was still consul, and the Populares were still in control. But for how long? He knew what men whispered, that Sulla would return, that when he did, there would be no mercy. The thought lingered like a shadow, even as the guests around him laughed and toasted the union.

'It's a good match,' said Marcus, his tone more serious now. 'Cornelia is strong, and her father...' He paused, glancing toward Cinna, who stood at the centre of a group of senators, his voice carrying above the din. 'Her father is the only thing keeping Rome out of Sulla's hands.'

Julius nodded.

'For now.'

A priest stepped forward, raising his hands to signal the start of the ceremony. The guests quieted, and Julius took a steadying breath before walking forward to stand beside Cornelia. The ceremony was simple, as all Roman weddings were, rooted in tradition, steeped in symbolism. Julius and Cornelia stood before the gathered guests, the flames of the household altar flickering between them. The priest began the Dextrarum Iunctio, the joining of hands, guiding Julius as he took Cornelia's right hand in his own. The warmth of her fingers surprised him. She was steady, not trembling, not hesitant. Whatever fear she felt, she hid it well.

'Gaius Julius Caesar,' the priest intoned, his voice carrying through the atrium, 'do you take this woman, Cornelia, to be your wife, to share in your home, your name, your fate?'

Julius looked into Cornelia's dark eyes, searching for any trace of doubt. There was none.

'I do,' he said firmly.

The priest turned to Cornelia.

'Cornelia Cinna, do you take this man, Gaius Julius Caesar, to be your husband, to share in his home, his name, his fate?'

For the first time, Cornelia smiled. A small, knowing smile, the kind that said she understood exactly what this meant.

'I do.'

The priest nodded and turned to the guests.

'Then let the gods bear witness, and let Rome welcome this union.'

A cheer rose from the gathered crowd as the final offering was made to Juno, goddess of marriage. The sacrificial cake, made of spelt, was broken and shared, and Julius placed a gentle hand on Cornelia's veil, lifting it away to reveal her face. She looked up at him, and in that moment, the politics faded, the alliances, the war to come, none of it mattered. There was only this. A wife, a husband, a promise.

As the sun began to set, the guests began to relax. The wine flowed freely, the scent of roasted lamb and honeyed almonds filling the air. Men of the Populares faction gathered in small groups, talking in hushed voices, their conversation flicking between celebration and the dark future ahead. Julius moved among them, Cornelia at his side, offering brief words to each senator, each general, each ally of her father's cause. He saw the way they watched him now, no longer as a boy, but as Cinna's son-in-law, as a man who had chosen his path.

Yet not all the guests were convinced. In a shadowed corner of the atrium, a group of older senators stood together, their conversations low and their expressions guarded. One of them leaned in to murmur to his companions.

'A bold move, this marriage. But will it be enough? Sulla is no fool and will see this for what it is, a challenge.'

Another man nodded.

'Cinna plays a dangerous game. Binding the Julii to his cause may strengthen his hand, but it also paints a target on the boy's back. Sulla will not forget this.'

A third man shook his head.

'Julius is no ordinary boy. He has his father's steadiness and his uncle's ambition. If anyone can navigate these waters, it's him.'

The first man snorted.

'Ambition is a double-edged sword, my friend. It can build empires or destroy them. We shall see which path young Caesar chooses.'

Their words were muted, meant only for each other, but the tension in their voices was palpable. They were men who had survived the shifting tides of Roman politics, and they knew better than to trust in the permanence of any alliance. Julius caught fragments of their conversation as he passed, but he did not linger. He had no need to hear their doubts; he carried enough of his own.

A heavy hand clapped onto his shoulder, and he turned to find Varius, grinning at him through his grey beard.

'A fine match, young Caesar,' said Varius, raising a cup in salute. 'Your father would be proud. And so would Marius.'

'Thank you,' said Julius. 'That means a lot to me.'

Varius's expression darkened slightly, his eyes flicking toward the city beyond the courtyard walls.

'The gods have favoured you today, boy. But do not mistake their favour for loyalty. They are fickle, and so is fortune. If Sulla returns, which he will, he will not see this marriage as a gift from the heavens, he will see it for what it is… a challenge.'

'Then let him see it,' said Julius. 'Let him see that I will not cower like the others, that I will not beg for his mercy or twist in the wind like a reed. If he takes my marriage as defiance, then he sees clearly. I will not unmake my vows to please a tyrant so let Sulla do as he will. I will do the same.'

Varius studied him for a moment, absorbing Julius's words. Then, slowly, a smile touched his lips, not of amusement, but of recognition.

'Good. Rome has enough men who bow their heads to cruel masters. It needs men who stand, men who defy the storm rather than be swept away by it. Perhaps the gods are fickle, but fortune favours those bold enough to seize it. Hold fast to your courage, Julius, one day, it may be all that stands between you and the abyss.' Without waiting for an answer, Varius raised his glass and turned away, leaving Julius staring after him.

A few moments later, a shadow crossed the courtyard, a messenger slipping through the revellers, heading straight Cinna and Julius's stomach tightened. Even on his wedding night, politics did not rest. Cornelia saw it too and she turned to him, her voice low enough that others could not overhear.

'We won't have much time, will we?'

Julius exhaled slowly.

'No. We won't.'

She nodded, accepting the truth without argument, and in that moment, he knew he had made the right choice. She understood. She had always understood.

As the night deepened, the feast continued, but the mood had shifted. The laughter was a little too loud, the toasts a little too fervent, as though the guests were trying to drown out the unease that lingered in the air. Julius and Cornelia moved among them, their hands clasped, their smiles practiced but genuine. They were a team now, bound not just by tradition but by a shared understanding of what lay ahead. In a quiet corner, Marcus leaned against a pillar, watching the scene with a wry smile.

'Well, Julius,' he muttered to himself, 'you've done it now. No turning back.'

Julius caught his eye and raised his cup in a silent toast.

Marcus returned the gesture without smiling.

'Gods help us all,' he said under his breath, and as the stars began to pierce the night sky, Julius felt the weight of the future pressing down on him. But he also felt something else, a flicker of hope, a spark of determination. He had chosen his path, and he would walk it, no matter where it led. For Rome, for his family, for Cornelia… and for himself.

Chapter Four

Rome – 83 BC

The air in the city was thick with fear, even before the news arrived. The birds flew in uneasy patterns over the Tiber, the temples were fuller than usual, and the streets were quieter, as if the city itself held its breath.

Then came the confirmation that most of the population had dreaded. Sulla was returning to Rome with an army of hardened veterans, men who had fought in the East and had learned to kill without hesitation. This was not a campaign, it was a reckoning and as the news spread, the panic took hold.

The Optimates, those loyal to Sulla and the ideals he stood for, met in closed chambers, sharpening their knives and making their lists while the Populares, those who believed in the rights of the people, looked to their leaders, seeking any means to resist.

At his family's domus, Julius sat with Aurelia and Marcus, a single oil lamp flickering between them, casting long shadows across the marble walls.

'How much time do we have?' asked Marcus.

'A few weeks,' said Aurelia, perhaps a month or two. It all depends if Cinna can join up with Carbo and stop him before he leaves Greece.'

'Cinna needs to act fast,' said Julius. 'If he hesitates, Sulla will take Rome before anyone can stop him.'

'And if he fights?' asked Marcus.

Julius hesitated. The truth was, not many thought Cinna was strong enough to withstand what was coming. He had power, but he didn't have Sulla's legions, the kind of men who had spent years fighting for their general and would die for him without question.

'Cinna needs support,' he said. 'If the Senate sides with him…'

Aurelia cut him off with a quiet laugh.

'The Senate will side with whoever holds the sword to their throats. You know that.'

Julius nodded.

'Then we must make them listen to reason.' He got to his feet and retrieved his cloak.

'Where are you going?' asked his mother.

'We're not done yet,' said Julius, 'there's a meeting of the Populares in the forum tonight. I'm going to see if there is anything we can do to help.' He turned to Marcus. 'Are you coming?'

'Wouldn't miss it for the world,' said Marcus and getting to his feet, followed Julius out of the door.

The wind whispered through the Vicus Longus, carrying the scent of the Tiber and the charred remains of burned-out torches. Rome felt different tonight. Uneasy, expectant, like a beast lying still before the pounce. Merchants closed their stalls earlier than usual and men who usually walked with confidence, cast furtive glances at everyone they passed, something was wrong.

Julius and Marcus headed towards the forum, the city tense and hushed as Sulla's return loomed. Julius thought of the man they feared, brilliant, ruthless, a patrician who had risen through cunning and cruelty. Sulla had saved Rome, then turned on it, his feud with Marius tearing the Republic apart. Now, with Marius dead and the Populares weakened, he would come not to rebuild, but to punish. His brilliance was undeniable, but so was his capacity for destruction.

The two young men continued, talking quietly amongst themselves but as they approached the forum, a voice cried out, splitting the night.

'*Cinna is dead!*'

Julius stopped mid-step. The words rippled outward like a wave, crashing through the streets. First, an echo, then gasps, then panic. A group of men at a street corner abandoned their dice game, scattering without a word. A merchant, still clutching a crate of figs, let it tumble to the ground and ran. Another voice echoed through the streets, louder this time.

'*Cinna's been murdered!*'

Julius spun sharply, his hand shooting out to seize the man's sleeve. The messenger, no more than a clerk by the look of him, was breathless, his tunic damp with sweat, his face pale with fear.

'What did you say?' Julius demanded, his fingers tightening.

The man flinched, yanking his arm free as though scalded. His eyes darted wildly, unfocused, like a cornered animal.

'They killed him!' he gasped. 'His own men, *his own soldiers!* They turned on him near Ancona. Beat him to death in the dirt!'

Julius stood rigid, the words hanging in the air, heavy and unreal. Lucius Cornelius Cinna, four times consul, the man who had defied Sulla and ruled Rome in his absence, was dead. The clerk swallowed hard, his breath uneven.

'There was a mutiny,' continued the clerk, his words tumbling over each other. 'He was about to set sail for Greece, to join Carbo against Sulla but the moment he stepped forward to speak, his men turned on him, struck him down before he could even draw his sword.'

Julius exhaled slowly, willing his thoughts into order. He had known Cinna to be ruthless, unyielding. The man had wielded power like a blade, cutting down opposition with the same brutality that Sulla had once shown his own enemies, but he had not been a fool. Had he truly misjudged his own men so badly? Whatever the facts, Cinna was gone and with him, the fragile hold the Populares had on Rome. The tide had turned.

'It's over, Julius,' said Marcus, cutting into his thoughts. 'We need to leave the city before Sulla arrives.'

Julius ignored him. His mind was already moving ahead, calculating the next step. Suddenly his eyes flew open, and he turned to face Marcus, his eyes full of fear.

'Marcus,' he gasped, 'we have to go back.'

'Where?' asked Marcus, as Julius turned to run.

'Cinna's house,' shouted Julius over his shoulder, 'Cornelia is there and if Cinna is dead, she is in danger.'

A few hours later, Julius sat in the shaded garden of Cinna's villa, watching Cornelia as she reached up and plucked a small fig from the low-hanging branch of an ancient tree. She turned it over in her fingers, her gaze distant, unreadable. The news of her father's death had reached her earlier that day, carried on the whispers of a city that had already begun to forget him. And yet, she had not wept, nor had she screamed. Instead, she had met the weight of loss with silence.

Julius admired that about her, the quiet strength, the way she held herself together even as Rome itself crumbled around her.

'I know why you are here,' she said at last without turning to look at him.

Julius leaned forward slightly.

'And why is that?'

'Because marrying me ties you to the Populares and to my father's memory.' She finally turned, meeting his gaze with clear, steady eyes. 'Even though both are doomed.'

'Do you think I would abandon you now?' asked Julius.

Cornelia exhaled, a slow breath that was neither relief nor resignation, simply understanding. She held his gaze, searching for something in him, and after a long pause, she shook her head.

'No,' she admitted. 'I do not. In fact, I think you are the only man in Rome foolish enough to dare defy Sulla.' She looked down at the fig in her hand, rolling it between her fingers as if testing its weight. Her voice, when she spoke again, was softer but no less resolute.

'You know I will not let my father's name die with him?'

Julius moved, closing the space between them in a single step. He plucked the fig from her fingers and tossed it aside. Then, gently but firmly, he took her hand in his own, his grip not just one of affection, but of purpose, of something unspoken but understood.

'I know,' he murmured. 'Because in this, we are one.' His grip
on her hand tightened, steady and unwavering. 'Whatever happens next, Cornelia, whatever fate or Rome or Sulla himself throws at us, we will face it together… always'

Chapter Five

Rome

The sun hung low over Rome, its light stained crimson as if the heavens themselves bled for the city. The walls had held for hours, manned by desperate soldiers and veterans loyal to the Populares. They fought with the ferocity of men who knew what awaited them if they failed, but Sulla's legions were relentless, hardened by years of war in the east and driven by the promise of plunder and vengeance. When the gates finally splintered and gave way, the tide of steel and fury poured into the streets like a flood unleashed.

The defenders, outnumbered and exhausted, were swept aside. Swords clashed, shields shattered, and the air filled with the cries of the dying. Those who could, fled, but there was no escape. Sulla's soldiers, their faces grim beneath blood-spattered helmets, moved through the city with brutal efficiency. They kicked in doors, dragged men from their homes, and cut down anyone who dared raise a hand against them. The streets ran red, not just with the blood of soldiers but with that of civilians caught in the chaos.

But it was in the shadowed alleys, the real terror began. Informers and Optimates, their faces alight with malice, pointed out those suspected of sympathizing with the Populares. Men were hauled into the open, their pleas drowned out by the roar of the mob, cast before the legionaries, who showed no mercy. Others were beaten to death on the spot, their bodies left as warnings to the rest. Women screamed, children wept, and the city that had once been the heart of the Republic became a slaughterhouse.

Amidst the carnage, Sulla rode through the streets on a white horse, his crimson cloak a stark contrast to the pale horror around him. His face was a mask of cold disdain, his eyes scanning the chaos as though it were beneath him. He did not flinch at the screams or the sight of his soldiers cutting down unarmed men. To him, this was not savagery but necessity. Rome had defied him, and now it would learn the price of defiance.

He paused at the foot of the Capitoline Hill, his gaze sweeping over the city he had once called home. The smoke of burning buildings curled into the sky, and the cries of the dying echoed like a dirge. Sulla's lips curled into a faint, humourless smile. This was not the Rome he had fought for, but it was the Rome he would reshape. Let the streets run red, let the Senate tremble… and let the people remember the cost of crossing Lucius Cornelius Sulla.

He spurred his horse forward, the clatter of hooves lost in the cacophony of destruction. Behind him, the rest of his legion followed, their swords ready, their eyes gleaming with the promise of more blood to come. Rome would bow, or it would burn. And Sulla would watch, unmoved, as the city he had come to claim paid its price in full.

For weeks, Rome had held its breath, preparing for the inevitable. But when Sulla finally revealed his vengeance in full, it was colder, crueller than any had imagined.

Each morning, lists appeared, nailed to the walls of the Forum, carved into tablets, inked onto parchments. The names upon them belonged to Rome's great men, senators, magistrates, equestrians, wealthy merchants, and some whose only crime was being suspected of disloyalty.

To be listed was a death sentence. No trial, no defence. Once a name was inscribed, a man ceased to be a citizen and declared an outlaw, stripped of every right and protection. Anyone could kill him. And the state would reward them for it… two talents of silver per head.

By midday, the first bounties were claimed. Men ran through the streets clutching sacks that dripped red, presenting their proof before the treasury, where cold-eyed clerks counted the rewards.

Rome had seen civil war, had seen blood spilled on its streets before, but this was different. This was not war, this was a purge, and it was only just beginning.

Every day, the lists grew longer. At first, Julius had told himself there would be limits. Sulla was brutal, yes, but he was no fool. He would strike his enemies, exact his revenge, then restore order. But there were no limits, there was only the killing and so, as neighbour killed neighbour, Rome watched in silence and the city turned on itself.

The villa was silent, not the silence of peace, but of fear, of voices lowered, of servants moving carefully, of a house that had begun to feel like a prison.

Julius sat at the table, staring at the flickering oil lamp. His mother sat across from him, her face set in the way it always was when she was holding back words, she knew she could not say. Beside her, sat Marcus. He had spoken little since arriving that evening, he didn't need to, the tension in the room spoke for him.

Cornelia stood near the window, her arms wrapped around herself, gazing out into the darkened streets. She had been quiet for days, but Julius knew the thoughts running through her mind. They were the same as his own.

'Your name will be on that list soon, Julius,' said Marcus. 'You're Cinna's son-in-law. That alone makes you a target.'

'You are also at risk,' said Julius quietly. 'Guilty by association, and for that, I apologise.'

'That is not your fault,' said Aurelia, 'but Marcus is right, we have waited too long. If Sulla orders your name written, we may not have time to escape.'

41

'We should have left when Sulla first landed in Italy,' said Marcus. 'Now the city is a prison. He controls everything, Senate, armies, the provinces.'

'Even if we ran,' said Julius, 'where would we go?'

'There is one way to stop all this,' Aurelia said quietly.

Julius turned to her before she could finish. He already knew what she would say.

'No.'

Cornelia finally turned from the window. She met Aurelia's gaze, something unreadable in her eyes.

'You want him to divorce me.' she said. It wasn't a question.

Aurelia hesitated.

'I want my son to live, 'she said, 'and if that is what it takes, surely it is a price worth paying.'

'And do you truly think that would save him?' asked Cornelia.

'It might,' interjected Marcus. 'You know what Sulla wants. He doesn't just want to destroy his enemies, he wants to erase them. But if Julius renounces Cinna's daughter, he might see it as submission. A sign that he is willing to bend.'

Julius gave a humourless laugh.

'Sulla does not want men who bend, Marcus. He wants men who kneel.'

Cornelia looked at him then, really looked at him. He could see the pain in her eyes, the anger, not at him, but at this, at the cruelty of it all. She opened her mouth but before she could speak, a sharp knock at the door shattered the silence.

Marcus's hand drifted toward his belt, where a dagger lay hidden beneath the folds of his tunic. Julius forced his legs to move, forced himself to breathe, as he strode to the door and unlatched it.

A single courier stood in the torchlight, a sealed scroll extended in his hand. He did not speak, he did not meet Julius's eyes. Julius took the parchment, and the courier hesitated for a fraction of a moment, just long enough for Julius to see the fear in his face, before turning on his heel and vanishing into the night.

He returned to the table and sat quietly, placing the scroll on its surface before looking at the waiting faces of those closest to him. Finally, with a deep sigh, he broke the wax seal and unfolded the scroll. The words were simple and as the others stared, he read them aloud.

'Lucius Cornelius Sulla Felix summons Gaius Julius Caesar to attend him at his villa.'

No threats, no accusations, just a summons. And yet, Julius knew what it meant.

He was being called to stand before the dictator to renounce his wife and beg for his life, or… to die.

'This summons is a trap, Julius,' said Marcus eventually. 'You know that don't you?'

'I know what it is,' said Julius.

'Then don't go. Flee the city, tonight. There's still time.'

'And where would I go? Become a fugitive? Live in hiding like a common criminal?' He shook his head. 'No. If I run, I am guilty. If I stand before him, I am still Gaius Julius Caesar.'

Marcus muttered a curse and sat heavily on a stool. 'Stubborn as ever.'

'My son,' said Aurelia, 'this is not the time for pride. You know what needs to be done.'

'It is not pride, Mother. It is principle.'

She studied him with those dark, searching eyes that had always unsettled him as a child.

'What does principle matter to the dead?'

'But I am not dead yet.'

Aurelia took his hand, squeezing it tightly.

43

'You are my only son, Gaius, and I will not lose you to this madness. You have to divorce Cornelia. If you do that, he may spare you.'

Julius stiffened at the mention of his wife.

'I will not divorce Cornelia, mother. Cast it from your mind.'

'But Gaius...'

'No,' he shouted. 'She is my wife, and I will not cast her aside to appease a tyrant.'

Aurelia exhaled, pressing her lips together.

'Then at least be careful. Sulla is no fool. If he has summoned you, it is not to hear your reasoning, it is to make an example of you.'

Before Julius could answer, Cornelia walked over and placed her hand on his shoulder.

'Gaius,' she said quietly. 'I do not want you to fight a battle you cannot win.'

Julius turned fully to her, taking her hand in his.

'You are my wife, Cornelia, and that will not change as long as I draw breath.'

'Even if it costs you everything?'

He stared into her eyes and squeezed her hand tighter.

'Even if it costs me everything.'

Marcus let out an exaggerated groan.

'Then we are all doomed.'

Julius shot him a look, but Marcus simply shrugged.

'I am just saying that I would rather face a legion alone than stand in a room with Sulla while refusing an order.'

Aurelia spoke again, her voice quiet but firm.

'Listen to me, Gaius. There are ways to navigate power without defiance. If there is a way to leave that chamber alive with your honour intact, take it. Do not mistake stubbornness for bravery.'

Julius met her gaze. He understood what she meant. There was no shame in playing the game, in surviving to fight another day. But this was different, this was not about politics; this was about the very essence of who he was.

'I will do what must be done,' he said at last.

Aurelia sighed but said no more. She knew that look in his eyes. No force in Rome, not even Sulla, would make him yield.

A heavy silence filled the room. Outside, the streets of Rome were alive with the murmurs of the city, but inside these walls, only the weight of the coming dawn mattered.

'It's late,' Cornelia whispered. 'You should rest.' She reached up, her fingers brushing his cheek. 'I will sit with you.'

Julius gave her a grateful smile and turned back to Marcus.

'If I do not return…'

'Don't finish that sentence,' Marcus interrupted. 'You will return, you have to. Who else would I drink with?'

Julius chuckled despite himself.

'Indeed.'

Marcus rose and stretched.

'Then let us drink tonight, while we still can. If Sulla's going to have you executed tomorrow, we may as well make sure you're too hungover to care.'

Cornelia rolled her eyes.

'You are insufferable, Marcus.'

'And yet you all keep me around.'

The tension in the room eased slightly. The weight of tomorrow remained, but for now, there was warmth. Julius looked around at the people who mattered most to him. He did not know what awaited him in Sulla's villa, but he knew one thing, he would not bow to a dictator, no matter the cost.

Julius had never been inside Sulla's villa before. Few had, and fewer still left with their fate unchanged. The estate sat on the Palatine Hill, overlooking the city like a throne above its subjects. It was not lavish in the way that other aristocratic homes were, Sulla had little taste for excess in decoration, but it radiated something far more potent. Power, control, fear.

The marble floors were cool beneath Julius's sandals as he was led through the atrium. The guards who flanked him did not speak, their presence alone was enough to remind him that he was not here as a guest. He was here to kneel, or to die.

At last, he was brought into a chamber lit only by bronze oil lamps, their glow flickering across the painted walls. A long table stood at the centre, scattered with documents, tablets, and a half-emptied wine cup. Sulla sat behind it, reclining in a high-backed chair, his pale blue eyes unreadable beneath a furrowed brow. He was older now, his face lined, his once-red hair turned grey, but there was no weakness in him. His body, still thick with the strength of a soldier, spoke of a man who had not been softened by age. Julius stopped before him, standing rigid, unbowed.

Sulla said nothing at first. He simply studied him, tapping one scarred finger against the table. The silence stretched, thick and suffocating.

'You look like your uncle,' he said finally.

Julius did not react. He knew which uncle Sulla meant. Gaius Marius, the man who had once been Rome's greatest general, Sulla's greatest enemy. The man who had butchered Sulla's allies in his absence and had ruled Rome through terror. The insult was deliberate.

Julius kept his voice even.

'Marius is long dead.'

'And yet his stink lingers in this city,' Sulla mused, pouring himself more wine. 'Just as Cinna's does. Tell me, boy, did you think I would not notice you? That I would not see the son-in-law of Cinna sitting in my city, wearing the name of the Julians, pretending he is above all of this?'

Julius met his gaze.

'I have raised no hand against you.'

'No. You have not.' Sulla swirled his cup, watching the wine catch the lamplight. 'But you married Cinna's daughter, tying yourself to the man who tried to wipe my name from history. Do you think I do not know what your kind whisper in their homes? That one day, the Republic will rise again, and another Marius will come?' He leaned forward. 'Tell me, Caesar. Is that man you?'

Julius could feel the weight of the guards behind him, the tension of the room pressing down on his shoulders. He knew what Sulla wanted. A denial, a plea, submission. He gave him none.

'Lucius Cornelius Sulla Felix,' he said. 'I am a Roman and have always served Rome to the best of my ability. I have taken no arms against you, nor have I conspired against your rule.'

Sulla studied him for a long moment. Then, he exhaled a quiet chuckle, shaking his head.

'You think yourself clever, Caesar. But cleverness does not save men from the lists.' He set his cup down. 'You have a choice. Divorce Cornelia and renounce Cinna's memory. Prove to me that you are not a threat.'

Julius's stomach twisted. He had known this demand would come, he had prepared himself for it. And yet, now that the moment was here, his blood boiled with fury. Sulla was not just asking for a divorce, he was asking for total submission, for obedience, and for a man who would kneel before him like all the others. His hands clenched at his sides, and he took a deep breath before responding.

'I cannot put aside my wife,' he said. 'I love her and will not betray our marriage vows. Neither will I sully her father's name. To do so now, after marrying into his family, will demean my own family's name. If you must kill me for loyalty and my own honour, then that is how it must be.'

Sulla exhaled through his nose, the faintest trace of amusement curling at the edge of his lips.

'You are a stubborn one, I'll grant you that.' He pushed himself up from his chair. Even now, surrounded by power, he carried himself like a soldier, every motion precise, every pause calculated. He stepped forward, stopping just short of Julius. He was not a tall man, but the weight of his presence was suffocating.

'Do you know why I summoned you here, boy, to my own villa?'

Julius met his gaze.

'To see if I would kneel.'

Sulla chuckled, shaking his head.

'No. If I wanted you to kneel, you'd already be in the Forum with a sword at your throat.' His expression hardened. 'I summoned you because I do not really care about your wife, only you. Cinna is dead. His daughter is nothing, but you, Caesar, you are not nothing.'

He let the words settle before continuing.

'I will not waste time with threats, for you know what I can do, and as long as you are in Rome, you are within my grasp. Today, you will leave here alive, but only because I allow it.' His pale blue eyes flickered with something unreadable. 'But that mercy has its limits, Caesar.' He turned away, and sat back down, reclining against the armrest. 'You have until tomorrow to announce your divorce. Do it and you live, refuse…' He shrugged. 'Well, the lists grow longer every day.'

Julius remained motionless. The warning was clear.

'Rome forgets the dead, Caesar, but it remembers the survivors so choose wisely.'

With a nod of Sulla's head, a guard stepped forward and the meeting was over.

Julius inclined his head, a gesture that was neither submission nor defiance, and turning on his heel, walked toward the doors. He did not rush, and he did not let them see his hands shake. As he stepped into the cold evening air, the weight of Sulla's ultimatum settled on his shoulders. He had one day. One day to decide if he would bow, or risk everything.

Later that night, the torches in the Julii domus flickered gently, their glow once again stretching long shadows across the marble floors. The hour was late, yet no one in the household had retired. The air was thick with unspoken words, with tension that clung to the walls like damp mist.

Julius stood at the centre of the atrium, his travelling cloak draped over one shoulder. His belongings, a modest bundle of clothes, a small sum of money, were packed. He was ready.

Aurelia stood before him, hands clasped tightly together. Cornelia, pale and silent, watched from beside her, her fingers gripping the edge of her shawl.

'I still don't like it,' muttered Marcus from the corner.

'Neither do I,' Julius admitted. 'But it is the only way.'

Aurelia stepped forward.

'You made the right choice, my son.'

Julius offered her a wry smile.

'I made the only choice that ensured I would live to make another.'

'That is wisdom, not cowardice.'

His gaze drifted to Cornelia. She had not spoken a word since he had announced his decision to leave. That troubled him more than he cared to admit.

'Cornelia…'

At last, she looked up, her eyes shimmering in the low light.

'You are leaving me.'

'Never,' he said, taking her hands in his. 'I leave Rome, not you.'

A tear slid down her cheek, but she quickly wiped it away.

'What if Sulla changes his mind? What if he comes for me in your absence?'

Julius stared. It was a fear he had not voiced, though it had haunted him since the moment he had made his decision, but Aurelia answered before he could respond.

'You are not the threat, Cornelia, my son is. Sulla is practical above all else, and with Julius gone, he will not waste his wrath on an innocent woman.'

'Where will you go?' asked Marcus. 'You cannot simply disappear.'

'We have family and allies in Etruria, I will go there until Sulla comes to his senses. He can't just kill anyone who disagrees with him else Rome will be an empty city in a matter of months.'

Aurelia stepped forward, reaching up to touch her son's cheek.

'Promise me something, Gaius.'

He met her gaze.

'Anything.'

'Only return when the time is right. Not before.'

A long pause. Then, at last, he nodded.

'I promise.'

He heard a rustling sound behind him, and he turned to see a servant carry a second pack into the atrium.

'That isn't mine,' he said with a frown.

'It's mine,' said Marcus. 'I'm going with you.'

Julius studied him for a moment. He should have known. Marcus had stood beside him in every fight, in every hardship since they had been young boys. To expect him to remain behind while he fled had never really been a real possibility.

'You know there is no need,' said Julius. 'With me gone, you are no longer complicit.'

'I know,' said Marcus, 'but I will go with you as far as Etruria. I just want to make sure you get out of Rome in one piece.'

Julius paused, staring at his lifelong friend.

'I've put up with you all these years,' he replied with a chuckle, 'I suppose a few more days won't make much difference.' He turned back and gave a kiss to both his mother and wife and, before, the tears could start, turned back to Marcus.

'Come,' he said, 'we have a long journey ahead of us,' and, after picking up a leather pouch containing letters of introduction and a small purse of silver from his mother, they stepped out into the cool night air.

The city was silent, as if holding its breath, as if it knew that tonight it was losing one of its own. The two young men walked quickly through the narrow, shadowed streets, keeping to the quieter paths. Patrols still roamed the city, and though Julius's name had not yet been written on Sulla's lists, it was only a matter of time.

As they neared the Servian Walls, the great stone gates loomed ahead, Rome's last barrier before the open road. Two horses waited for them in one of the many stables just beyond the archway and the stable master was an old Populares supporter, a man who had served under Marius and Cinna. He said nothing as they approached, simply nodding and holding the reins out to them, the arrangements already made. Julius ran a hand along the horse's flank before mounting, the animal shifting beneath him, restless.

He looked up for one last look at the walls of Rome before turning to Marcus.

'Ready?'

Marcus gave a single nod, and, with a flick of the reins, they rode out into the darkness, heading north toward exile, toward the unknown.

Chapter Six

Rome

he Via Flaminia stretched endlessly before them, its ancient stones bathed in the pale glow of full moon. The road had carried consuls, generals, and armies to the far reaches of the Republic, but tonight, it carried only a fugitive and his friend.

Julius pulled his cloak tighter around his shoulders, the damp chill of early spring settling into his bones. They had been travelling for two days but Etruria was still days away, and every mile brought new dangers. Sulla's patrols roamed the countryside, hunting the last remnants of Cinna's allies, ensuring that no trace of the old regime remained, and though it was likely that no message had reached them yet regarding his fate, they didn't want to take any unnecessary risks.

'I don't like this,' muttered Marcus, scanning the darkening fields on either side of the road. 'Too many places for men to hide.'

'You worry too much,' said Julius.'

'It's my job to worry,' replied Marcus. 'You were the one who told Sulla himself that you wouldn't crawl before him. And now we ride his roads alone hoping his men don't slit our throats in the dark.'

A cold wind swept across the fields, rustling the olive trees lining the roadside. In the distance, a faint glow of torchlight flickered against the horizon, a camp straddling the road.

'That looks like a checkpoint,' said Marcus. 'I heard Sulla's men have been checking travellers heading out of the city.

Julius exhaled slowly. It was to be expected. The dictator's grip on Rome was absolute, but he still had enemies beyond the city. If he was securing the roads, it meant he was still hunting. Still purging. He straightened in his saddle, eyes locked on the torch-lit crossing before them.

'What do we do?' asked Marcus.

'We keep riding,' said Julius. 'If we turn back now, they'll know we have something to hide.'

'And if they ask who we are?'

'As far as they know we are just Roman citizens, travellers heading to Mevania on family business.'

'Mevania? Who do you know in Mevania?'

'Nobody,' said Julius, 'but I'm not going to tell them where we are really heading, am I?'

'Fair point,' murmured Marcus.

Julius urged his horse forward. If Sulla's men meant to stop him, they would have to see through a Julius Caesar who did not flinch. And he did not intend to flinch.

The torches burned bright in the darkness, casting their flickering light over the road. Ahead, the checkpoint stood like an iron gate between them and freedom, a small outpost of legionaries, stationed where the Via Flaminia narrowed between two steep embankments.

Julius and Marcus slowed their horses, joining a small line of merchants, travellers, and farmers waiting to pass through. The air was tense. No one spoke. The only sounds were the clank of armour, the occasional whimper of a nervous traveller, and the low murmur of an official consulting his scrolls.

The legionaries were battle-hardened, their faces lined with scars. These were not the soft soldiers of Rome's garrisons, these men had seen war, and they had survived. And that made them dangerous.

Julius tightened his grip on the reins, forcing himself to breathe evenly. Ahead, a man stood in front of the soldiers, arguing vehemently. His voice was loud enough to carry, his gestures growing desperate.

'There must be some mistake!' he shouted as a legionary pulled him off the road. 'I am no enemy of the state, I am a loyal Roman. I support Sulla, I always have!'

The Centurion in charge stood watching, his hands resting on the pommel of his gladius. He did not move, did not react, as though the man's pleas were nothing more than the chatter of insects.

Eventually he turned to an official standing just behind him, a scribe in a dull grey tunic, holding a scroll in one hand and a reed pen in the other. The official scanned the list, his finger trailing down the parchment.

Julius and Marcus watched in silence until finally, the official turned his head and muttered something they couldn't hear.

The Centurion gave a single nod, then turned back to the struggling man.

'Take him.'

The soldiers dragged him away, pulling him toward the embankment as the man's protests broke into something shriller, pleading.

'No, wait, please, I have money! I have a family! Please…please!'

The Centurion followed and drew his gladius, the moonlight glinting off the steel as he pressed the tip of the blade against the man's stomach.

The man sobbed a final desperate plea, but his protestations fell on deaf ears and as everyone watched in horror, the Centurion thrust his gladius into the victim's soft flesh.

The man gasped in agony, his eyes wide with shock. The gladius twisted, then withdrew, leaving him to crumple onto the ground, his blood soaking into the thirsty earth.

Julius's fingers tightened on the reins, his breath quickening with barely contained fury, but before he could move, a hand clamped down on his wrist.

'Don't,' hissed Marcus. 'There's nothing you can do.'

The Centurion wiped his blade clean, sheathed it, and turned back to the line as if nothing had happened.

'Next.'

Julius and Marcus eased their horses forward, the hooves striking against the stone road with measured rhythm. The Centurion turned to face them, his expression hard and impassive. He was a veteran, that much was obvious, not just from the scar running down his jaw but from the way he held himself, the way he seemed to command fear without raising his voice. He stepped forward, eyes flicking from Julius to Marcus before settling on their horses, their quality unmistakable.

'Names,' he said flatly, looking back up.

Julius forced his body to relax, though his pulse hammered in his throat. Fear was weakness, and weakness invited suspicion.

'I am Gaius Julius Caesar, travelling to Mevania, and this is my cousin, Marcus Antonius Gracchus.'

The Centurion's eyes narrowed slightly at the names, but he said nothing. Instead, he turned to the scribe who had sealed the previous man's fate. He was already running his finger down the parchment.

Julius stood still, his heartbeat loud in his ears. Beside him, Marcus remained silent, his hand twitching near his belt, as if resisting the urge to rest it on his dagger.

'Purpose of travel?' the Centurion asked.

'Family business,' said Julius.

The Centurion's lips twitched slightly, whether in amusement or scepticism, Julius couldn't tell.

'Family business,' he repeated before gesturing vaguely toward the road behind them. 'You came from Rome?'

'Yes.'

'And yet you travel at night with no servants, no guards?'

Julius gave a small, well-practiced smile.

'The heat of the day disagrees with me,' he replied, 'and as for guards and servants, these are tough times, Centurion, and they cost money.'

The Centurion didn't return the smile. He glanced at their horses again, fine animals, too fine for a casual journey.

'You seem well-equipped for a simple family visit.'

'We are taking them to my uncle.' said Julius smoothly. 'He is a horse trader and asked me to deliver them.'

The Centurion studied him. He wasn't an idiot, he was probing, testing for cracks in their story. But Julius had spent enough time visiting Rome's courts to know when to talk and when to hold his tongue. The Centurion held his gaze for a long moment before turning to Marcus.

'And you? What's your business in Mevania?'

'The horse trader is my father,' said Marcus, embellishing the lie, 'and I haven't seen him for a long time.'

The Centurion stared, then turned to the scribe, waiting for a decision. The official consulted his scroll again, his finger trailing painfully slow over the names. He frowned slightly, then looked up.

'Their names are not here.'

Julius barely resisted the urge to exhale. Obviously, any updated list containing his name had not yet reached the outpost. The Centurion gave them both another long, searching look before finally stepping back.

'You are free to go but if I was you, I would start travelling in the day. There are many desperate men at large, and the likes of you would not last a minute against them.'

Julius gave a curt nod.

'We will. Thank you.'

He glanced across at Marcus before setting off at a measured pace, resisting the urge to gallop until the checkpoint was well behind them and only when the torches had faded into the distance did they both dare to breath normally.

'That was close,' said Marcus.

Julius didn't respond immediately. He was staring ahead, his mind racing. His name was not on the list… yet. But how long would that last? Sulla's reach extended farther than Rome, and this journey was only just beginning.

Chapter Seven

Etruria

The Via Flaminia stretched before them, a straight, unwavering line of stone and dust, cutting through the rolling hills of Etruria. The road was wide enough for two carts to pass side by side, its surface worn smooth by centuries of travellers. The edges were lined with milestones, each one marking the distance from Rome, a silent reminder of the world they had left behind.

To their left, the landscape rolled gently into golden fields and olive groves. To their right, the distant silhouette of a walled town sat atop a hill, its terracotta rooftops glowing in the fading light. Thin wisps of smoke curled from chimneys, and even from a distance, they could hear the faint hum of a market winding down for the evening.

Julius reined in his horse and reached beneath his cloak, pulling out a small parchment. The edges were worn and creased from the journey, the ink slightly smudged. He unrolled it carefully, scanning the directions written in his mother's precise Latin script. Marcus slowed his own horse beside him.

'What does it say?'

Julius's eyes flicked over the words.

'Past the town, take the third turning off the road, towards the low hills.' He looked up, scanning the terrain.

'About another mile,' he said, and urged his horse forward, leading them past the outskirts of the town. A few farmers and merchants walked the roadside, their heads lowered, their thoughts on the evening ahead. No one paid the two young riders much attention, just another pair of dust-covered travellers.

A mile past the town, they turned off the road and onto a track barely wide enough for a cart. The hills rose around them, covered in a patchwork of olive groves, vineyards, and low stone walls and the scent of wild thyme filled the air. The further they rode, the quieter the world became as the distant sounds of the town faded, replaced by the rustling of the wind through the trees.

An hour passed, and then, as they crested a gentle rise, they saw the villa they sought nestled against the edge of a small olive forest, its whitewashed walls glowing in the evening sun. The red-tiled roof was partially obscured by the surrounding trees, but it was unmistakably the place described in his mother's letter. It was not a grand estate, but neither was it a simple farmhouse.

Julius pulled out the parchment again, double-checking the details.

'This is it,' he said and nudged his horse forward. They rode down the hill and into the courtyard, the sound of their horses' hooves echoing against the stone.

The courtyard lay still, save for the faint rustling of the olive trees in the evening breeze. The air smelled of hay and the lingering scent of smoke from a fire long since burned out.

Julius and Marcus dismounted, their boots thudding onto the stone slabs. Marcus, ever cautious, let his fingers rest near the hilt of his dagger, his eyes sweeping the villa's darkened windows and the surrounding tree line. Something felt wrong.

The place was certainly lived in, Julius could see the stacked firewood against the villa's outer wall, the faint outline of fresh cart tracks on the slabs, but the silence was unnatural. No servants, no welcoming voice, no sign of movement save for the slow sway of the trees.

Then, as they watched, the barn door creaked open and two figures emerged, each holding a pitchfork.

The older man was thick-set and broad-shouldered, his tunic streaked with dirt and sweat, his grip firm on the wooden handle of his weapon. The younger one, perhaps his son, was leaner, but his stance mirrored his father's. The boy's knuckles whitened around the shaft of the pitchfork, his dark eyes flicking between the two strangers.

'Who are you?' asked the older man, his voice edged with

suspicion. 'What are you doing here?'

Julius kept his posture calm, though his mind was already calculating. The moment could turn dangerous in an instant. If they had the wrong villa and these men were loyal to Sulla, revealing their identities could doom them both. But if they had reached the right place, caution would only waste time. He chose his words carefully.

'We are travellers,' he said calmly. 'Seeking shelter for the night.'

The man's eyes narrowed.

'Travellers don't ride into private courtyards uninvited.'

Julius could feel the tension in the air, the coiled readiness of men prepared to defend their home. The wrong word here, the slightest misstep, and they might be forced to fight their way out. He reached slowly beneath his cloak, his fingers brushing against the parchment hidden there. This was a risk, but there was no other way.

'I am seeking Titus Varro,' he said at last. 'My mother sends her regards.'

'Your mother?' His voice was cautious, suspicious. 'What's her name?'

'Aurelia Cotta,' replied Julius. 'I believe you knew her.'

The man stiffened slightly. His son, still gripping his pitchfork, glanced up at him, searching for guidance. Julius saw the faintest flicker of recognition in the older man's eyes. The name meant something to him, but that was not the same as trust.

'Aurelia's son?' he asked, voice low.

Julius gave a single nod.

'I can prove it.'

Slowly, deliberately, he lifted his arm and offered the note to the man, the wax seal that bore the mark of his family, broken, but still clear.

A long pause followed, then, at last, the man reached for it. His fingers were rough, scarred by years of labour, but they handled the parchment carefully. He broke looked at the seal and unfolded the note, his eyes scanning the words written inside. His lips moved slightly as he read. Eventually the tension in his shoulders eased and he lowered the pitchfork.

'Come inside,' he said. 'You'll be safe here. Lucius, take their horses.'

He turned toward the villa's entrance, while his son moved toward the horses, taking the reins, though he still cast wary glances at their unexpected guests.

Julius met Marcus's gaze briefly before nodding and following the man inside.

The villa's interior was simple but well-kept. Stone walls lined with wooden beams, a central hearth, and a long table with sturdy benches.

Titus motioned for them to sit.

'You've had a long journey. I'll get you something to eat.'

Julius and Marcus lowered themselves onto a bench and a few minutes later, Titus returned with a wooden tray carrying bread, olives, and a bowl of lentil stew. A jug of watered wine followed, the scent of sour grapes filling the air.

Marcus wasted no time, tearing a hunk of bread and dipping it into the stew. Julius, though hungry, kept his focus on Titus. The older man sat across from them, staring at the two young men

'Tell me,' he said, 'what's happening in Rome?'

'Sulla is cleansing the city,' said Julius, finally breaking off a piece of bread. 'His proscriptions grow worse by the day. The Forum is filled with heads on spikes, and his men hunt down anyone who stood with Marius. Senators, knights, even merchants suspected of disloyalty, all dead. We barely made it past the roadblocks.'

Titus sighed.

'That's why I was cautious outside. Sulla's spies are everywhere.' He tapped the table lightly. 'You may trust a man for years, but the promise of gold or a clean record can change him in an instant. One word from the wrong mouth, and the next thing you know,' he slid a finger across his throat.

Julius nodded grimly and dipped the bread into the soup. He had seen it happen too many times already.

'Your father was a good friend to me,' continued Titus, 'and I will gladly help but you can't stay here.'

Julius looked up.

'You mean to turn us away?'

'Not exactly.' Titus took another sip of wine. 'This place is safe for now, but if anyone saw you arrive, word will spread. I know somewhere better, but we will wait until morning. You'll stay here for the night and at first light, we'll find you somewhere safer.'

Julius studied him for a moment, weighing his options. He had no reason to distrust the man, his mother had sent him here after all. Still, in these times, trust was a luxury. Finally, he gave a slow nod.

'Very well.'

Titus pushed back his chair and stood.

'You need to rest while you can. When you've eaten your fill, I'll take you to your room.'

Ten minutes later he led them down a narrow corridor lit by a single oil lamp. The room was small but clean, with two simple wooden beds with woollen blankets folded at the foot of each. A narrow window let in the faint sound of crickets outside.

'It's not much,' said Titus, 'but it's better than the ground.'

'We've slept in worse places,' said Marcus.

Titus nodded, lingering in the doorway.

'Lock the door behind you, I'll wake you at dawn.'

Once he had left, Marcus closed the door, sliding the wooden bolt into place before dropping onto one of the beds with an exaggerated groan.

'Gods, finally. A real bed.'

Julius sat on the edge of his own, removing his boots, his mind still racing. They had a place to sleep for the night, but the real question was could they trust Titus, or would they wake to the sound of Sullan soldiers surrounding the villa. It was a question that really needed answering, but for now he was just too tired and within minutes, both men were fast asleep, their fate in the hands of a stranger they had only just met.

Chapter Eight

Etruria

A soft knock on the door stirred Julius from sleep. He sat up, blinking against the faint glow of a lantern filtering through the cracks in the wooden door.

'Wake up,' a voice whispered from the other side. 'It's time.'

Marcus groaned beside him, shifting under the woollen blanket.

'Already?' he muttered, rubbing the sleep from his eyes.

Julius swung his legs over the side of the bed, his muscles aching from the many days of hard riding. There was no time for comfort, and he rose, fastening his cloak as Marcus reluctantly followed.

Outside the room, the villa was silent, the world beyond still trapped in the grey hush of predawn. A lone servant waited in the corridor. He motioned for them to follow, and they were led to the kitchen, where the warm scent of fresh bread filled the air.

Titus was already seated at the wooden table, alongside his wife, a woman with kind but tired eyes. Julius and Marcus took their seats as a modest meal was placed before them, bread, cheese, and a bowl of barley porridge.

They ate in silence, each man lost in his own thoughts. Outside, the first faint stirrings of dawn were beginning, though the sky beyond the small kitchen window remained dark.

After a while, Titus broke the silence.

'Once you are done, Lucius will take you into the hills. There's a place there, not far, but far enough. You'll be safe there.'

His wife placed a small leather pack on the table, carefully tied with twine.

'Enough food for a couple of days,' she said softly. 'We will send more when we can.'

Julius took the bundle with a grateful nod.

'Thank you.'

Titus reached into his belt and produced a small leather purse, the weight of it unmistakable as he set it down in front of Julius. Silver.

Julius stared at it, frowning.

'I can't take this.'

You can, and you will, said Titus. I served alongside your father, he was like a brother to me. He gave a small, knowing smirk. 'If it eases your pride, you can pay me back, when you can.'

Julius hesitated, then picked up the purse and tucked it into his cloak. Before anything more could be said, the door creaked open, and Titus's son stepped inside.

'The horses are ready,' he said.

Julius and Marcus rose, gathering their cloaks around them. A final nod was exchanged, a silent understanding passing between them.

'Thank you,' said Julius, his voice quieter than usual. 'I will never forget your kindness.'

Titus clapped him once on the shoulder.

'Just go, and make sure you stay ahead of Sulla's men.'

They stepped out into the cold predawn air, where their horses waited, saddled and ready. The sky above was still deep blue-grey, the first hints of dawn barely touching the eastern horizon. The air smelled of dew and pine, the distant hoot of an owl the only sound breaking the quiet.

Julius and Marcus mounted up. They exchanged final glances with Titus and his wife, offering grateful farewells, then, with a final nod from Titus's son, they turned their horses toward the forested hills.

The path westward was rough, barely more than a hunter's trail, winding between patches of dense oak and pine. For hours, they travelled in near silence with only birdsong echoing through the trees.

By midday, they had reached higher ground, where the trees

thinned, and the valley below stretched wide and distant. From here, they could see Etruria, hazy in the far-off heat. It looked peaceful from this distance, a stark contrast to the bloodshed and chaos of Rome.

They rode on, the terrain growing steeper, until finally, in the late afternoon, they emerged into a clearing. A small hut stood nestled against the edge of the trees. It was simple but sturdy, made of stone and timber, its roof thick with dried thatch. Nearby, a stream trickled over smooth rocks, cutting a path down toward the valley.

Lucius dismounted.

'This is it, he said, you'll be safe here.'

Julius slid from his horse, taking in the surroundings with a pragmatic eye. The location was good, elevated with a clear view of the valley below. If anyone came looking for them, they'd see them first. Marcus, however, wrinkled his nose.

'Gods, it stinks.'

'It's used by goat herders,' said Lucius. 'The stream will give you fresh water and you can hunt for fresh meat. There are plenty of deer and hares up here, but I'll come every few days with supplies. Stay out of sight, and don't do anything stupid.' He mounted his horse without waiting for a reply and rode back down the trail, leaving them alone in the silent clearing.

Julius walked toward the hut's door, giving it a firm push. Inside, the stench of goats was overwhelming. The floor was layered with old straw, droppings, and the remnants of whatever filth the previous occupant had left behind. Marcus stopped at the threshold, staring in disgust.

'You know,' he said with a sigh, 'it's amazing how much I suddenly miss Rome.'

For the next hour, they worked in silence, dragging old straw and filth outside, sweeping the floor with makeshift brooms of pine branches, and chasing out two startled rats that had taken up residence in the corners. By the time they were done, the air was mercifully fresher, though the faint scent of goat still clung stubbornly to the walls.

Marcus collapsed onto the now-clean floor, wiping his forehead.

'That was the worst hour of my life,' he moaned.

Julius ignored him, rolling out his sleeping mat near the wall. His mind was already turning, calculating their next move. Marcus watched him for a moment, then shook his head.

'You're already planning, aren't you?'

'We can't stay here forever,' replied Julius, sitting down onto his makeshift bed. 'Sulla will fall one day, but we need to be ready for when it happens.'

Marcus looked across and sighed.

'I don't know how you do it, Julius, I really don't We just spent the afternoon shovelling goat shit, and you're already plotting your return to Rome.'

Julius glanced over.

'That's because I don't intend staying in these hills any longer than I have to.'

Marcus shook his head and stretched out on his own mat.

'Well,' he said, 'when you march triumphantly into the city as a conquering hero, remind me to get a proper bed. That is, if you don't get us both killed before then.'

Julius lay back, staring at the roof above.

'I can't promise that,' he said quietly, 'but I'll certainly try my best.'

Miles to the south, on the outskirts of Rome, Lucius Cornelius Sulla sat at a heavy cedarwood table, one hand resting on a long scroll of names, his proscriptions. The names of men already hunted, executed, or exiled were marked in thick strokes of ink. Some had been crossed out entirely, others remained. His sharp eyes scanned the list, pausing halfway down and he read the name aloud, *Gaius Julius Caesar*. He exhaled slowly and looked up at the stern-faced officer standing before him.

'Any sight of him?' he asked.

The officer shook his head.

'No, Domine. No trace.'

A muscle in Sulla's jaw twitched. He had allowed the boy to live against his better judgment now the little bastard had fled, and Sulla did not tolerate defiance.

'Forget the others for now. Focus on Caesar. I want him found. Assign extra men if needed but I want him dragged back to Rome. If he resists, kill him.'

The officer gave a curt nod.

'It will be done, Domine,' said the officer, and turned sharply to stride from the chamber.

By midday, a century of legionaries moved through the Subura, the district where Julius's family resided, the air thick with the sounds of soldiers hammering on doors, barking questions at terrified residents.

In the atrium of the Julii villa, Aurelia and Cornelia sat in the cool shade, their hands resting lightly in their laps. They did not move, they did not speak. Before them, loomed a grizzled Centurion, his patience wearing thin.

'Where is he?' he demanded again.

Aurelia met his gaze without blinking.

'I told you, I do not know.'

The officer scowled and took a step closer.

'Do you know what happens to those who defy Sulla?'

Cornelia's hands clenched in her lap, but Aurelia remained unmoved.

'We are not defying Sulla,' she said calmly. 'We simply do not know where my son is.'

The Centurion's lips curled into a sneer.

'Lies. Perhaps I should drag you to the Tullianum. Maybe after a few hours in a cell, you'll remember something useful.'

A tense silence fell over the room but before Aurelia could respond, a soldier burst into the atrium, breathing hard from exertion. He saluted swiftly before speaking.

'Domine, someone has talked. A merchant's slave heard rumours of two young men leaving Rome many nights ago. Heading north to Etruria.'

The Centurion turned back to face the two women.

'We're done here for now,' he said, 'but don't think this is over,' and with the heavy sound of sandals on marble, he turned away, leaving the two women alone in the gloom.

Aurelia waited until the last man was gone, listening for the final clash of iron gates as they closed. The villa was silent once more and only then did she exhale and turned to a nearby servant.

'Bring me a parchment and a reed pen,' she ordered. 'I need to send a letter.'

The girl bowed quickly and hurried away.

Aurelia's face remained calm, but her mind was already calculating the next move.
Julius had probably made it to Etruria by now, but Sulla's reach was long, and she needed to make sure her son stayed ahead of it.

Chapter Nine

Etruria

The wind rattled the wooden shutters of the hut as Julius and Marcus sat in silence. Outside, the forest stretched dark and endless, the trees swaying beneath the weight of the coming storm. Two weeks had passed since they had first arrived in the hut, but that arrangement had just come crashing down when Lucius had brought them devastating news.

'*Sulla's men are in the town. They are looking for you by name.*'

Marcus broke the silence first, rolling his dagger between his fingers.

'So, that's it then. No more food, no more supplies. No more friendly faces.'

Julius exhaled slowly, his eyes still fixed on the fire.

'We knew this couldn't last forever.'

'Aye,' muttered Julius. 'But I was getting used to fresh eggs.'

Julius didn't smile, Lucius had risked too much for them already. Now, he and his family would have to pretend they had never harboured fugitives and if Sulla's men had any suspicions, they wouldn't hesitate to make an example of them.

Marcus stretched his legs out with a sigh.

'It's only a matter of time before someone gives us up, Julius. If we stay here, we're as good as dead.'

'Then we don't stay,' said Julius, simply.

'You say that like we've got somewhere to go.'

'We do,' replied Julius, reaching into his tunic and pulling out the small piece of parchment. 'One last contact. One last address.'

Marcus sat forward, frowning.

'Who?'

'A man named Merula. He was an old ally of my father and Marius.'

'And where exactly is this *Merula*?'

Julius ran his finger along the rough map scrawled beneath the name.

'Deep in the Sabine Hills. South-east of here, near Amiternum.'

Marcus let out a slow breath.

'That's at least eighty miles, Julius, and we can't take the main roads. We should go north, away from the Sullan patrols.'

'I know,' said Julius, 'but we have no allies in that direction. If we keep to the mountain paths, we should keep ahead of them.'

Marcus studied him for a long moment. Then he gave a small, resigned shake of his head.

'Gods, I must be mad for following you.'

Julius smiled and looked toward the bolted door. Outside, the wind had picked up, the first drops of rain tapping against the thatched roof.

'At first light, then?'

Marcus nodded, knowing neither would get much sleep that night.

'First light it is.'

The first light of dawn was little more than a grey murmur on the horizon when Julius pushed open the wooden door of the hut. The storm had passed in the night, leaving the ground slick with rain. The wind had quieted, but a lingering chill still clung to the morning, curling about his exposed hands as he stepped outside.

Marcus was already tending to the horses, brushing them down and checking the straps of their saddles. The beasts had been restless through the storm, and the tired lines on Marcus' face told Julius that his friend had spent more time calming them than sleeping.

'They're as ready as they'll ever be,' muttered Marcus, tightening the last of the buckles. 'If we push them, we might cover twenty miles before we have to stop.'

Julius nodded, his mind turning over the risks, the possibilities. Sulla's men were getting closer, their net tightening. They had to move fast.

Marcus adjusted his cloak and pulled the hood over his head.

'Are you sure about this Merula?'

Julius hesitated. His mother had spoken of him once or twice, an old friend of his father, a loyal Marian, but years had passed, and in these dangerous times, a man's allegiances could shift like the tides. Still, it was a chance. Their only chance.

'I'm sure enough,' he said. 'If he's loyal, he'll help us. If not…' He left the words hanging in the cold morning air.

Marcus grunted, swinging himself up into the saddle.

'If not, our heads will be on spikes above the forum in days.'

Julius mounted his own horse, tightening his grip on the reins.

'Then let's make sure we stay ahead of them.' With one last glance at the hut that had sheltered them, he nudged his horse forward, leading the way into the misty forest before them.

Back in Rome, the kitchen of the Julii villa was filled with the warm scent of fresh bread and crushed herbs, but neither woman had the appetite to eat. Outside, Rome bustled as it always did, the sounds of merchants haggling, of sandals scuffing against cobbled streets, of carts rattling over stone. But inside these walls, a much quieter war was being fought.

Aurelia dipped her reed pen into a jar of black ink, her movements deliberate and controlled. She had always prided herself on her ability to remain calm in moments of crisis, but this was different. This was her son's life.

She wrote carefully, the names forming a neat list in dark, flowing Latin. Across from her, Cornelia sat with her hands folded, her brow furrowed in worry.

'It's only a matter of time before they catch him,' Cornelia murmured.

Aurelia's pen did not pause, but her lips pressed together tightly.

'I know,' she admitted. 'Which is why we must act now.'

Cornelia glanced at the unfinished list, biting her lower lip. 'And if we fail?'

Aurelia set the pen down and met her daughter-in-law's gaze.

'We will not fail, Cornelia. It is not an option.'

Cornelia sighed, but she said nothing more and for a long time, the only sound in the kitchen was the quiet scratch of ink on parchment. Finally, Aurelia leaned back, inspecting the list with a critical eye. Cornelia reached for it and began to read aloud.

'Quintus Lutatius Catulus... Marcus Aemilius Lepidus... Gaius Aurelius Cotta...' There were more but she read the rest in silence. Finally, she looked up and frowned. 'This isn't enough.'

Aurelia knew she was right. The names on the list were influential, but influence meant little in the face of fear. Rome belonged to Sulla now, and men who once walked with pride and ambition now stepped carefully, afraid to attract his notice. Many of these names would hesitate, some would refuse. Others might even betray them to save themselves. But they had to do something. Cornelia's voice was tense when she spoke again.

'Sulla has the power of life and death over Rome. We need more than this.'

Aurelia stared at her daughter in law, her mind working before finally, her lips curved slightly, a slow, knowing smile forming at the edges.

Cornelia caught the change immediately.

'What is it?'

Aurelia's eyes glittered in the lamplight.

'Sometimes,' she said smoothly, 'it takes a woman's touch.'

Cornelia's frown deepened.

'What does that mean?'

Aurelia rose from her seat with deliberate grace, brushing her hands against the fabric of her fine but modest tunic. She moved to the corner of the kitchen, where a bronze mirror hung upon the wall. Adjusting the golden pins in her hair, she regarded her own reflection for a moment.

'Where are you going?' Cornelia asked, suddenly uneasy.

Aurelia turned, fastening her cloak with a simple brooch.

'Start reaching out to those on the list, Cornelia. Call in favours, remind them who Julius is, and who he will become.'

Cornelia stood, gripping the parchment tightly.

'And you?'

Aurelia picked up a thin silver bracelet, fastening it around her wrist.

'A single man may hold complete control over Rome, Cornelia,' she said, adjusting her cloak, 'but never underestimate the power of the women who whisper in his ear.'

Cornelia's stomach tightened. She had no idea who Aurelia was planning to visit, but something told her that Sulla himself would not like it. Aurelia gave her one last glance, then stepped toward the doorway, disappearing into the dim corridors of the villa.

Back in the north, the days stretched endlessly for Julius and Marcus as they pressed toward the Sabine hills. Forced onto hidden paths to evade Sulla's patrols, their journey wound through dense forests of twisted oaks and ancient boulders, silent remnants of a time before Rome. Travel was slow, supplies were scarce, and scavenging had become their way of life. The road itself felt like a prison, each day blending into the next and by the time they neared their destination, the weight of exhaustion was matched only by the fragile hope that relief was finally within reach.

Julius reined in his horse at the crest of a hill, gazing down at the river below.

'There's the river,' he said. 'The house is half a day's ride north of the bridge.'

'Then let's get moving,' said Marcus. 'I can almost taste a hot meal already.'

They nudged their horses forward, the thought of safety driving them onward. But as the hours passed and they finally arrived at the estate Julius' mother had directed them to, all hope withered.

The villa was a ruin. Its walls stood blackened by fire, its roof collapsed. The once-proud courtyard fountain was choked with ash, and the olive groves, once teeming with life, lay abandoned, their soil scarred by the imprint of heavy boots, Roman boots.

There were no bodies. No signs of life. Whoever had lived here was either dead, captured, or long gone.

Julius remained motionless atop his dust-covered horse, his expression unreadable as he took in the destruction.

Marcus swung down from his horse, kicking at a fallen roof tile, a small cloud of ash rising into the air.

'So, what now?' he asked.

Julius didn't answer immediately. He simply stared at the ruins, the weight of their situation pressing down on him. They were fugitives, Rome was closed to them, and now, even its outskirts offered no refuge.

Eventually, with no choice but to keep moving, they turned their horses southward, hoping to find shelter deeper in the Sabine hills.

Days blurred into nights as they wandered the hills, moving from one abandoned farm to another. Each place they found was the same, empty, desolate, stripped of anything useful, their owners obviously Populares supporters discovered by Sulla's henchmen.

The cold settled deep in their bones, hunger gnawed at their resolve, and the silence of the wilderness pressed in on them like a heavy shroud. The isolation was relentless, the nights stretching long and uneasy.

As they camped in a ravine beneath the skeletal branches of bare trees, Julius stared into the darkness, his senses sharpening. The usual sounds of the night, distant owls, the whisper of leaves, had changed. Something was out there.

He exchanged a glance with Marcus, who had also gone still, his hand drifting toward the hilt of his sword. The fire flickered low, casting shifting shadows across the rocks. The sounds weren't those of animals, they were footsteps, careful and deliberate… they were not alone.

Julius reached for his dagger just as the first figure emerged from the darkness but within moments, they were surrounded.

The men wore mismatched tunics, their cloaks patched and weathered, but their bearing was unmistakable. Soldiers. Not legionaries, not anymore, but still dangerous. Their hands rested on the hilts of their weapons, and their eyes gleamed with suspicion. The leader glanced at their meagre camp, then at Julius and Marcus, his gaze lingering.

'Fugitives?' he asked, voice rough with disinterest, though his posture was anything but relaxed.

Marcus straightened, his fingers twitching near his sword.

'We're travellers,' he said evenly.

The man snorted.

'Is that so? Doesn't look like you've had much luck on the road.' He cast a slow look at their dirty cloaks, the half-eaten scraps of bread beside the fire. 'Not many honest men sleep in ravines these days. There are more and more rats scurrying from Sulla's justice, though.'

The implication was clear. Julius could feel the weight of Marcus' readiness beside him, his body tensed like a coiled spring, waiting for the inevitable fight. He raised a hand.

'We don't want any trouble.'

The leader smirked.

'No one ever does.' He nodded to his men, who shifted closer, hands poised over their weapons.

There was no doubt now, these men didn't know who he was, but they suspected enough. If they took them back to the wrong camp, if the wrong officer asked too many questions, their lives would be worth nothing. Julius reached into his cloak, moving slow.

'Perhaps we can come to an arrangement?'

The leader arched a brow but didn't stop him. Julius withdrew a small leather pouch, the weight of it lighter than he would have liked. He untied the cord, letting the dull gleam of silver catch the firelight, what remained of the purse given to him by his mother back in Rome.

A silence stretched between them and the men shifted, their wary expressions flickering with interest.

Julius tossed the purse to the leader, who caught it easily, weighing it in his palm. He glanced at his men, then at Julius.

'You've bought yourself a day,' he said eventually. 'After that, if we see you again, you're fair game.'

Julius inclined his head, masking his relief.

The leader gestured to his men, and just as swiftly as they had come, they melted back into the darkness.

Marcus exhaled sharply.

'That was close.'

Julius watched the shadows fade before responding.

'We need to move. Now.'

'To where?' snapped Marcus. 'We are running out of options and Sulla's men are everywhere.'

'There is one more place,' said Julius. 'Somewhere even Sulla cannot reach.' He turned to stare at his lifelong friend. 'We head east.'

Marcus stared back.

'East?' he said, 'to Greece?'

'No.' replied Julius. 'To Asia Minor, Bithynia to be exact. Nicomedes of Bithynia owed my father a favour once. I think it's time he repaid it.'

Marcus stared at him in disbelief.

77

'You're talking about leaving Italy and going to the East, where Rome has more enemies than friends? Where the first Roman noble spotted without an army ends up dead.' Marcus shook his head in astonishment. 'That's your plan?'

'It's better than running in circles through these gods-forsaken hills, waiting to be caught and executed,' snapped Julius.

'You're serious about this, aren't you?' said Marcus.

'Yes.'

'And if it goes wrong? If we end up in chains, or worse?'

Julius exhaled, watching the fire flicker.

'Then we die trying to take control of our fate. Instead of waiting for it to take us.'

Marcus let out a low laugh, shaking his head.

'Gods, you always were ambitious, but this is something else altogether.'

A long silence stretched between them as the wind stirred the branches above, whispering through the darkened hills. Finally, Marcus sighed.

'Fine,' he said, 'let's go to the East but I need to sleep. At least let me have one last night of suffering in these hills.'

'We can't,' said Julius. 'You heard what he said. In one day, we will once again become quarry, but this time, they know where we are. We have to go now.'

Marcus sighed and looked towards his tethered horse before muttering something about 'damn madmen with grand ideas' before bending to pack his bedroll.

Chapter Ten

Sulla's Villa

Aurelia and Cornelia stood before the man who ruled Rome with an iron will, their hands clasped, their backs straight. They had come as mothers, as wives, but most of all, as women who would not let their futures be dictated by fear alone.

On the heavy wooden table between them, parchments lay scattered, their wax seals broken. They bore the names of some of Rome's most powerful families, senators, knights, generals, even those who had once fought at Sulla's side. Each one pleaded for mercy for Gaius Julius Caesar.

Sulla had read them all, one by one, his face growing darker with every page. His fingers, calloused from war, crumpled the edge of one parchment, his teeth grinding behind thin, pale lips.

With a snarl of rage, Sulla seized the petitions in his hands and flung them across the chamber. The parchments scattered like falling leaves, some landing at Aurelia's feet.

'This is an insult!' he roared.

Cornelia flinched, her nails digging into her palms. But Aurelia did not move.

Sulla's gaze burned into them, his fingers digging into the arm of his chair.

'Do you take me for a fool? Do you think I rule Rome with a soft heart?' His voice was venom. 'You waste the ink of senators, the breath of nobles, for a boy who is nothing!'

'He is not nothing,' replied Aurelia. 'He is his father's son, a man of Rome, a man of…'

'A man of trouble!' Sulla snapped, rising to his feet. He leaned forward, pressing his fists into the table. 'Take your pathetic letters and go. Before I decide to put your names on the lists beside his.'

Cornelia stepped back, blinking rapidly, her composure fraying. But Aurelia remained steadfastly in place.

'You are still here?' said Sulla ominously. 'You are playing a dangerous game, woman.'

Cornelia hesitated, looking back.

'Mother, come, we have to go.'

Aurelia lifted a hand without taking her eyes off Sulla.

'You go. I have unfinished business here.'

Cornelia's breath caught.

'But… '

'Go,' Aurelia said again, her voice calm but commanding.

Cornelia's gaze darted between her mother-in-law and the dictator, but she knew Aurelia well enough to obey when she used that tone. Slowly, she stepped toward the doors.

Sulla's fingers twitched against the table. He had stood on battlefields, watched cities burn, executed thousands with the stroke of his pen. And yet, before him now stood a single woman who refused to bow, beg or break.

When the doors finally closed behind Cornelia, Sulla exhaled sharply, shaking his head.

'By the gods… you are either the bravest woman in Rome or the most foolish.'

Aurelia met his gaze without hesitation.

'I am neither,' she said. 'I am just a mother.'

Sulla let out a short, sharp laugh.

'And what, pray, do mothers think they can teach me in this situation?'

Aurelia stepped forward, her voice steady, measured.

'That Rome was built by men like you,' she said, 'but it will outlast you. And the sons you choose to spare will be the ones who decide what your legacy will be.'

Sulla's smirk wavered, a silence stretching between them. Aurelia let it linger just long enough before she spoke again, her tone soft but unyielding.

'Julius is young, and has a lot to learn, but he is no fool. Neither is he a threat to you, unless you make him one. Even your own men whisper of his potential. He has a mind as sharp as a legionary's blade, and a tongue that could stir an army to follow him into the underworld itself. What better servant to Rome than a man with both the intelligence to command and the wisdom to wait?'

Sulla's fingers tapped idly against the armrest of his chair. He said nothing.

'You have already won Rome, Sulla,' she continued. 'No one questions that. But even the greatest victories require careful hands to shape what comes after. And one day, perhaps, a man like Julius may yet serve you, not in exile, not in death, but by strengthening the Republic you claim to protect.'

The room was silent, save for the distant crackle of torches until eventually, a sound made them both look again towards the ornate door and Sulla narrowed his eyes as a figure stepped inside. A hush fell over the chamber, as if even the gods had paused to listen. In front of them stood the most powerful woman in Rome, the Virgo Maxima.

The High Vestal Virgin moved with quiet authority, her white robes flowing like water over marble, the sacred fillets of wool woven into her hair gleaming in the lamplight.

No one spoke. No one dared, and the weight of her presence settled over the room like a blade held just above the throat.

She did not look at Sulla first, she turned to Aurelia and smiled, but when she finally turned to the dictator to speak, her voice was like wind through the temple halls, soft, ethereal and undeniable.

'Lucius Cornelius Sulla,' she said, 'I have come to speak of mercy.'

The words seemed to suspend time itself.

Sulla exhaled sharply, his jaw tightening, but he did not interrupt as the Vestal took one step closer.

'You have saved Rome,' she murmured, 'and you have purged its enemies. You have restored order, and you have won your war.' She paused. 'But Rome is still bleeding.'

A shadow flickered in Sulla's eyes.

'You are the Republic's sword,' she continued, 'but Rome is not a blade alone. It is stone, it is law, it is sacrifice and it is people. And now the gods look down upon you to see how you manage so many parts.'

Sulla's fingers stilled.

'This boy, Gaius Julius Caesar, is but a single thread in the great tapestry of Rome. He is ambitious, yes. But youth is a thing not yet formed, Sulla. A thing still malleable. It is a sad fact that violence has its place, but so too does mercy. And when both have passed, only legacy remains.'

She took a slow step back, her expression lightening just a fraction.

'You are Rome's ruler, and the decision is yours alone to make, but know this, we, the Sisters of Vesta, stand with the petition and hereby beg your pardon of Gaius Julius Caesar.' With that, she smiled one last time, turned, and glided out of the chamber, her robes once again whispering softly against the marble, the doors closing behind her with a soft but resolute thud.

Outside the Chamber, Cornelia watched as the priestess passed, her breath catching in her throat until minutes later, Aurelia emerged from the chamber.

Cornelia rushed to her side.

'Mother,' she gasped, her words tumbling out. 'What happened in there? How did you get the Virgin to come? Did he agree? Where are you going?'

Aurelia turned, her voice light, triumphant.

'I am going to write more letters,' she said. 'Hundreds of them.'

Cornelia's heart pounded.

'You mean… ?'

Aurelia nodded.

'We did it, Cornelia, Sulla has pardoned my son. Now we just need to spread the word.'

Chapter Eleven

The Road to Brundisium

The Via Appia had carried them south for days, winding through the countryside, past olive groves, vineyards, and quiet towns that seemed untouched by the violence consuming Rome. But as they crested the final hill, the world opened up before them, and for the first time, Julius laid eyes on the greatest port in Italy. Brundisium.

It sprawled out along the coastline, its harbour bristling with warships, their tall masts standing like a forest of wood against the slate-grey sea. The city itself was a maze of white-stone buildings, its docks stretching into the waters where triremes, quinqueremes, and merchant vessels jostled for space. Even from this distance, he could see the flicker of signals from ships waiting to dock and the constant movement of soldiers and sailors on the piers.

Julius had been to Ostia, Rome's primary port on several occasions. It was a city of commerce, of grain shipments and traders from every corner of the Republic. But Brundisium was something else altogether. Here, legions had departed for Greece, for Africa, for the far reaches of the known world. Here, fleets had been built to crush Carthage, to battle Mithridates, to enforce Rome's will upon the waves. Every plank of wood, every stretch of rope, every nail hammered into these docks had played a part in conquest.

Julius could taste the salt in the air, could hear the deep, groaning creak of ships shifting in the water. Legionaries patrolled the stone breakwaters, their cloaks snapping in the wind, their eyes sharp as they watched every soul who entered the city. It was beautiful… and it was terrifying.

Marcus let out a low whistle beside him.

'By the gods…'

Julius didn't answer. He was still taking it in, the sheer scale of it. The might of Rome, gathered here on the water. But as they rode closer, the awe gave way to unease.

The gates of Brundisium were shut, and outside, stretching along the road, was a vast camp of the desperate and the exiled. Thousands, of people gathered outside the city walls. Not an army, not merchants, but the homeless, the destitute and the starving.

Julius tightened his grip on the reins as they approached, his eyes scanning the crowd. Women clutched thin-wrapped bundles to their chests, old men sat hunched in the dirt, and children with hollow faces moved between the makeshift tents of tattered cloth, their haunted eyes searching for anything to ease their hunger.

Some were Marians, once loyal to the faction his uncle had led, now stripped of their homes and citizenship by Sulla's vengeance. Others were farmers and artisans, men who had lost everything when Sulla had seized their land and given it to his veterans. A few still wore the tatters of legionary tunics, men who had fought in wars but had returned to find their loyalty rewarded with exile.

A Roman woman, her once-fine stola now stained with dust and filth, grasped at Marcus's horse as they passed.

'Please,' she rasped. 'My husband… they took him… I have nothing…'

Marcus jerked the reins, pulling back, there was nothing he could do. The woman stumbled away, and a boy, her son, perhaps, rushed forward to steady her.

'Julius,' he muttered, shifting uneasily in his saddle. 'What is this?'

Julius did not answer immediately. He could only stare. This was not Rome. This was not the Republic he had been raised to believe in, this was something else.

'Come,' he said quietly. 'Let's see if we can find a way inside.'

They continued through the makeshift camp, the stink of unwashed bodies and rotting food thick in the damp sea air. The crowd parted sluggishly as they passed, weary faces glancing up only briefly before looking away. Hope had long since left this place and Marcus shifted uneasily in his saddle.

'This is madness,' he said. 'Why are the gates closed? Brundisium is a port, not a fortress.'

Julius's eyes flicked to the walls. Legionaries stood on the battlements, their red-crested helmets stark against the grey sky. The gates, massive, solid timber, reinforced with iron, stood firmly shut, barring entry to all but the most privileged.

As they neared the entrance, they saw a raised platform, surrounded by a small group of men, petitioners, travellers, merchants, even former soldiers. At the centre of the platform, another Roman official sat on a stool, draped in a fine but travel-worn toga, a wax tablet resting on his lap. His hair was neatly oiled, his posture straight-backed. But it was his expression that struck Julius most, he looked bored, as if he had spent the entire morning listening to pleas he had no intention of granting.

Julius and Marcus dismounted, handing their reins to a boy too weak to be a threat but too desperate to be ignored.

'Watch them,' said Julius, pressing a coin into the boy's palm.

The boy clutched the money greedily, but his wide eyes stayed fixed on the city gates, the legionaries, the official on the stool. Julius followed his gaze. Something was wrong.

They moved toward the front of the platform, standing just behind a man in a tattered cloak, his voice rising in frustration.

'You don't understand, I have family inside! I was born here! I just need to…'

The official on the platform sighed loudly, rolling his shoulders as if this plea, this moment, was nothing more than an inconvenience. He barely lifted a hand, a small, lazy flick of the wrist, but the command was clear.

Two legionaries stepped forward, dragging him back from the platform. He struggled at first, pulling against them, but there was no escape from Roman discipline, only the inevitable realisation that he was utterly powerless.

'Please,' he gasped. 'Please, my wife…my children…'

The official didn't even look at him. He was already turning away, speaking in a low voice to the legionary standing nearby, just as another soldier launched a clenched fist into the pleading man's gut, sending him sprawling to the floor. He gasped and tried to crawl away, his fingers digging into the dust, but a boot crashed into his side, the sound of a breaking rib joining his scream of pain.

The official sighed again, waving for the next petitioner.

Julius exhaled slowly, forcing himself to think. A man had just been severely beaten, his only crime asking to enter his own city, and the official hadn't even bothered to watch. Marcus leaned in, recognising the warning signs in his friend's eyes.

'We are not here to die in the dirt outside Brundisium, Julius. Get control of yourself.'

Julius blinked hard, tearing his gaze away from the crumpled figure on the ground. They still had to get inside but if they waited their turn like the others, if they pleaded for permission like beggars, they could share the same fate.

His resolve hardened and his eyes flicked to the walls, to the man standing above them, the one who had not spoken but who had watched everything with cold detachment. His cloak was heavier than the others, his helmet more ornate. He carried himself like a man who commanded men, not simply one who followed orders. A higher-ranking officer.

Julius turned to Marcus.

'I think I know how we're getting in.'

Marcus frowned.

'How?'

Julius nodded toward the officer above them.

'We speak to the man who actually makes decisions,' and without waiting for an answer, he stepped forward, away from the line, away from the desperate, heading directly for the gate.

Two legionaries at the base of the gates stiffened as Julius approached.

'Get back in line.'

Julius didn't stop.

'I will speak with your officer,' he said.

The legionary's hand moved to his sword.

'No one speaks with the Tribune,' he said. 'Take your petition to the official.'

Julius let out a short breath, feigning amusement.

'Then perhaps you should let him know I am here, and he can decide that for himself.'

The legionary hesitated, eyeing Julius more closely now. A man dressed well, speaking with authority, unafraid, not the usual kind of refugee they were used to dealing with. Above them, the officer on the wall looked down with interest. For a moment, no one spoke, then the officer lifted a hand, giving a simple flick of his fingers and the legionaries stepped aside.

Julius felt Marcus exhale beside him, half in relief, half in disbelief. The climb up the stairway was short, but Julius could feel the weight of a hundred stares on him as they ascended. The moment they stepped onto the wall, the Tribune turned to face them. He was older, perhaps in his mid-forties, his face weathered by years of war. His armour was polished but practical, marked with campaign scars, and his cloak bore the deep red of senior rank. This was no politician's soldier, this was a man who had killed and had bled for Rome.

Julius knew his type. Men like this respected strength, confidence. Anything less was weakness.

'You have my attention,' said the Tribune. 'Now, tell me why I shouldn't have you thrown back into the mud with the others.'

Julius didn't flinch. He met the man's gaze, squared his shoulders, and spoke.

'I am Gaius Julius Caesar,' he said calmly. 'A citizen of Rome, and a son of the Julii, one of the oldest families of the Republic. I am neither a refugee nor a traitor. I travel east on family business, and I will depart from this port, with your permission or without it.'

The officer studied Julius for a long moment, his gaze flicking briefly to Marcus before settling back on him. There was no warmth in his expression, no immediate decision. Only calculation. Then, slowly, he exhaled through his nose.

'You've chosen a poor time to travel, Julius Caesar,' he said at last. 'Rome is split in two, and there are many men who have yet to decide where their loyalties lie.'

Julius met his gaze without blinking.

'Rome's politics are for Rome to settle,' he said evenly. 'My fate lies in the East. And I will get there, one way or another.'

A flicker of amusement crossed the officer's face.

'Bold words for a man on the wrong side of a closed gate. Do you not see the problem?'

'Then open it,' replied Julius. 'And the problem will be solved.'

The officer's mouth twitched slightly, not quite a smile, not quite approval. He let the silence stretch a moment longer, perhaps waiting to see if Julius would flinch. He didn't and at last, called down to the waiting guards.

'Let them through.'

Julius heard Marcus exhale sharply beside him, but he kept his own expression even. This was how Rome worked, on confidence, on the ability to convince men of power that you, too, belonged among them.

The heavy doors groaned as they were pulled apart, revealing the streets of Brundisium beyond. The officer called down as the two young men descended the stairway.

'You're lucky I'm feeling generous, Julius Caesar. Stay out of trouble.'

Julius inclined his head, not in gratitude, but in acknowledgment. Then, without another word, he and Marcus stepped forward, passing through the gates of Brundisium.

89

Chapter Twelve

Brundisium

Brundisium smelled of salt, tar and sweat. The docks were a tangle of ropes, sails, and restless men, a constant churn of movement and noise that never seemed to settle. Julius and Marcus made their way through the chaos, leading their horses carefully between stacked crates and sleeping beggars. The ships in the harbour ranged from grand Roman war galleys to smaller merchant vessels, their wooden hulls creaking against the tide. The city pulsed with activity, a lifeline of trade and war.

'This place is madness,' muttered Julius, sidestepping a pair of drunken sailors stumbling toward a brothel.

'It's Rome's greatest port,' said Julius. 'What did you expect?'

'Something a little less likely to get me stabbed,' quipped Marcus.

They found lodgings near the docks, a two-story insula wedged between a bakery and a brothel. The landlord, a thin, sharp-eyed Greek, barely looked up from counting his coins before tossing them a key and directing them to a cramped room overlooking the water.

Julius dropped his pack beside the rough cot, stretching his arms.

'Sleep can wait,' he said. 'We need to find a ship.'

Marcus gave a tired sigh but nodded.

'A drink first, then?'

Julius nodded.

'Now that sounds like wisdom.'

The taberna was dirty, loud and reeked of saltwater, its patrons a mix of dockworkers, sailors, and men who had nowhere else to go. Oil lamps flickered against the dirty walls, illuminating a scene of drunken arguments, whispered dealings, and the ever-present hum of trade.

A pair of whores laughed near the entrance, their painted faces catching the light as they leaned toward a group of sailors. A dice game in the corner nearly erupted into violence before the bartender, a scarred Numidian with one good eye, threw another round of drinks on the table.

Julius and Marcus pushed through the throng, navigating the packed room with careful steps. At the bar, a thick-armed man with sun-darkened skin muttered something to a younger Roman in a trader's tunic. Julius caught only fragments of their conversation, mentions of ships, bribes, and routes avoiding Sullan patrols.

'The mood is strained,' muttered Julius, glancing around, 'we need to be careful. Rome is at war with itself, and that war doesn't stop at the city gates.'

The conflict between Sulla and the remnants of the Populares in Greece cast a long shadow over Brundisium. This city also belonged to Sulla, but its docks were filled with men who had no loyalty to Rome, only to coin. Julius turned to the bartender.

'We need passage east' he said quietly, 'is there anyone in here willing to take passengers to Asia Minor?'

The Numidian stared at the two young men before answering.

'You are strangers around here,' he said, noting the way they were dressed, 'and anyone with any sense is staying clear of the Aegean right now. If you have any sense, you'd return to where you came from.'

Julius was about to respond when a shouting match erupted behind them. Two men, a Roman veteran and a Greek merchant, were squared off, fists clenched. The Roman, his face ruddy from too much wine, kicked the table over and stepped forward.

'Thermus should have finished the job!' he snarled. 'Purge every last one of you Marian bastards!'

The Greek sneered.

'And yet your precious general still fights in Greece. Maybe

Mithridates will gut him for us.'

The Roman lunged and as the room erupted into chaos, Julius grabbed Marcus's arm, pulling him back out of the way, and, as cups shattered, and men surged toward each other with fists and knives, the bartender just casually continued to wipe his counter.

'Welcome to Brundisium,' he said with a sigh. 'What can I get you?'

Days later, Julius and Marcus sat at a table in a different taberna, this one quieter, but no less tense. They had spent days asking questions, feeling out the shifting allegiances of Brundisium, and had found nothing but distrust and danger. Passage east was scarce, war had made sure of that. But one way or another, they had no choice. They had to leave.

Julius ran a finger over the rim of his cup, staring at the dark liquid inside as if it held the answer. It didn't.

'We need to make a decision,' he said quietly, 'we've waited long enough.'

'But if we decide wrong,' said Marcus. 'we'll end up with our throats slit in an alley. Every captain we've spoken to is either too afraid to take passengers or demands coin we don't have. The ones who might take us are smugglers or worse.'

'Do you have a better idea?' asked Julius. 'Brundisium is Sulla's, and you can be sure his allies have eyes and ears on every street. We have to do something before it's too late.'

'I know,' said Marcus, placing his cup back on the table. 'But rushing onto the first ship could get us both killed.'

Julius frowned, staring back at his friend.

'Us?' he said. 'What do you mean us? As soon as we find a ship, you are going back to Rome.'

'I'm not going back to Rome,' said Marcus without looking up from his cup. 'I'm coming with you.'

Julius blinked, then let out a short laugh.

'Don't be ridiculous, Marcus. 'This isn't your fight. You have a future in Rome. You can…'

'Do what?' Marcus cut in, looking up. 'Wait for Sulla's men to decide I'm an inconvenience? Watch from the shadows as the Senate tears itself apart?' He shook his head. 'No. My future isn't in Rome, Julius, not anymore.'

Julius studied his friend carefully. Marcus had always been practical, cautious, the voice of reason in moments of recklessness. But now, now he had the look of a man who had already made his choice.

'You don't have to do this,' he said quietly.

'Oh yes I do,' said Marcus. 'Someone has to look after you.'

Julius didn't speak for a long moment. Then, finally, he reached out and clasped Marcus's wrist, gripping it tightly before responding.

'Then I'll just have to make sure we make the right decisions.'

A movement to their right caught Julius's eye as a man, seated alone in the shadows, shifted in his chair. He raised his flask to his lips, took a swallow, and then, slowly pushed back his chair before walking towards them.

As he neared, the smell hit them, salt, stale sweat, cheap wine, and something rancid clinging to his breath. His teeth were crooked and yellowed, his skin roughened by years at sea, and when he finally spoke, his voice was thick, slightly slurred, but not entirely unfocused.

'You two have loud tongues for men looking to stay unnoticed.'

Marcus's hand shifted beneath the table, fingers hovering near his dagger. Julius kept his face impassive, but his muscles coiled with readiness.

The man snorted, as if amused by their wariness, and pulled out a chair. Without waiting for an invitation, he dropped into it heavily, setting his flask down with a dull thud.

'I overheard your conversation,' he said, rubbing at the scruff on his chin. 'You need a ship east and lucky for you, I have one.'

Julius and Marcus exchanged a glance, as the man leaned forward.

'I am Captain Nikias, and my ship, the *Heron*, leaves for Ephesus in two days' time. If you want passage, then I am your man.'

Julius studied him carefully, his instincts fighting against the sudden glimmer of opportunity. The man looked like a drunk, but beneath the grime and the ale-stained tunic, he had the bearing of someone who had spent a lifetime at sea.

'And what do you gain from this, Captain?' Julius asked smoothly.

Nikias grinned, revealing his row of uneven, yellowed teeth.

'I gain coin,' he replied, 'and you gain a way off this cursed dock before your questions get you killed.' Nikias took another swig from his flask and wiped his mouth on the back of his hand. 'You have money, yes?'

'Possibly,' said Julius, thinking about the full purse he still had from Titus.

'Then why are you waiting?' replied the captain. 'Let's agree a price and in two days, you'll be on your way to Ephesus. After all, it doesn't look like you have many other options.'

The taberna's oil lamps burned lower, their flames flickering with the salty breeze that slipped in through the cracks in the wooden shutters. The night had settled deep, but the drinking and shouting in the far corners of the room never fully ceased. A brawl had broken out near the entrance at some point, but the bartender hadn't bothered to intervene.

Julius barely noticed, his attention was fixed on Captain Nikias, who now sat sprawled across his chair, one arm draped over the backrest, his flask half-empty, his grin ever-present. The man had the look of someone who had spent more time on the sea than on land, his skin darkened and leathery from sun and salt, his fingers thick with calluses from years of rope and rudders.

For the past hour, he had regaled them with stories, storms that had split ships in half, pirates that had chased him through the Aegean Sea, and narrow escapes from greedy Roman customs officials looking for extra coin. Some of it was true, most of it was utter nonsense. But it was entertaining enough that even Marcus, usually suspicious of men like Nikias, began to smirk between sips of wine. But Julius was less interested in tales of the sea than he was in war. He leaned forward slightly, resting his forearms on the table.

'Tell me about Mithridates,' he said, cutting through the captain's latest boast about outrunning a Carthaginian galley that supposedly still haunted the western Mediterranean.

Nikias glanced at him, then let out a slow breath, scratching his beard.

'Ah. That's what you're after.'

Julius shrugged.

'I prefer history over ghost stories.'

Nikias chuckled.

'Fair enough.' He took another long swig from his flask, then sat back and wiped his mouth on his sleeve. 'Mithridates,' he began, 'is the greatest enemy Rome has faced since Hannibal. The man's outlived three Roman generals, and even now, he's still standing. If Sulla hadn't come for him, he'd still have half of Asia Minor under his rule.'

Julius's gaze sharpened.

'Start from the beginning.'

Nikias took a deep breath and shifted in his seat.

'You want the full story, eh? Fine. It started over ten years ago. Rome had control over much of Asia, and Mithridates, king of Pontus, was supposed to be a loyal client king. But the man wasn't content with just ruling his own lands. He wanted everything.' He leaned in, his voice lowering slightly. 'He began pushing his borders, taking land that Rome claimed as its own. The Senate warned him, but he ignored them. Then, four years later, he did something no one thought possible.' He paused, swirling the last of his drink.

'He slaughtered every Roman and Italian in Asia Minor.'

Julius and Marcus exchanged glances.

'Eighty thousand dead,' Nikias continued. 'Men, women, children. They were dragged from their homes and butchered in the streets. Roman merchants were hunted down. Senators' families burned alive and every Italian settler in the region wiped out on his orders.'

Julius stared, fascinated at the story. He had heard whispers of the massacre before, but never in such detail.

'Rome couldn't ignore that,' Nikias continued. 'But Rome had its own troubles, the civil war between Marius and Sulla was just beginning. The Senate sent an army east, led by that fool Archelaus but Mithridates crushed them. He marched through Greece, took Athens, and the Greeks welcomed him as a liberator.'

'Then Sulla came,' said Marcus.

'Aye, Sulla came,' replied Nikkia. 'The war turned quickly after that. He stormed Athens, defeated Mithridates' generals and forced the bastard into retreat. Within three years, Sulla had him cornered. They signed a peace treaty, but only because Sulla had to return to Rome.'

Julius nodded. He knew the rest. Sulla had abandoned the East to deal with his enemies in Italy, but Mithridates had never been truly defeated.

'And now?' he asked.

'The region is still unstable,' said Nikias. 'Mithridates still rules Pontus, licking his wounds, rebuilding his armies and Rome is distracted with its own chaos.' He gestured vaguely toward the docks. 'That's why men like me are making a fortune. The garrisons in Asia need supplies, Rome is stretched thin, and every legionary stationed in Ephesus knows it.'

Julius sat back, processing. The East was far from secure so if he was heading to Asia Minor, he would be entering a world still on the brink of war.

Marcus took a slow sip of wine.

'So that's why you're sailing there? To profit off Rome's instability?'

Nikias nodded.

'A man must eat.'

Julius studied him for a long moment. The captain was rough, unpolished, and reeked of ale, but he was also a survivor, a man who knew how to navigate war-torn waters, how to read the shifting tides of power. The kind of man who could get them where they needed to go.

The conversation drifted after that, back into talk of pirates, storms, and old grudges between rival captains, but finally, Nikias drained the last of his flask and smacked his lips.

'Two days, lads,' he said, standing up, 'we leave at dawn.'

The Heron was no Roman war galley, sleek and disciplined, but a merchant vessel built for endurance rather than speed. Her hull, made of seasoned pine and strengthened with iron nails, groaned with the weight of amphorae, sacks of grain, and crates of olive oil bound for Ephesus. Unlike the great triremes of the navy, she had only a single bank of oars, reserved for emergencies when the wind failed, or danger loomed. Most of the time, she relied on her broad, square sail, which hung heavy with the wind, carrying them steadily eastward over the restless waters of the Adriatic.

Julius and Marcus had been given a space near the stern, a cramped corner where they stowed their meagre belongings between coils of rope and sealed barrels, but they were not the only passengers. Among them were two mercenaries, hardened men who spoke little but kept their weapons close. One, a Gaul with a craggy face and a broken nose, sharpened his blade each evening as if in prayer. The other, a silent Greek, bore the scars of a dozen battles and never sat with his back exposed. They were heading east, drawn by the promise of work, whether in Mithridates' armies or in Roman service, they had yet to decide.

A medicus, grey-haired and severe, occupied a shaded corner

of the deck, murmuring over a scroll of Galen's writings. He had the look of a man who had spent years mending the wounds of soldiers and sailors alike, his hands stained with the residue of herbs and old blood.

Then there was the philosopher, a man who, from the moment Julius first noticed him, seemed set apart from the rest.

His name was Aulus Crispus, a Roman of equestrian birth, dressed in a simple yet finely woven woollen cloak, his tunic belted with the casual ease of a man who had long abandoned the vanities of public life. His face was lined with age and thought, but his eyes were keen, always watching, the sea, the crew, the shifting balance of men and fate aboard the ship. He carried little with him: a leather pouch of coins, a writing tablet, and a handful of scrolls, his only true weapons, guarded with a quiet intensity that rivalled a soldier's grip on his sword.

He, like the others, was just another passenger on the Heron. But fate had a way of binding strangers on the same road, their paths crossing for reasons they could not yet see.

The voyage was monotonous, yet unpredictable. At dawn each day, the deck stirred with the first sounds of the crew. Nikias, often hungover, barked orders from the stern while his men hoisted the sail or checked the rigging. The wind dictated their pace, sometimes sending them gliding over the waters with ease, at other times leaving them stranded in stagnant, breathless heat.

Meals were simple, dried fish, hard bread, and watered-down wine, eaten in the shade of the sail or against the wooden railing where the sea spray cooled their skin. At night, some men gambled with dice near the prow, while others slept wrapped in their cloaks, lulled by the steady creak of the ship's timbers.

Each day was the same and the monotony began to take its toll, but for Julius, the philosopher became an unexpected source of interest.

Aulus Crispus spoke in measured tones, quiet, always

choosing his words carefully, and yet there was something in his manner that suggested he had once moved among Rome's elite, perhaps even in the Senate itself.

'You ask too many questions,' he said one evening, as Julius pressed him on Mithridates and the politics of the East.

'And yet you keep answering them,' Julius replied with a smirk.

Crispus exhaled, amused.

'Curiosity is a dangerous thing in a world ruled by ambition. Knowledge is a tool, but it can be a weapon as well. The wrong knowledge in the wrong hands can topple a kingdom.'

Julius leaned back, arms crossed.

'And what about the right knowledge?'

Crispus studied him.

'That depends on the man who wields it.'

Julius found himself drawn to the man's perspective, his ability to untangle the web of power that stretched from Rome to the farthest reaches of the East and while Marcus kept to himself, watching the crew and the other passengers with quiet suspicion, Julius spent more and more time talking with Crispus, debating the nature of war, the weakness of the Republic, and the lessons of past conquerors. And each evening, as the sun dipped low over the horizon, Crispus would pose a single question.

'What do you truly want, Julius?'

And each evening, Julius would stare back at the philosopher, unable to come up with an answer.

It was during one of their evening conversations when Crispus stared at Julius, his eyes probing but not judgemental.

'You had a tutor in Rome, didn't you?' he asked.

Julius nodded.

'Of course. Every boy of my position did. Rhetoric, law, philosophy… They made me memorise Plato's Republic and recite Aristotle's lessons on demand. But none of it felt real. It was just words on a wax tablet, something to impress a senator at a dinner party.'

Crispus chuckled.

'Ah, the curse of youth. You were taught philosophy as if it were poetry, something to admire, but not to live by.' He stretched out his legs, adjusting his cloak against the cool sea breeze. 'But you're older now and you're far from Rome. So, tell me, Julius, what do you remember of those lessons?'

Julius leaned against the railing, reaching back into his memories.

'That a just man is superior to an unjust one. That wisdom, courage, moderation, and justice are the pillars of virtue. That a Republic should be governed by reason, not ambition.'

Crispus laughed, shaking his head.

'Spoken like a man who still believes the Senate follows its own rules.' He looked out over the water. 'And do you believe any of that?'

Julius hesitated. Did he?

'Perhaps once,' he admitted. 'Before I saw men like Sulla bend the Republic to their will. Before I learned that power is not given to the most virtuous, but to the most ruthless.'

Crispus studied him for a moment, then nodded.

'Then let me teach you philosophy as it is meant to be taught, not as a game of words, but as a way of understanding the world around you. We will leave Plato and Aristotle in their dusty scrolls and speak only of what is real.'

Julius raised an eyebrow.

'And what is real, Crispus?'

The philosopher smiled.

'Pain. Hunger. Fear. The certainty that every man you meet will act in his own self-interest, no matter what fine words he dresses it in. Tell me, when was the last time you saw a truly selfless act?'

Julius frowned. The question was not difficult, but the answer was.

'I…' He stopped and thought, scouring his memory… Nothing.

Crispus nodded, as if that proved his point.

'Philosophy, real philosophy, is not about how men *should* act. It is about how they *do* act. Understand that, and you will never be surprised by betrayal. Never be caught unprepared by ambition. And most importantly, you will never lie to yourself about what men are capable of.'

Julius frowned and met his gaze.

'And yet you call yourself a philosopher, not a cynic?'

Crispus grinned.

'Because knowledge is power, Julius, and power, used correctly, is the only true virtue left in this world.'

Julius watched him, feeling something stir within him. This was not the philosophy of idle scholars in marble halls. This was something else, something sharper, something… *useful.*

The following day, the wind changed. It came in a sudden shift, a cool breath against the humid air, carrying with it the scent of rain and something deeper, something raw and untamed. The Heron, which had sailed smoothly for days, now creaked uneasily beneath them, her wooden frame groaning like an old man sensing trouble in his bones.

Julius stood near the stern, eyes on the horizon. The sky had darkened, thick with clouds that moved like gathering armies, swallowing the light. Far in the distance, the first flash of lightning split the sky, illuminating the rolling expanse of the Adriatic.

Nikias stood at the helm, his usual drunken slouch replaced by a rigid, alert stance. He chewed his lip, gaze fixed on the storm, his hands clutching the rail. Then, with a sudden bark of orders, the entire ship came alive with movement.

'Get the sail down! Double-check the lashings!'

Sailors scrambled up the rigging, pulling at ropes with frantic urgency. Others rushed to secure the crates of cargo, tying down barrels and amphorae, cursing as the wind picked up. The Heron's mast creaked ominously as the sail was reefed, the fabric snapping wildly in the growing gusts.

Julius and Marcus exchanged a glance. They had heard about the danger of sea storms and the fear was clear on their faces. Nikias caught them watching and marched over, his face grim.

'You two, below deck. Now.'

'How bad is it?' Marcus asked, though the answer was already written in the captain's face.

'Bad enough,' Nikias muttered. He turned and shouted toward the rest of the passengers. 'All of you, get below deck! Secure yourselves however you can, lash yourselves to the beams if you must. If you're lucky, we'll see land again in two days. If not…' He left the sentence unfinished and turned to continue his work.

Another flash of lightning ripped across the sky, closer now. The sky rumbled, deep and menacing and the waves began to churn, rolling higher with every breath.

Julius hesitated, watching the captain's unease, watching the way the sailors moved, men who had spent their lives on the sea, men who should have been accustomed to such storms. But there was something else in their eyes. Fear.

Nikias grabbed him by the shoulder.

'*Move!*'

The wind howled through the ship's rigging like a thousand voices wailing in the night, a piercing shriek that drowned out even the thunder's roar. The hull groaned under the force of the waves, each impact shuddering through the timbers as if the sea itself were trying to rip the ship apart plank by plank.

Below deck, darkness reigned. The only light came from a single oil lamp, swinging wildly from its hook, casting jagged shadows that lurched and twisted with every violent tilt of the ship. The passengers clung to whatever they could, knuckles white with desperation, but it was a losing battle and as a monstrous wave slammed into the Heron's side, sending her plunging into the trough of the next surge, Julius felt himself wrenched from his precarious refuge, his grip torn away as he was hurled across the deck. He crashed into the wooden beams, pain exploding through his shoulder, the impact rattling his very bones.

Further along the deck, a rope snapped with a sharp, whip-like crack and the sudden release sent a stack of crates toppling amongst the passengers. A scream of pain echoed in the darkness and for a brief, terrible moment, no one moved. The deck was a treacherous, shifting battlefield, where any misstep could mean being thrown to the mercy of the storm. But then, through the chaos, one figure pushed forward, the medicus.

He fought his way toward the trapped man, stumbling, slipping, the floor slick with seawater pouring in through the seams. Each step was a battle against the storm's fury but eventually he fell to his knees beside the injured man, his hands scrabbling at the heavy crates.

'Someone help me!' he shouted over his shoulder. 'He's trapped.'

Julius paused before forcing himself forward. His muscles screamed in protest and the moment he let go of his support, the ship pitched violently again, sending him sprawling, but he gritted his teeth, regained his feet, and pressed through the chaos, to reach the medicus.

The trapped man, a trader from Rome, grimaced in pain, his breath coming in shallow, panicked gasps, his ribs crushed beneath the weight. Another wave hit and the ship tipped so sharply it felt as though it might capsize, but the crates slid an inch... just enough.

Julius shoved his shoulder beneath the edge of the largest one, grunting against the strain and as his fingers dug into the wood, the rough surface biting into his skin, the medicus grabbed the trader under the arms, and with one final, desperate pull, dragged the man free.

103

They staggered, half-crawling, toward a slightly more sheltered corner of the hold, dragging the trader with them. The man gasped, clutching his ribs, his face pale as the medicus immediately set to work, pressing cautious hands against his chest.

'His ribs are broken,' he shouted, 'but I don't think the lungs are pierced. There's not much we can do during this storm, we just have to pray to the gods and ride it out.'

Julius nodded, swallowing down the bile rising in his throat. The storm was not letting up, it was growing worse. The ship was being torn apart, but down here, beneath the deck, all they could do was endure.

The Heron shuddered again, and they all looked up in fear as a giant crack pierced the howling wind, a sound that could only mean one thing… the mast was breaking.

The Heron was no longer a ship, it was a plaything of the gods. Waves the size of fortresses tossed her like driftwood, sending her lurching skyward one moment and plummeting the next. Each impact sent a fresh groan through her battered timbers, and with every shudder, it seemed less likely she would hold together. The crew fought desperately, hauling at ropes, screaming orders that were lost to the wind, but it was useless. The Heron was at the mercy of the storm, and the storm had no mercy to give.

Below deck, Julius, Marcus, and the others held on as best they could. Every roll of the ship sent crates crashing, water sloshing across the planks, bodies slamming into wood. The injured merchant drifted in and out of consciousness, his breathing laboured, while the medicus did what he could with nothing but his hands and his knowledge.

Hours passed, though they felt like eternity and then, the gods answered the many prayers that had been sent up in their name. The winds began to ease, the rain, though relentless, softened and the waves lost some of their fury. The storm was passing.

Above deck, the sailors, their faces pale with exhaustion, took what little control they could. The main mast was splintered, the sail torn to ribbons, but Nikias and his men worked tirelessly, lashing together a makeshift rigging, patching what they could to drag the ship back from the brink, and by dawn, the Heron was once again limping eastward.

Several days later the ship drifted into Ephesus like a wounded beast. The docks, bustling with traders and sailors, turned to watch as the ship crawled into place, her hull battered, her mast jury-rigged, her crew barely standing. Nikias, dark-eyed with exhaustion, let out a breath it seemed he had been holding for days.

'We live,' he muttered. 'Somehow.'

Julius and Marcus gathered their things, their bodies aching from the ordeal and as they moved toward the gangplank, Julius turned back to the captain.

'You got us here,' he said. 'Despite the odds.'

Nikias snorted, rubbing at the salt-stained scruff on his chin.

'I'd say it was skill, but that'd be a lie. The gods let us live… *this time.*'

Julius gave a nod of respect.

'Then let us hope they favour you the next time as well.'

'I'll need more than their favour, my friend,' said Nikias, 'I'll need another ship.'

Julius nodded and turned to leave. But before he could step off the dock, a voice called out behind him.

'Wait!'

Julius turned. The injured merchant lay on a stretcher, carried by two men. His face was pale, his breathing ragged, but his eyes were sharp with determination. He lifted a trembling hand, beckoning them closer. Julius approached, Marcus at his side.

'You saved my life,' said, his voice weak. 'I am a man of honour and do not forget such things.'

Julius shrugged.

'You would have done the same.'

The merchant winced before answering.

'Perhaps.' he said, pausing before continuing. 'If fate allows, I don't know when, and I don't know how, but one day, our paths will cross again, and when they do, I will repay my debt in full.'

Julius met his gaze for a long moment, then nodded. He didn't believe in debts.

But he did believe in fate.

Chapter Thirteen

Ephesus

Ephesus was a city of contradictions. It bore the mark of Rome's rule, yet its spirit remained Greek. Statues of Artemis, the city's patron goddess, stood proudly in its streets, her many-breasted form a symbol of fertility and protection. But alongside the old temples were newer Roman buildings, basilicas, bathhouses, and an amphitheatre that echoed with Latin as well as Greek. Traders called out in both tongues, hawking fine cloth from the East, wine from Italy, and spices from lands beyond the Black Sea.

The streets, still lively even as the evening deepened, bore scars of the past decade. Only seven years earlier, Mithridates VI of Pontus had turned this city against Rome, leading its people in the slaughter of every Roman citizen within its walls. Thousands had died in a single night. Now, the city bowed once more to Rome, but the tension lingered, old resentments, buried just beneath the surface.

Julius and Marcus felt it, even as they moved cautiously through the bustling avenues. They had arrived, but what now?

They found lodgings behind a small shop, a cramped room that smelled of dust and stale grain, but it was dry and safe, and after the ordeal at sea, that was enough. Still, uncertainty gnawed at them.

'Now that we're here, what exactly do we do?' muttered Marcus, stretching out on the thin sleeping mat.

Julius sat cross-legged, elbows resting on his knees.

'We find out who holds power. Then we decide, but first, let's see if we can find something hot to eat.

Ten minutes later, they walked outside and deeper into the city's heart. Eventually, they found small kapeleion, a dimly lit establishment tucked between a bronzesmith's workshop and a stall selling dyed fabrics.

Smoke curled from an open hearth at the back, where a bearded Greek turned skewers of lamb over the coals, the fat sizzling

107

as it dripped into the fire. The scent of roasted meat and spiced wine filled the air, mingling with the murmur of voices.

Julius and Marcus ducked inside, their eyes adjusting to the gloom. The place was half-full, sailors hunched over clay cups, a group of merchants debating grain prices in low voices, and a pair of men rolling knucklebones near the entrance. A serving boy, barefoot and quick, appeared with a tray of cups.

'Wine? Meat? Bread?' he asked in fluent but unpolished Latin.

Julius glanced at Marcus, who rubbed his chin thoughtfully.

'Something hot,' said Marcus immediately. 'I'm done with dried fish and stale bread.'

Julius turned to the boy.

'Lamb, bread, olives and wine, but not the kind that peels the skin from your throat.'

The boy snorted as if he'd heard the request a thousand times before and darted away, weaving between the tables. Julius leaned back, glancing around the room.

The kapeleion was exactly the kind of place where deals were made, where men whispered of war and opportunity. Somewhere among the low voices and the shifting lamplight, someone was probably planning their next move. Rome ruled here, but not all accepted it.

Their meal came and Marcus wrapped a pile of lamb in a flatbread before taking a huge bite, his eyes half closing in ecstasy. Julius laughed and did the same, and for the first time in many days, both men finally relaxed. More food came and they were on their second jug of wine when a voice called out from across the street.

'Well, look who survived the storm.'

Julius and Marcus glanced up to see the two mercenaries from the Heron standing at the entrance to the kapeleion. Without waiting for an invitation, the Gaul slid onto the bench opposite them, motioning for wine.

'I'd ask how you're enjoying Ephesus,' he said, but it looks like you are doing just fine.'

'Just glad to have our feet on solid ground.' said Julius. 'All we have to do now is figure out what happens next.'

'Good luck with that,' said the Gaul. He looked across at his comrade. 'We're going to sell our swords to the Roman general.'

Marcus raised an eyebrow.

'And not Mithridates?'

'I may fight for coin,' said the Gaul, 'but I'm not a fool. Mithridates turned this whole province into a butcher's yard, and I'll not serve a man who slaughters civilians for no reason. No, we'll fight for Rome and besides, Rome always pays its debts.'

Julius leaned forward.

'Which Roman general?'

'Marcus Minucius Thermus,' said the Gaul, taking a piece of gravy-soaked bread from Marcus's platter. 'He's besieging Mytilene on Lesbos. A proper fight, from what I hear but he needs men, the kind who don't ask too many questions.'

Julius exchanged a glance with Marcus. Thermus was a Sullan commander, sent to secure Rome's grip on Asia, but if there was any place to make himself useful, to make himself known, it was there. He turned back to the mercenary.

'When do you leave?'

The Gaul wiped his mouth on his forearm.

'We are signing up tomorrow. Are you thinking of joining?'

Julius said nothing. But the thought was already forming.

Two jugs of wine later, Julius and Marcus watched as the two mercenaries strode into the night, disappearing among the throngs of late-night drinkers and merchants closing their stalls. The eatery around them was still busy, clay cups clinking, men laughing too loudly, the occasional argument over a game of dice, but Julius heard none of it. His thoughts were already at the agora, standing before the recruiting officers, his name being written down, the weight of a sword in his hand.

109

'This could be our chance, Marcus,' he said quietly.

Marcus exhaled sharply and leaned forward, his forearms resting on the table.

'Our chance for what, Julius? You came here to seek your father's old friends, not to march straight into a war. We aren't soldiers, Julius. We don't owe Rome anything and I'm not about to get myself killed in some war over an island I've never set foot on.'

Julius tilted his head, studying his friend.

'If you think this is just about Mytilene, it isn't. It's about more than that. It's about Rome. It's about putting ourselves in the path of something bigger. If we just drift from one city to the next, what are we? Nobody. But if we stand with Thermus, if we fight alongside him, we become part of the story. We *matter*.'

Marcus stared at him, then let out a dry laugh, shaking his head.

'Julius, you sound like a man trying to convince himself, not me.'

Julius opened his mouth to respond, but Marcus cut him off.

'And even if you're right, even if this does lead to something greater, have you thought about what we'd actually be doing? Fighting and killing for coin? Selling ourselves to whatever Roman general needs another sword? That's not glory, Julius, that's desperation.'

Julius's smirk faded. He leaned back and his brow furrowed. Marcus wasn't wrong, and yet, something inside him resisted the idea of walking away. He had felt it back in Rome, the pressure of standing in the shadow of greater men. He had sworn that his name would mean something, but it wasn't enough. Not yet.

'You don't have to come, you know,' he said after a long pause.

Marcus scoffed.

'Don't be ridiculous. I'm not letting you march off with a pack of cutthroats on your own. But let's think before we act. We don't have to decide right now, let's just sleep on it.' He pointed a finger at Julius. 'But no promises.'

Julius nodded.

'No promises.'

Marcus drained the last of his watered wine, then pushed back his chair to stand up.

'Come on,' he said, 'let's get some rest.'

Chapter Fourteen

Ephesus

The streets of Ephesus were alive with movement, yet Julius barely noticed. His mind was fixed ahead, on the decision already made. Marcus walked beside him, but his steps were less certain, his expression shifting between doubt and quiet frustration.

'We could still turn around, you know,' he muttered. 'Go back to that dusty little room, get some rest, think it through properly.'

'And then what?' asked Julius. 'Spend another day wandering the streets like lost traders? There's no decision left to make.'

Marcus shook his head.

'No, see, that's the thing. You act like this was decided long before we even spoke to those mercenaries. But I remember the conversation, Julius. You weren't sure.'

Julius turned his head slightly, giving Marcus a sharp look.

'I only thing I wasn't sure of was if you'd come.'

That stopped Marcus in his tracks. He frowned, then hurried to catch up, his voice quieter now.

'You mean to tell me that you've known all along you were going to do this?'

Julius gave a small shrug.

'Not all along. But it was always an option.'

Marcus sighed.

'By the gods, Julius. You say I overthink things, but you don't think at all. You just… decide. And when you do, there's no talking you out of it.'

Julius finally stopped walking, turning to face his friend properly.

'Because there's nothing to talk about, Marcus. Look at where we are. Look at what's happening around us. Rome is still at war, the East is still unstable, and men like us, men with ambition but no power, either step forward or get swept away.' He paused. 'And I will not be swept away.'

Marcus studied him for a long moment.

'And that's what this is about, isn't it? Not the pay, not the war. It's about being noticed.'

Julius shook his head.

'Noticed? No, Marcus. It's about being remembered.'

The Roman presence in Ephesus was impossible to ignore, but in the agora, it was unmistakable. Beneath the shade of a columned portico, a makeshift recruitment post had been set up with a wooden standard, bearing the insignia of Legio VI Ferrata planted in the ground. Behind it, two officers in worn but well-kept military tunics sat behind a long table alongside a scribe scratching names onto a parchment with an inked stylus.

Surrounding them, a small contingent of soldiers stood in formation, eyes scanning the crowd with the wary expressions of men who had seen real battle. They weren't here to impress. They were here to find men who could fight.

A line had already formed, a mix of seasoned warriors, drifters, and the desperate. Some were veterans, their faces set with the kind of grim certainty that only came from knowing what battle truly was. Others were young, hungry, and reckless, eyes burning with dreams of glory, coin, or simply escape.

The process was quick, brutal, and impersonal. Each man stepped forward and gave his name and a Centurion looked them over, asking a few direct questions:

'Where have you fought before? Are you in debt or fleeing Rome? Will you swear loyalty to Rome and its commanders?'

There were no flowery oaths, no inspiring speeches, this was a recruitment drive for spare bodies for the fight, not for men looking to join the ranks of the legion. If they passed this stage, the Centurion grabbed their hands and forearms, testing their grip, their strength, the stability of their stance. Too weak? Too sickly? Dismissed. There was no room for cripples and cowards.

All those accepted, dipped a second stylus into an ink pot and marked their name on a scroll. Payment, equipment, and orders would come later but first, they were expected to prove they were worth it.

Julius and Marcus stood at the edge of the line, watching in silence. Ahead of them, the Gaul and his companion stepped forward. The officer barely glanced at them before making a mark on the wax tablet, recognising the presence of battle-hardened men.

'Report at dawn. You'll receive your assignments tomorrow. Next.'

The mercenaries stepped away and as they passed, the Gaul smirked towards Marcus and Julius.

'Your turn, Romans.'

Julius felt his pulse quicken. He glanced at Marcus, but Marcus wasn't looking at him, his eyes were locked on the table, on the officer waiting for them. The moment had come. No more talk. No more hesitation.

'Names?' said the Centurion.

'Julius Gaius Caesar and Marcus Antonius Gracchus'

The Centurion repeated the cursory checks that had applied to all the others. To him, they were just another pair of restless young men, likely aristocrats from Rome who had fallen on hard times. He waved to the scribe.

'Mercenary detail. Put them with the others.'

The scribe dipped his stylus but before he could write their names, Julius spoke sharply, the single word almost a command.

'*No!*'

The scribe paused, his scarred brow lifting slightly as he glanced up. Marcus stiffened beside him, sensing something shift in the air. Julius stepped forward.

'I will not sign up as a mercenary. I will be a Roman officer, or nothing.'

A slow, unnerving silence followed. The men behind them shifted, glancing at one another, half amused, half curious.

The Centurion stared at Julius for a long moment, then let out a short, dry laugh.

'Is that so? And are you trained, then? Have you fought in a legion before?'

Julius met his gaze without flinching.

'No.'

The Centurion's smirk widened.

'Then you're mercenaries.' He gestured at the scribe. 'Put them down and move them along.'

'I am of the gens Julia,' interrupted Julius, 'and demand that I am treated accordingly.'

This time, the Centurion paused properly, and Julius pressed the moment.

'My aunt was married to Gaius Marius and my father was a praetor. My family traces its line back to Venus herself, and yet you would sign me as a common sword-for-hire?'

Marcus stared at his friend, astonished by his tone, by his sheer audacity.

The Centurion leaned forward slightly, eyes narrowing.

'And what would you have me do, then? Make you a general? Shall I hand you a legion today?'

Julius didn't blink.

'Men of my age and station are often recruited as trainee officers in the legions, as well you know. I assume Thermus is not so flush with such men that he can afford to turn away well-connected Romans.'

The Centurion said nothing at first. He merely studied Julius, weighing his words.

Then, slowly, he sat back, exhaling through his nose.

'Hah. You've got some nerve, boy.'

The scribe hesitated, stylus hovering over the tablet, waiting for the Centurion's decision. Julius stood motionless, his heart hammering, but his expression never wavered.

Around them, the sounds of the agar carried on, orders being shouted, the occasional grunt of approval or dismissal, but in that moment, none of it mattered. Finally, after what felt like an eternity, the Centurion exhaled sharply and nodded.

'Fine. You've got a name, and that means something. But it's not my place to give you rank, it's up to Thermus whether you're worth anything more than a foot soldier. Especially considering you've never held a sword in real battle.'

The scribe, stylus still poised, hesitated. The Centurion flicked a hand.

'Write his name down. Potential officer, pending authorisation.'

Julius allowed himself the faintest ghost of a smile as the Centurion turned his gaze to Marcus.

'And you? What's your story?'

Marcus opened his mouth, but before he could speak, Julius cut in smoothly.

'He's with me.'

Marcus's head snapped toward him, eyes widening.

'Julius…'

Julius didn't stop. His voice remained even, controlled.

'A man of my station requires a servant. I assume Thermus does not expect a Roman of my lineage to travel alone. He will accompany me as staff, or neither of us will go.'

Marcus's jaw dropped as the Centurion stared at Julius for a long moment. Then his gaze flicked to Marcus, taking in his well-made tunic, his carefully kept hair, the lack of scars on his hands. His lip curled slightly.

'A servant, is he? Looks a bit soft for a servant.'

'He is capable,' said Julius smoothly, 'and entirely loyal.'

Marcus made a strangled noise in the back of his throat but, miraculously, said nothing.

The Centurion glanced between them once more, then gave a short, dismissive snort.

'It's not my problem. If Thermus doesn't like it, he can send you both back to Rome.' He gestured at the scribe. 'Put his name down under staff alongside the other. We'll see what Thermus decides.'

Julius stepped forward and signed his name onto the scroll. Still looking half-stunned, Marcus followed suit and as he straightened, the Centurion leaned back in his chair.

'Report to the General's villa at the far end of Ephesus tomorrow morning. I will ensure his staff know you are coming.'

Julius gave a short nod, then turned on his heel. Marcus hesitated for a brief second, then followed. Only when they were clear of the recruitment post, weaving through the crowded agar, did Marcus finally find his voice.

'A *servant?* A bloody servant, Julius?'

Julius smirked, eyes still fixed ahead.

'It worked, didn't it?'

Marcus muttered something under his breath that was almost certainly an insult, but he said nothing else.

Julius allowed himself a small, satisfied breath. They were going to see Thermus,
and this was only the beginning.

Later that night, Julius and Marcus sat in the same kapeleion, the sun casting long shadows across the dusty stones of the ancient street. Around them, the daily rhythm of Ephesus continued as if nothing had changed, merchants haggling, artisans calling out their wares, slaves scurrying past with hurried steps, but for them, everything had.

Marcus sat in stubborn silence, his jaw set, staring silently out over the passing population.

'Oh, come on Marcus,' sighed Julius eventually, 'are you really going to sulk?'

'Sulk?' Marcus rounded on him, forcing Julius to flinch. 'You signed me up as your bloody servant!'

Julius met his indignant gaze, trying to suppress his need to laugh.

'It was necessary,' he said. 'We needed passage, and that Centurion was never going to take two unproven young men as officers, no matter how impressive our family trees are. This way, we will get there, and once we do, I'll make it clear you're not my servant.'

Marcus narrowed his eyes.

'And if Thermus decides I should stay a servant? That would be an interesting turn of events, wouldn't it? 'Oh, Julius, where's your servant, Marcus?' 'Oh, he's back at the camp, polishing my boots.'

Julius suddenly snorted with laughter, spitting out a spray of wine.

'Oh, Marcus,' he gasped, clapping his friend on the shoulder. 'You'd make a terrible servant. You complain too much.'

Marcus grumbled something under his breath but finally let out a reluctant sigh.

'Fine. But you owe me for this.'

'I'll buy you the finest wine Lesbos has to offer,' said Julius. 'Assuming, of course, we don't get killed first.'

'You're not helping,' said Marcus and picked up his own wine to end the conversation.

They continued their meal and when finished, headed back to their lodgings, but as they rounded a corner, a familiar figure emerged from the crowd.

'Crispus,' called Julius, recognising the philosopher. 'Over here.'

Crispus smiled and walked toward them, his simple woollen cloak draped over one shoulder, a scroll tucked beneath one arm.

'So, have you found a purpose yet?' asked Crispus with a smile, 'or are you just getting lost in bigger places?'

Julius grinned.

'A bit of both,' he replied. 'We have signed up for the campaign in Lesbos. Thermus is leading a campaign there and we intend to join him.'

Crispus nodded slowly, his eyes narrowing slightly as he processed the information.

'A Roman army,' he said eventually, 'a Sullan commander, and a man with ambition. That's a dangerous combination.'

'That depends on who you ask,' replied Julius. 'From my perspective, it is an opportunity.'

Crispus glanced at Marcus, then back at Julius.

'And tell me, did you talk your way into a position of command, or did you simply demand one?'

Marcus snorted.

'Oh, you should have seen it. He went straight to the recruiter and demanded an officer's rank.'

Crispus chuckled.

'Of course he did. And did they give him one?'

Julius smiled.

'Not yet. But they will.'

Crispus studied him for a moment, as if searching for something beneath the confidence, beneath the ambition. Finally, he nodded.

'Then I'll watch your progress with interest.'

119

Julius and Marcus exchanged a final few words with the philosopher before saying their goodbyes and continuing down the street toward their lodgings. But just as they walked away, Crispus's voice called after them, repeating the same question that he had asked Julius every night on the ship.

'Gaius Julius Caesar,' he called, making both young men turn around to face him. 'I still haven't had my answer so will ask you one more time. Have you decided what you want yet?'

Julius stared back. For a moment, he just stood there, looking around at the buildings, the people, the city soaked in Greek tradition but ruled by Roman will. Then, slowly, he turned back, to meet the philosopher's gaze, realising he finally knew his path.

'Yes, I have,' he said with conviction. 'I want Rome, Crispus, I need Rome. But more importantly, Rome *needs* me… They just don't realise it yet.'

Crispus watched him for a long moment, his expression unreadable. Then, with a quiet chuckle, he turned and walked away.

Julius stood there for a breath longer before turning back toward the lodgings, but this time, Marcus didn't say a word, he just stood there staring in shock at the back of his oldest friend as he walked away.

Chapter Fifteen

Ephesus

The grand villa loomed ahead, set apart from the bustling streets of Ephesus by high stone walls and a gated courtyard. Beyond the gate, the villa's columned façade gleamed in the moonlight, its design a blend of Roman authority and Greek elegance.

Julius and Marcus approached cautiously, their boots scuffing against the worn marble steps leading up to the entrance. Two legionaries, their polished cuirasses glinting in the torchlight, crossed their spears to bar the way. Behind them, more guards stood at intervals, hands resting on the hilts of their gladii.

A Tribune in a crested helmet stood at the gate, holding a wax tablet. He barely glanced up before speaking.

'Name and business?'

Julius straightened.

'Gaius Julius Caesar. I seek an audience with Marcus Minucius Thermus.'

The Tribune finally looked at him, scanning his face before running a finger down the list. After a moment, he gave a small nod.

'You're expected. Follow me.'

The guards stepped aside, pulling open the heavy gate. Julius and Marcus exchanged a brief glance before stepping through.

Inside, the villa's courtyard stretched before them, white gravel crunching beneath their feet, fountains trickling in the warm night air. Slaves in muted tunics moved quietly between the columns, their heads bowed.

The Tribune led them through a series of corridors, past frescoed walls and bronze oil lamps, until they reached a small, sparsely furnished waiting room. A single wooden bench stood against one wall, opposite a large doorway shrouded with a heavy curtain. Several other men waited in silence, each waiting their turn for an audience with the General. The Tribune gestured to the bench.

'Wait here. You will be called.'

Without another word, he turned and disappeared through the curtain, leaving them in the dimly lit chamber.

Julius waited in silence, not sure what to expect. Marcus shifted beside him, arms crossed, his boot tapping lightly against the floor. Men came and went and then, then, at last, the curtain stirred, and a servant entered, dressed in a simple tunic. He looked around the room before settling his gaze on Julius.

'Gaius Julius Caesar?'

Julius stood. Marcus moved to rise as well, but the servant lifted a hand.

'Just him. You will wait here.'

Marcus frowned but said nothing. The servant turned and led him through the curtain, down another short corridor, and into a large chamber lit by bronze lamps and a central brazier.

Inside, a group of Roman officers stood in discussion, their words clipped with the confidence of men accustomed to command. Their cloaks were edged in purple, their belts gleamed with polished bronze, and though they spoke easily, there was an intensity to them, men accustomed to war, men who weighed every word. But one man stood out among them.

Marcus Minucius Thermus.

He was older than Julius expected, his features weathered but strong, his bearing commanding. He spoke in a measured tone, gesturing to a map unfurled across a wooden table and as he talked, the others listened without question.

Julius waited, hands at his sides, his heartbeat steady. He had learned long ago that patience was indeed a virtue.

Thermus continued his discussion, not looking up. Only several moments later did he pause, letting silence settle over the group. Then, finally, he turned. His eyes, sharp and assessing, fixed on Julius.

'You must be Julius Caesar,' he said. 'Is your father of the same name?'

'He was, Dominus, alas he has passed now.'

'Didn't he once serve in Bithynia?'

Julius nodded.

'He did, for many years.'

Thermus stared at Julius for a long moment, his expression unreadable. Then, with a curt motion, he turned to the gathered officers.

'Leave us.'

There was no hesitation. The men dipped their heads in deference, murmuring quiet acknowledgments as they filed out. The heavy door closed behind them, sealing the chamber in silence.

Thermus gestured to a low wooden chair near the brazier.

'Sit.'

Julius obeyed, settling onto the seat as a servant appeared, carrying a tray. A cup of wine was poured without a word, the deep red liquid catching the firelight. Thermus took a cup for himself but did not drink. Instead, he studied Julius, fingers tapping idly against the rim of his cup.

'Your father,' he said at last. 'Tell me, was he truly a friend of Nicomedes, the King of Bithynia?'

Julius met his gaze without flinching.

'He was, Domine. My father often talked about him.'

Thermus exhaled, nodding slowly as if confirming something to himself. He leaned back, weighing his words.

'Understand this, Caesar, I do not make a habit of entertaining young men who turn up at my door, full of ambition and fine words, expecting an officer's commission.' His eyes flicked over Julius, assessing. 'But your name means something and perhaps you have something I can use.'

He took a slow sip of wine, letting the words settle between them. He let out a slow breath before speaking again.

'We sail for Mytilene within weeks,' he said eventually. 'The city defied Rome, and it will suffer for it. I have the men I need, almost. But not enough ships and that is a problem. My fleet is too small for a full assault and if we cannot blockade the harbour, the Mytileneans will simply resupply and drag this war out. We need ships to surround Lesbos and choke the city into submission.'

Julius listened, waiting as Thermus took another sip of wine.

'Nicomedes, however,' continued the general, 'has ships and plenty of them. The problem is, he is no friend of mine and I doubt he'd even grant an audience if I sent an envoy.'

He fell silent again, drumming his fingers against the arm of his chair. His eyes narrowed slightly as he studied Julius. Then, as if coming to a decision, he leaned forward.

'I'll make you a deal, Caesar. You will go to Bithynia as the head of a Roman delegation. You will use your family's name, your father's connections, whatever it takes, to persuade Nicomedes to release a fleet of ships to aid our campaign against Lesbos.' He let the weight of the words settle. 'If you can do that, I will consider your commission.'

Thermus watched Julius carefully, expecting hesitation, a flicker of doubt, a moment's pause. This was no simple task. A king's favour was not won easily, nor were his ships lightly given, but Julius did not hesitate.

'I accept,' he said simply. 'When do I go?'

Thermus's brow lifted slightly, caught off guard by the young man's certainty. He had expected negotiation, perhaps even refusal, but there was nothing in Caesar's eyes except conviction.

'You seem sure of yourself,' he mused.

'That is because I am.'

A beat of silence stretched between them, then Thermus let out a quiet breath, shaking his head with the faintest trace of amusement.

'Very well,' he said. 'You have your chance. Drink up, Caesar, and may the gods go with you.'

Chapter Sixteen

The Road to Bithynia

Julius, Marcus and six Roman envoys made up the delegation, their horses laden with provisions as they set their course north. The first days passed without trouble as the Via Sacra stretched through rolling hills, olive groves and vineyards. Farmers called to one another across the fields, and the road teemed with life, merchants leading loaded donkeys, traders guiding carts heavy with goods, and travellers moving between distant towns.

By the third day, they reached Pergamum and its great acropolis, a crown of stone and marble dominating the plains below, stopping only long enough to rest their horses and refill their waterskins before pressing on.

Soon, the landscape changed. The once-gentle hills gave way to sparse forests, where blackened ruins stood as silent reminders of Mithridates' war and charred beams jutted from the earth like broken ribs, the scars of past battles still fresh upon the land.

That night, as they camped beside a swollen river, Marcus sat hunched in his cloak, his gaze shifting warily toward the shadowed trees.

'These roads aren't safe,' he muttered. 'We've seen no patrols for days.'

Julius, tightening a saddle strap, didn't look up.

'That's why we ride hard, Marcus, and don't linger.'

'I preferred Ephesus,' said Marcus. 'At least there you could get a hot meal and if someone wanted to rob you, they did it in the open.'

The next morning, they set off again, but the rain came swiftly, turning the road into a river of mud. The horses struggled, hooves slipping, and the wheels of passing carts sinking deep into the sludge.

Balbus, the officer in command of the roman delegation, urged his mount alongside Julius, rain dripping from his sodden cloak as he scowled at the churning road.

'At this rate, we'll be lucky to reach Cyzicus before the next Saturnalia.'

Julius wiped the water from his brow, unimpressed.

'Unless you've found a way to control the weather, we ride on.'

Balbus grunted but gave a nod.

They pressed forward, the rain finally easing as they neared the coastal plains. The sea emerged on the horizon, a glimmering stretch of blue against the storm-dark sky and by the time they rode into Cyzicus, its harbour was alive with movement with trading vessels jostling for space alongside Bithynian warships, their banners snapping in the wind.

They stared at the harbour below. Sailing across the Propontis would save time, but the storm clouds thickening over the water made the decision for them.

'We take the land route,' Balbus declared, watching the restless waves. 'I've no interest in drowning before we reach Nicomedia.' Julius and Marcus gave no argument and decision made, they turned east, passing through Lampsacus to follow the coastline, and at last, after twelve gruelling days, they finally caught sight of their destination. Nicomedia lay ahead.

'We made it,' muttered Julius, his voice laced with satisfaction.

'Just about,' said Marcus. 'Another night on the road and I'd have started talking to my horse.' He shifted in the saddle, stretching the stiffness in his shoulders. 'I'll never complain about a Roman road again.'

Julius smiled, but his eyes were already scanning the horizon. The city stretched along the Propontis, its streets alive with movement, merchants calling their wares, sailors unloading cargo, slaves hauling amphorae of oil and wine. It was a Greek city at heart, despite its Roman ties, and it was impossible to ignore the towering palace of King Nicomedes which dominated the heights above.

A voice behind them broke the moment.

'Enjoy the view while you can,' said Balbus, riding up alongside them, 'it's not often you get to walk into a king's court.'

Julius turned to face him.

'Let's hope we walk out just as easily.'

'That depends entirely on how well you talk, Caesar. The king holds Rome in favour when it suits him, but kings can be fickle.' He fixed Julius with a hard look. 'Thermus gave you this mission, but make no mistake, our lives rest on how well you handle it.'

Julius nodded.

'Then I won't fail.'

The officer kicked his horse forward, and for the first time in a long time, Julius felt the slightest flickering of doubt in his chest.

The gates of the palace compound loomed before them, flanked by towering stone walls and a row of ceremonial guards standing rigid in polished armour. Their helms gleamed under the midday sun, but their expressions were far from warm.

As Julius and his companions reined in their horses, an official stepped forward, his robes immaculate, his face carefully composed. He studied them for a long moment before offering the barest inclination of his head.

'You are expected,' he said, his tone devoid of warmth. 'Follow me.'

No further pleasantries were exchanged and as the delegation was ushered through the gates, their horses were taken by waiting attendants offering neither words nor smiles. This was not a warm welcome, it was merely a formality.

The official led them through the winding streets of the palace complex, past towering columns and manicured gardens, until they arrived at a separate building within the grounds, a grand

127

structure of marble and carved wood, its entrance guarded by statues of long-forgotten kings.

Stepping inside, the contrast was striking. Where the gates had been cold and uninviting, the interior was a display of wealth and power. The floors gleamed with polished stone, murals of past victories stretched across the walls, and the air carried the rich scent of myrrh and spiced wine.

A team of silent servants awaited them, bowing before leading them through the corridors. Each man was shown to a private chamber, the rooms draped in fine silks, their beds piled with soft cushions. It was luxury, but it was also calculated, an unspoken message that their hosts held the power here.

After taking time to wash away the dust of the road, they gathered in a spacious dining hall. At its centre a long table stretched before them, already adorned with ornate jugs of deep red wine, silver platters piled high with ripe figs and olives, and steaming bowls of spiced meat.

As they settled into their seats, the doors swung open once more and a procession of servants entered, moving with quiet precision, each bearing trays laden with roasted lamb, fresh bread still warm from the ovens, and delicate pastries glistening with honey. The scent of cinnamon and citrus filled the air as they set the dishes down with practiced grace, pouring wine into goblets before retreating soundlessly to the edges of the room.

Then, behind them, the same official who had greeted them at the gates stepped inside, his expression as unreadable as ever.

'His Majesty, King Nicomedes IV Philopator, remains occupied with urgent matters of state,' he announced. 'However, he sends his regards, and a feast to honour your arrival.'

With a final, shallow bow, he turned and left, leaving them alone with the feast before them.

Julius glanced at Marcus, who raised an eyebrow, already reaching for his goblet.

'Well,' muttered Marcus. 'At least we won't starve while we

are here. Do you think they always eat like this?'

Julius reached for his goblet.

'Nicomedes isn't a fool,' he said. 'He's survived too long in this region to be anything less than shrewd and all this is simply a message to inform us how powerful he still is.'

Balbus, seated across from them, leaned back in his chair, swirling own his wine before taking a slow sip.

'Powerful yes,' he said. 'But not without cost. You weren't here when Mithridates came through. I was.'

'What was it like?' mumbled Marcus through a mouthful of stew.

Balbus set his cup down, his expression darkening.

'It was chaos,' he said simply. 'When Mithridates made his move, Bithynia was one of the first to suffer. Nicomedes had been Rome's ally for years, and he'd been a thorn in Mithridates' side. The old king had taken his chances before, trying to expand into Pontus, relying on Rome to prop him up, but Mithridates was patient. He waited, gathered his strength, and when he finally struck, it was with an army that outnumbered anything Nicomedes could field.'

Marcus frowned.

'I heard the Bithynians barely put up a fight.'

Balbus scoffed.

'They didn't stand a chance. Nicomedes fled, his army crumbled, and Mithridates swept across the region like a storm. It wasn't just Bithynia, the whole of Asia bled. Ephesus, Pergamum, every city that had once knelt to Rome was turned against us.' He exhaled sharply, gripping the stem of his goblet. 'And then came the massacres. Eighty thousand Romans and Italians, slaughtered in a single night. Every man, woman, and child Mithridates could find. No mercy, no exceptions.'

A heavy silence settled over the table, the crackle of torches along the walls the only sound. Julius broke it first.

'And yet, Nicomedes is still here. His throne intact.'

129

Balbus nodded slowly.

'Because we took it back for him. Sulla sent Lucullus and Fimbria east, and Mithridates was driven out. Nicomedes was restored, but make no mistake, he knows he sits on that throne because Rome wills it. Without us, he is nothing.'

Marcus drained his goblet and set it down with a thud.

'Then let's hope he remembers that when we ask for his help.'

The following days blurred together in a haze of waiting. Each morning, they sent word to the king, and each afternoon, the answer was the same, Nicomedes was occupied with affairs of state but would receive them as soon as he was able. The message was always polite, always carefully worded, but after nearly a week, it had become nothing more than a thinly veiled dismissal.

At first, Julius had held his patience. Nicomedes was a king, after all, and kings did not simply drop their affairs to accommodate visitors, even those from Rome. But as the days dragged on, that patience soured into frustration. The lavish quarters that had seemed a symbol of hospitality now felt like a comfortable cage. Servants attended to their every need, but no one answered their questions.

By the tenth day, even Marcus, who was usually content so long as there was good food and wine, had grown restless. He sat near the window, his boot tapping rhythmically against the marble floor as he scowled at the city beyond.

'This is a waste of time,' he muttered. 'If he hasn't seen us by now, he has no intention of doing so.'

Balbus, seated across the room, gave a weary sigh.

'Kings don't rush, Marcus. And certainly not for us.'

'Then perhaps we should leave,' said Marcus. 'If he won't see us, that is answer enough.'

Julius had been silent until now, but his frustration had been building with each passing day, each repetition of the same tired excuse. He had spent his life watching men like Sulla and Marius, men who took action when action was needed. And now, with their purpose hanging in limbo, he found himself wondering what either of them would do in his place. The answer was obvious.

A knock at the door interrupted his thoughts, and as expected, the official entered with his usual air of stiff politeness. He offered a short bow and delivered the same message they had heard countless times before.

'His Majesty remains occupied but sends his regards. He assures you he will receive you at the earliest opportunity.'

Julius stood abruptly and without hesitation, crossed the room to follow the official as he turned to leave. The man barely made it past the threshold before Julius reached out and seized his arm.

The official froze, his body going rigid beneath Julius' grip. He turned slowly, eyes narrowing with a mix of shock and growing anger.

'Unhand me,' he said.

Julius held his grip a moment longer, just long enough to make his point, before releasing him.

'This has gone on long enough,' he said. 'My father was a friend to Nicomedes, a loyal ally. Tell the king that the son of Julius Caesar has travelled hundreds of miles to see him, and if he has any regard for his memory, then he will see us immediately.'

The official smoothed his sleeve where Julius had grabbed him, his expression darkening.

'Careful, boy,' he warned. 'You may be important in Rome, but here, you are merely a guest. And guests who overstep their welcome often find themselves in far less… comfortable accommodation.'

The words hung in the air like a threat, but Julius didn't flinch. He met the man's gaze, refusing to back down, but he could see that he had already pushed too far. The official's jaw was set, his posture stiff with barely contained fury. Without another word, he turned sharply on his heel and strode out, his robes billowing behind him.

Julius watched him go, his mind racing. He had forced the issue, but had it worked? Or had he just made things worse?

Chapter Seventeen

The Palace of Nicomedes

The next morning, the knock came at the door again, but this time it was different, firmer, more deliberate. The official stepped inside, his usual mask of cool indifference firmly in place, but there was something else in his posture now.

'His Majesty will receive you at noon.'

Marcus let out a sharp breath, grinning as he clapped Julius on the back.

'Finally,' he said. 'I was beginning to think we'd grow old in this place.' But the messenger wasn't finished.

'The king has indeed granted an audience,' he said, raising his voice, 'but only for Gaius Julius Caesar.'

The relief in the room changed in an instant.

'Only him?' Balbus demanded, his brows drawing together. 'We are a Roman delegation. We came together…'

'And yet, His Majesty has requested only him,' replied the messenger. 'It is not a negotiation. He may come alone, or not at all.'

Julius studied the messenger's face. There was no room for argument here, no possibility of pressing the issue. Nicomedes had made his terms clear. He turned to his comrades.

'We've waited long enough,' he said, 'I'll go and see what I can do but if I there are problems, I will argue for your attendance.' Before anyone could respond, he turned back to the messenger. 'Tell the king it will be my honour,' he said and watched as the messenger turned away to return to the palace.

Several hours later, Julius left their quarters and walked across to the palace entrance. Behind him, Marcus stood by the entrance, watching him go but his eyes narrowed slightly as he let his gaze drift upward, drawn by a subtle shift in the light.

There, on one of the smaller balconies, half-concealed

133

behind an ornate curtain, a figure stood watching. The man was dressed in a flowing robe of deep purple, the hem embroidered with gold and even from this distance, Marcus could tell the cloth was of the finest weave, the cut unmistakably regal. He had never seen Nicomedes before, but he needed no introduction. That was the king, and his gaze was fixed firmly on Julius.

The palace doors swung open, and Julius stepped inside, his breath catching in his throat. He had seen wealth before, marble halls, golden statues, the extravagant villas of Rome's elite, but this was something else entirely.

The floor beneath him was a single sheet of polished onyx, so smooth it reflected the towering columns that lined the entrance hall. Mosaics of gods and heroes stretched across the vaulted ceiling, their eyes seeming to watch him as he passed and massive braziers burned with perfumed oils, filling the air with the scent of myrrh and jasmine. The very walls shimmered, inlaid with lapis lazuli and bands of pure gold.

Servants lined the hall in perfect silence, their heads bowed as Julius was led forward. Not a murmur passed between them, only the whisper of their silken robes as they shifted to make way. He had expected some acknowledgment, some wary glances or whispered words, but instead, there was only quiet reverence, as if he were stepping into a temple rather than a royal court.

At the base of a grand staircase, his escort stopped, and a servant stepped forward, bearing a folded cloth draped over his forearms. With careful hands, he unfurled it, a cloak of shimmering gold fabric, impossibly light, yet rich enough to be worth a fortune.

Julius hesitated, but the servant moved with quiet efficiency, settling the cloak over his shoulders before stepping back with a deep bow. The guards gestured for him to move, and he ascended the stairs before heading through an immense set of gilded doors.

The audience chamber stretched before him, cavernous and vast. The walls were draped in deep purple, embroidered with golden lions and serpents and at the far end of the hall, seated atop an ornate throne unlike anything Julius had ever seen, was Nicomedes IV of Bithynia.

Julius forced himself to move forward, his footsteps echoing in the vastness of the chamber. His palms felt clammy against the gold-trimmed fabric of his borrowed cloak. He stopped at the foot of the throne and inclined his head slightly, waiting.

For a few moments there was nothing, no words, no acknowledgement, then, to Julius's surprise, Nicomedes rose and without warning, reached forward... and embraced him.

Back in the courtyard, Marcus pushed open the heavy wooden door and stepped back into their quarters, heading to the room where he shared meals with the rest of the delegation.

Balbus was already there, seated at a small table, a jug of wine before him. He looked up before pouring a measure into two cups, sliding one across to Marcus as he took the seat opposite him.

Marcus accepted it, taking a slow sip before exhaling. Something sat uneasily in his mind, a nagging discomfort he couldn't quite place. He stared into the dark red liquid, swirling it idly before finally speaking.

'Something's bothering me,' he admitted. 'But I don't know what.'

Balbus didn't react, simply taking a measured sip of his own.

'We've been sitting around for almost two weeks,' he said evenly. 'That would make any man uneasy.'

Marcus studied him for a moment. There was something too casual in his tone, too dismissive ... and he had avoided meeting Marcus's stare.

'Do you know something,' asked Marcus, setting his cup down. 'Is Julius in danger?'

For a moment, Balbus didn't answer. Then, with a quiet sigh, he shook his head.

'No,' he said. 'He isn't in any danger. But there are...

rumours.'

Marcus frowned.

'What kind of rumours?'

Balbus hesitated, then let out another sigh.

'Nicomedes has a reputation,' he said. 'He's known for his attraction to men, young men, in particular. And you have to admit, Julius is a particularly handsome young man.'

A silence stretched between them, then, Marcus burst out laughing.

Balbus looked at him, unimpressed, but Marcus only shook his head, grinning as he took another swig of wine.

'Gods, I thought you were going to tell me something serious.' He wiped his mouth, still grinning. 'You had me ready to storm the palace.'

Balbus didn't share his amusement.

'It's not nothing, Marcus,' he said.

'Oh, it is,' said Marcus, still shaking his head. 'Believe me, there are no concerns on that score. I've known Julius my whole life and if there's one thing I know for certain, he is a ladies' man through and through. Now, if you don't mind, I'm going to finish this wine and enjoy the fact that our greatest concern is a king's wandering eye and not an assassin's blade.'

Later that night, Julius found himself dining with the king deep in the bowels of the palace. A long table of dark cedar stretched the length of the room, its surface polished to a mirror sheen, inlaid with bands of gold and mother-of-pearl, but despite its size, only two places were set, Nicomedes at the head, Julius immediately to his right.

Soft candlelight flickered against the deep purple tapestries lining the walls, their golden embroidery glinting in the dim glow and braziers burned with fragrant oils, filling the air with the warm scent of cinnamon and cloves.

Servants moved in near silence, bringing forth an endless

array of dishes. Platters of roasted lamb, garnished with pomegranate seeds and drizzled in honeyed wine, fresh fish, their skins crisped with fragrant herbs, and warm bread, dusted with sesame.

Julius accepted a goblet of dark wine, taking a measured sip. The moment stretched, unhurried, before he finally spoke.

'My father,' he said, setting the goblet down. 'I believe you knew him well?'

Nicomedes leaned back in his chair, his expression touched with nostalgia.

'I did,' he said with a nod. 'Gaius Julius Caesar was a man of quiet strength. A soldier, yes, but more than that, a diplomat when it mattered. Rome sent him east in my father's time, long before I took the throne. He negotiated trade agreements, calmed border disputes, and though he spoke for the Senate, I always felt he carried himself as his own man.'

Julius listened intently as Nicomedes continued, his words rich with detail. He spoke of his father's dealings in Bithynia, of nights spent in council chambers, of battles fought on distant shores where Rome's influence stretched thin. There was admiration in his voice, but also familiarity. Nicomedes had not simply met his father as a Roman envoy, he had known him as a man.

The conversation flowed easily as the night wore on. The wine loosened their words, and soon, they spoke of more than just the past, they talked of politics, philosophy, and of the changing world beyond Rome's reach. Finally, Julius sighed and placed his goblet down on the table.

'Your Majesty,' he said, without looking up, 'there is something we must discuss, the reason I am here.' He allowed the words to settle before looking up to meet the king's gaze. 'Thermus needs a fleet.'

Nicomedes paused mid-motion, before slowly lowering his cup.

'And he sent you to ask for it,' he said eventually, 'because I was a friend of your father.'

Julius did not look away.

'Yes,' he admitted, 'but you too have known war and know that any hesitation can be the difference between victory and disaster. Mytilene is a threat and if left unchecked, it could become something worse. However, it could take months for Thermus to amass the ships he needs, but if you could loan him some of yours, the threat could be ended before it spirals into something larger. I did not come here expecting gifts, majesty, or to use my father's name as a lever, I came because I knew you would listen. Not just to me, but to reason.'

The words hung between them and Nicomedes reclined slightly, running a hand over the stem of his goblet. His gaze did not waver, but something in his posture shifted, as if weighing the request against something unseen.

Julius held his breath until the king finally nodded.

'I will consider it,' he said, 'but not tonight. 'For now, let us just enjoy the evening.'

Julius accepted the answer for what it was, an opening, not a promise. He inclined his head slightly, then reached for a piece of bread, tearing it apart before dipping it into a bowl of seasoned oil. The mood remained warm, the conversation lightening again as the night stretched on. They spoke of Rome, of the men who ruled it, of the world beyond their borders and as servants refilled their goblets, and laughter punctuated their words, for the first time in weeks, Julius felt at ease.

The days stretched into weeks, each one identical to the last. Marcus and the others remained confined to their quarters, unable to leave the palace grounds, their only news of Julius arriving through carefully worded messages.

'He is well and will return when the negotiations are over.'

The same words, repeated over and over again, yet never accompanied by details. No explanations, no assurances. Just enough to keep them waiting, powerless.

Marcus paced the courtyard in frustration, boots scuffing against the sun-warmed stones. The city bustled beyond the palace walls, but here, within the gilded confines of their guarded residence, time moved like a stagnant river. He had never been good at waiting. Balbus sat nearby, sharpening a dagger against a whetstone.

'Four weeks,' muttered Julius, stopping in front of him. 'Four damned weeks. This is getting ridiculous.'

'Maybe he enjoys fine wine and soft cushions more than you thought,' replied Balbus.

'He wouldn't just forget us,' said Marcus with a scowl. 'There's something wrong.'

'These things take time, Marcus,' replied Balbus. 'And besides, there nothing we can do. He's where he needs to be. We are where *we* need to be. It will all sort itself out in time.'

Marcus let out a frustrated breath.

'And what do you suggest we do in the meantime? Sit here like prisoners?'

'You could learn something useful,' said Balbus.

'Like what?' asked Marcus.

Balbus glanced towards the row of gladii hanging from hooks embedded into the wall.

'You could learn how to fight.'

Marcus followed his gaze before turning back to face him. 'Are you serious?'

'Deadly,' said Balbus. 'You are a young man in a country beset by war. It's about time you learned how to defend yourself.'

The training began in earnest the very next morning. The courtyard became their battleground, the air filled with the clash of steel, the scrape of boots against stone, and the occasional burst of laughter from their fellow travellers whenever Marcus fumbled a parry or stumbled over his own feet.

At first, he was hopeless, his strikes too slow, his stance too rigid. Balbus toyed with him, deflecting his attacks with ease and punishing every mistake with a sharp slap from the flat of his blade.

'You're thinking too much,' Balbus barked one morning after disarming Marcus for the third time. 'Your enemy isn't going to wait for you to work out your next move. Again!'

And so it continued, day after day. The sun rose, the swords clashed, and Marcus fell, again and again. His hands blistered, his muscles ached, and yet Balbus never let up. If he was slow, Balbus made him quicker. If he hesitated, Balbus pressed harder.

Then, something changed. The awkwardness began to fade, his grip steadied, and his footwork improved. He stopped flinching at every strike and started meeting them with his own. The bruises still came, but now they were earned in battle rather than in clumsiness.

As the weeks passed, something hardened in Marcus. The frustration of waiting, the helplessness of their situation, the uncertainty of Julius' absence, it all boiled beneath the surface. He fought harder, more aggressively. His swings became sharper, his attacks faster and he stopped holding back.

One evening, as the last light of day painted the courtyard gold, Balbus raised his sword for another round. Marcus met him head-on, but this time, something was different. His anger was raw, his blows ferocious. He forced Balbus back step by step, the sheer force of his assault driving the veteran onto the defensive. The spectators who had once laughed at his clumsiness were now silent, watching as Marcus fought with something close to real skill.

Then he lost himself in it and with a guttural roar, Marcus swung wildly, aiming for Balbus' head. It was a powerful strike, fast, reckless and deadly. But Balbus was still better and ducked under the swing before stepping inside his opponent's reach and driving his fist straight into his Marcus's lower back.

The impact sent Marcus sprawling and he hit the ground hard, the dust rising around him. The world spun as he lay there in agonising pain, face down, his breath ragged. He coughed, spitting dirt from his mouth and shaking his head as he tried to make sense of what had just happened.

As his focus returned, he stared at pair of ornate boots, planted firmly in the dust before him. Marcus blinked, his heartbeat still pounding in his ears before slowly, he raised his gaze and squinted at the man standing before him. It was Julius.

'Are you finished?' asked Julius.

Marcus exhaled, wiping dust from his chin.

'I think so.'

Julius nodded.

'Good. Now get up. We're getting out of here.'

Chapter Eighteen

Ephesus

The dock at Ephesus was alive with motion, the scent of salt and fish thick in the air as gulls wheeled overhead, crying out above the din of sailors and merchants. The water beyond the piers shimmered beneath the midday sun, reflecting the rows of ships moored along the harbour, Roman triremes, merchant galleys, and sleek Bithynian vessels, their prows carved with the likenesses of sea creatures.

Julius and Marcus moved through the throng, stepping aside as dockworkers hauled crates of grain and dried fruit up gangplanks, their bare backs glistening with sweat. Nearby, a group of soldiers in battered tunics laughed among themselves as they leaned against a stack of barrels, sharpening their gladii in preparation for the coming campaign.

'Not a bad sight, is it?' said Marcus, nodding toward the sea. 'Ships from Bithynia, already on their way to Lesbos. You did well, Julius, though what you did to make Nicomedes see sense is beyond me.'

'Those are only half of them,' said Julius, changing the subject. 'The rest are already on their way to Lesbos to join with Lucullus.'

'I still can't believe Thermus actually rewarded you for it?'

'You sound surprised,' said Julius.

'Oh, I *am* surprised,' said Marcus. 'Thermus handing out honours like a senator handing out bribes? That's rare enough. But making you a Contubernalis and letting us join the campaign? I thought we'd be stuck counting grain shipments in Pergamum.'

Julius exhaled, his expression growing more serious as they walked.

'The truth is, he didn't have much choice. He needs every ship and every man he can get. And after Nicomedes' support, denying me would have been… ungracious.'

Marcus gave him a sideways glance.

'So, what you're saying is, you made it impossible for him to refuse.'

'Something like that,' replied Julius with a smile.

They reached the pier where their assigned vessel was moored, a sturdy Roman supply ship, its hull painted in the red and gold of Thermus' forces.

'Well, there she is,' said Marcus. 'Our home for the next few days.'

Julius pulled his cloak tighter around his shoulders, the memory of their last voyage that had nearly ended at the bottom of the sea still raw.

'You look like a man walking to his own funeral,' said Marcus.

'After the last voyage, can you blame me?' muttered Julius. He cast a wary glance towards the ship, its deck already packed with supplies, animals, and men. 'That thing doesn't look much better than the last one.'

'At least this one isn't sailing through the heart of a storm,' said Marcus. He slapped Julius on the shoulder. 'And if it does, I'll personally throw you overboard to lighten the load.'

Julius scowled but said nothing and turned his attention to the motley gathering of warriors waiting to embark.

There were legionaries, not many, but they moved with the crisp discipline of Rome, their segmented armour polished, short swords resting comfortably on their hips. These men were professionals, their expressions impassive as they checked their gear and ignored the chaos around them. The rest? A rabble of adventurers, mercenaries, and exiles.

A group of Thracians stood near the gangplank, towering men with thick beards and tattooed arms, their curved rhomphaia blades strapped across their backs. They eyed the Romans with amusement, muttering in their own tongue. Nearby, a knot of Greek hoplites adjusted their bronze helmets, their spears bound in cloth, shields slung over their shoulders. They looked clean, well-fed, probably veterans of some city-state's war, looking for the next opportunity to sell their swords. And then there were the desperates, half-starved wanderers clutching rusted weapons, runaways, criminals, and men with no better prospects than war.

The crew of the ship were a sullen, sunburnt lot, moving about their duties with sluggish efficiency. The captain, a wiry Greek with a permanent sneer, barked orders at his men while chewing on an olive pit.

'Roman passage?' asked the captain as Julius and Marcus approached the gangplank. His gaze flicked over their fine cloaks, their expensive boots, and he smirked. 'Ah, noble volunteers. Off to see some real blood, are we?'

Julius handed over the token that guaranteed their place.

'We're here to fight, not sightsee.'

The captain inspected it lazily, then tossed it back.

'Hope you don't mind the smell of goat,' he said, 'your kind usually pays extra for comfort, but Thermus isn't funding a pleasure cruise.'

Julius stepped past him without another word. Onboard, the deck was a chaotic mess of cargo, men and animals. A pair of donkeys brayed in protest, tied beside stacks of grain sacks, the smell of seaweed, and wet fur lingering in the air.

Julius found a spot near the railing, watching as the rest of the passengers filed aboard. The legionaries took a disciplined position near the mast, standing apart from the rest, the Thracians settled in a group, already gambling with dice, while a pair of the Greeks muttered prayers to their gods.

Marcus leaned against the rail beside him, stretching his arms.

'A fine collection of Rome's finest.'

Julius exhaled, bracing himself as the sailors loosened ropes and the oarsmen took their places. The captain barked orders, and as the ship began to drift from the dock, Ephesus shrunk behind them, the hills and temples fading in the morning mist.

The wind filled the sails, pushing the heavy merchant vessel northward across the wine-dark sea. The coast of Asia Minor stretched to their right, rugged cliffs and olive-covered hills rising from the water. Beyond the horizon to the left, unseen but ever-present, lay the open Aegean, a graveyard for the unprepared.

Julius stood near the prow, the steady motion of the ship unsettling his stomach, but he focused on the horizon, willing himself to ignore it.

Marcus leaned against a coil of rope beside him, chewing on a strip of dried meat.

'This isn't so bad,' he said between bites. 'Better than the last voyage.'

Julius gave him a sidelong glance.

'That's not exactly high praise.'

A gruff laugh interrupted them. One of the sailors, a thickset man with a bald head had been listening. He spat over the side and smirked.

'You boys still wet behind the ears, then? Had a rough crossing, did you?'

'Let's just say we're hoping this one stays calm,' said Marcus.'

The sailor shook his head.

'It's not the sea you need to worry about,' he said. 'It's what's waiting for us when we get there.' He gestured toward the northern horizon, where the island of Lesbos lay somewhere beyond the haze. 'Mytilene's not some backwater town, you know. The city has strong walls and is heavily defended. The bastards are dug in, and they've still got friends out there.'

Julius followed his gesture.

'You mean ships?'

The sailor nodded.

'Aye. Some of their fleet's still hiding along the coast, trying to break our blockade. Not that they've had much luck, Lucullus has them boxed in tight, especially since Nicomedes sent his ships. That was an immense stroke of luck.'

Marcus drew a breath to inform the sailor it was Julius's doing, but Julius gave him a look that made him shut his mouth.

'Ever seen a proper naval battle, lads?' continued the sailor.

'Not yet,' replied Marcus. 'We've spent more time trying not to drown.'

'Then you'll want to stay close to the deck when we pass Lesbos. You might just get a show.'

'How many ships does Lucullus have?' asked Marcus.

The man scratched his beard.

'Enough. Last I heard, he's got at least thirty warships patrolling the coast, Liburnians, triremes, even a few quinqueremes. They may be getting old now, but they are still fast and deadly. If anything, bigger than a fishing boat tries to slip through, his boys burn it or sink it.'

Marcus let out a low whistle.

'And the Mytileneans?'

The sailor shrugged.

'They had an impressive fleet once, but most of it is now at the bottom of the sea. The rest are holed up in hidden coves, trying to find a way out before Lucullus strangles them completely. They do come out occasionally, to get supplies or to target lone ships without any escorts, but to all intents and purposes, they are done. They just have no answer to our navy.'

Julius glanced toward the open sea. Somewhere out there, Roman warships prowled the waters, their oars cutting through the waves like sharpened knives.

'So why haven't they surrendered yet?' he asked.

The sailor laughed.

'Because they're Greek, lad. Proud bastards, too stubborn to lay down their arms until their sails come crashing down about their heads.'

A sudden shout from the mast cut the conversation short. A lookout had spotted something in the distance. The sailors moved quickly, peering ahead. Far on the horizon, barely visible through the morning haze, were the distant sails of a Roman squadron, moving in tight formation northward towards Lesbos.

The black-painted hulls of the warships cut through the water like hunting beasts and even at this distance, Julius could see the rhythmic flash of oars, the disciplined movement of Rome's navy. Things were getting real and for the briefest of moments, he wondered just what he had gotten himself in to.

Beyond the horizon, far to the north, a Liburnian warship cut through the waters of the Aegean, its oars moving in perfect rhythm. The sea was calm, but the tension on board was anything but. Every man on the deck knew that an enemy fleet was out there, somewhere beyond the horizon, trying to slip past Rome's blockade and it was their job to stop them.

Tribune Aulus Septimius stood at the prow, his cloak pressed against his back by the sea breeze. He had commanded warships before and fully understood the patience of naval warfare, the long, empty hours spent scanning the horizon, the sudden fury of combat when an enemy was finally sighted. He had seen fleets burn, men drown, and the ocean turn red with blood, but there was no glory in war at sea. There was only the hunt, the kill, and survival.

Boots thudded against the deck behind him, but he did not need to turn to know who approached. Centurion Decimus Cordus halted beside him, a veteran of the legions. Cordus commanded the ship's complement of marines, the classiarii, men trained to fight in the brutal, cramped chaos of a naval battle. Unlike the sailors, whose weapons were short, curved blades meant for slashing ropes and rigging, Cordus and his men carried the standard Roman gladius, their movements drilled for boarding actions and close-quarters combat.

'No sign of them,' said Septimius, his eyes still fixed on the horizon.

'Not yet,' Cordus answered, calmly, 'but if they're out there, we'll find them.'

Septimius finally turned to face him. The Centurion stood like a statue, his arms folded behind his back, his feet planted firmly as if the shifting deck did not exist beneath him. There was no unease, no wasted movement. Everything about the man spoke of discipline.

'The men?' Septimius asked.

'They are ready,' said Cordus. 'We drill three times a day, the oarsmen are in rotation and every marine is armed, armoured and waiting. We can board at a moment's notice.'

Septimius gave a short nod.

A sharp blast of a horn from the aft deck cut through the air and every sailor turned, snapping to attention as the ship's captain emerged.

Nestor, a Greek who had served under Rome for years, strode to the command deck, his face set in stone.

'Trim the sail,' he ordered. 'We hold our course to the eastern pass. If they come, we intercept. No ship gets through.'

The sailors moved at once and as they started pulling at the ropes to adjust the canvas, the Roman warship pressed on, silent and watchful, a lethal blade of the Republic, poised to strike at a moment's notice.

Chapter Nineteen

The Aegean Sea

The sea stretched out like polished glass beneath a cloudless sky, the steady creak of wood, the rhythmic splash of oars, and the occasional murmur of conversation the only sounds as the three Roman supply ships sailed northward towards Lesbos.

Julius stood near the prow, watching the horizon. The voyage had been smooth, the winds favourable and for once, the sea felt almost welcoming. Marcus stretched out beside him.

'I could get used to this,' he said.

'Let's not tempt the gods,' muttered Julius, enjoying the calm.

Moments later, as if responding to his warning, a voice called out across the decks.

'Sails on the horizon!'

Heads snapped up and conversations stopped as the captain and crew rushed to the rails, squinting into the distance.

Julius followed their gaze, expecting to see the squadron they had seen a few days earlier. At first, he saw nothing, just the endless blue where sea met sky, then, faint and distant, he spotted two dark shapes, their sails full, their prows slicing cleanly through the water.

The older sailors muttered curses, their hands tightening on the railings. One of them turned to the captain, his face grim.

'They're Mytilenean warships,' he said.

The ships weren't large, no bigger than triremes, but to a fleet of defenceless merchant vessels, they were death itself. These weren't lumbering grain carriers weighed down with supplies, these were sleek predators, built for speed, for boarding, for the kill.

Julius felt his stomach tighten.

'Can we outrun them?' he asked.

The captain shot him a glare.

'We'll try.'

The sailors moved fast, adjusting the sails, shifting the weight of the cargo. The other two ships followed suit, veering slightly to catch the wind.

Julius and Marcus watched in silence as the enemy ships grew larger with every passing moment.

'It's no use,' muttered Julius, as the Mytilenean ships closed the gap. 'They're too fast.'

The captain, realising there was no way he could outrun them, turned to his men.

'Arm yourselves! Prepare to repel boarders!'

The order sent a ripple of urgency through the deck and the few legionaries on board, formed a line, drawing their gladii, adjusting their shields. Julius drew his own sword. His hands were steady, but his pulse was a hammer in his chest. Marcus stood beside him, his own heart racing, but unlike Julius, as his hand found the now familiar hilt of his gladius, somewhere, deep inside there was the faintest flicker of excitement.

The rest of the men stood in uneasy silence, gripping whatever weapons they had managed to find. Some clutched rusty swords or dented shields, but most held makeshift weapons, fishing knives, wooden clubs, even lengths of rope weighted with iron hooks, and
Julius could see the fear in their faces.

'Stand ready!' shouted the captain, and fight like you have never fought before. If they take this ship, we all are all dead men anyway.'

The men shifted uneasily, exchanging nervous glances. Then, suddenly, without warning, the enemy ships veered away. Shouts of confusion rippled across the deck and Julius blinked in disbelief, watching as the two Mytilenean warships turned sharply, their sails shifting.

'What in Hades?' he muttered. Then, they saw it. From the east, a Roman war galley surged closer, its hull cutting through the waves with terrifying precision. The crimson-painted prow bore the snarling face of a wolf, sunlight gleaming off its bronze plating. Its oars drove the water into a white froth, each stroke in perfect unison, propelling it forward with incredible speed.

Julius felt the shift in the air. Where before there had been dread, now there was something else... awe. A sailor let out a ragged laugh, his voice filled with relief.

'It's one of ours!'

Not far away, close enough to hear the shouts of alarm, the Mytileneans panicked and though the first ship caught the wind, its sail snapping taut as it turned sharply to flee, the second wasn't so lucky.

The war galley's speed increased, the prow dipping slightly as the ram was aimed at the vulnerable enemy hull. It was going to hit and every man on the supply ship watched in silence as the sea itself seemed to tremble beneath the oncoming impact.

When it came, the collision was thunderous as the bronze ram punched through the enemy hull like a spear through flesh. The enemy ship lurched sideways, men screaming as they were thrown from their feet. Some tumbled overboard, vanishing beneath the churning foam while others staggered, grasping for ropes and railings, their faces twisted in panic.

'Ad gladios!' Centurion Cordus bellowed on the attacking ship, his voice cutting through the chaos, and the classiarii surged forward like unleashed hounds, vaulting across the shattered prow with practised ease. Their iron-shod caligae thudded against the enemy deck, shields raised, gladii flashing in the sunlight and they struck without hesitation, without mercy.

The Mytileneans barely had time to react. Those closest to the impact were still reeling, clutching at minor injuries or trying to right themselves, but the Romans were already upon them.

The first rank of classiarii hit hard, driving their shields into the enemy line before stabbing low, gladii ripping through cloth and flesh with brutal efficiency.

A Mytilenean officer, his bronze helmet askew, raised his curved sword in a desperate swing but a Roman marine caught the blow on his shield, twisted his wrist, and slammed the boss into the man's face. Teeth snapped, blood spraying, and before the officer could even fall, the Roman rammed his sword into the man's throat.

Julius and Marcus stood at the rail of their supply ship, watching in stunned silence. The precision of the Romans was terrifying. There was no chaos in their ranks, no reckless lunging or wild slashes. They moved as one, shields overlapping, swords stabbing in quick, efficient thrusts.

A Mytilenean tried to retreat, scrambling backwards, only to be cut down by a gladius to the chest. Another warrior, face contorted in rage, charged forward with a spear but he barely took two steps before a Roman pilum took him in the chest, driving clean through him, and he fell backwards, gasping like a fish on dry land.

Some of the Mytileneans tried to fight. They roared their defiance, swinging their weapons in desperate arcs, but the Romans were relentless and within a few moments, the deck became a slaughterhouse.

'By the gods,' muttered Marcus. 'They are... *magnificent.*'

It was over in minutes and the last few Mytileneans, realising the futility of resistance, dropped their weapons and raised their hands in surrender. The deck was a charnel house, bodies sprawled in pools of blood, the air thick with the copper stench of death.

Centurion Cordus stood amid the carnage, his sword dripping red, his face unreadable. He surveyed the bloodbath with the gaze of a man who had seen it all before. He gave a short nod, the fight was done.

The Roman marines moved quickly, securing prisoners and finishing off the wounded. There was no celebration, no cheering, just the methodical efficiency of men who had done this a hundred times before.

Julius swallowed hard. The battle had been short, brutal, and utterly decisive and the Romans had dominated. He had always known Rome's strength lay in its legions, but today, he had seen another face of its power, one forged in the blood and steel of the classiarii. And it was terrifying.

The war galley came alongside the merchant vessel with practised ease, its oars retracting in perfect synchrony as grappling lines were thrown across and secured. The crew of the merchant ship, still reeling from the near-disaster, moved quickly to assist, steadying the gangplank as it was laid between the vessels.

Cordus stepped across first, his movements as deliberate and controlled as they had been in battle. His bloodied gladius was sheathed, but his gaze remained sharp, scanning the faces of the men before him. Behind him followed Tribune Septimius, his red-crested helmet marking him as a high-ranking officer of the classiarii.

The merchant captain stepped forward and clasped the officer's forearm in greeting.

'Gratitude is not enough, Tribune,' he said, his voice tight with relief. 'Without your intervention, we would have been fish-bait before the hour was done.'

The Tribune inclined his head slightly.

'You were fortunate,' he said, 'the Mytileneans are getting desperate. We have sunk or captured half a dozen of their raiders in the last fortnight, yet they still come.'

Julius, standing nearby, took in the Tribune's words with a frown.

'They must be running low on supplies,' he said.

'Exactly,' said Cordus. 'They know they cannot hold out forever, so they seek to do as much damage as possible before the end. Their commanders have given up on honourable engagements, now they are little more than pirates, striking at whatever they can reach.'

The merchant captain exhaled sharply.

'I've sailed these waters for years, but never has it been this bad.'

The Tribune studied him for a moment before giving a short nod.

'We will escort you the rest of the way to Lesbos. Thermus has already sent his forces ashore at the port of Pyrrha so by now, it should be under Roman control.

A visible wave of relief washed over the merchant crew. The knowledge that a war galley would guard them was an unexpected blessing and the tension that had gripped the ship began to ease.

Marcus wandered to the edge of the deck, his gaze fixed on the war galley alongside. His eyes traced the lines of its hull, the oars now resting just above the water, the great bronze ram slick with blood and sea foam. He paced along the rails, drinking in every detail, the disciplined ranks of marines still standing at attention, the neatly coiled ropes, the great mainsail emblazoned with the red insignia of the Republic.

Julius walked over, noticing his friend's fascination.

'Are you admiring the ship, or the men who command it?'

Marcus turned, eyes gleaming.

'Both. Look at them, Julius. Every man knows his place, and every movement is precise. And that ship, it moves like a hunting beast. I have seen many vessels in my time, but never one like this.'

'Perhaps you should trade your horse for an oar.'

'Perhaps I should,' mused Marcus. 'The land has its charms, but there is something about the sea… the way it can be tamed by those who understand it. In another life I might have taken to a ship like this.' His gaze drifted back to the war galley, watching as its crew moved with disciplined ease, preparing to escort them towards Lesbos. The journey was not yet over, and danger still lurked on the horizon, but for now, at least, they were not alone on the water.

The war galley parted ways with the merchant vessels as they neared Lesbos, slipping away into deeper waters like a predator returning to its hunt. The merchant ships pressed on, their sails full, but the relief of their narrow escape had long faded. The men on board were silent now, staring ahead as the coastline unfurled before them, revealing a scene that sent a chill through even the most hardened among them.

As they rounded the final headland, the harbour of Pyrrha sprawled beneath a sky thick with smoke. The stench hit them first, a foul mixture of burning timber and rotting flesh. The bay was crowded with ships, some intact, others reduced to skeletal ruins, their blackened masts jutting from the waves like the bones of the dead. A few drifted aimlessly, abandoned, their hulls scarred with scorch marks and studded with arrows.

The docks were no better. What should have been an orderly port of trade was instead a shattered ruin. Empty crates and broken supply boxes lay in heaps, thrown aside by desperate hands. Blood stained the wooden planks, some dried into dark smears, some fresh, pooling beneath the wounded who lay sprawled across every available surface.

There were too many of them. Soldiers with missing limbs, their wounds hastily wrapped in blood-soaked bandages. Men groaning, shivering with fever, their skin slick with sweat as infections took hold. Others did not even moan, they simply lay there, eyes wide and unblinking, their faces frozen in the final moments of agony.

Shouts rang out through the thick air. Legionaries barked orders, their voices hoarse with exhaustion, trying to impose discipline where there was none. Dockworkers struggled to move barrels of water and sacks of grain, but the sheer mass of bodies, both living and dead, made every effort slow and inefficient. A group of medics rushed past, carrying a stretcher with what had once been a man. His lower half was gone, severed by some terrible wound, and yet he still clung to life, his lips moving in silent, desperate prayer.

Beyond the chaos of the docks, through the smoke that curled above the shore, the city of Mytilene loomed. Its massive walls gleamed faintly under the sun, their golden hue undisturbed by the carnage unfolding far below. It was untouched, defiant, standing as a cruel reminder that the war was far from over.

Julius and Marcus stood near the prow of their ship, neither speaking as they took it all in. Around them, the other men aboard the merchant ship had fallen into uneasy silence, their previous relief swallowed by the grim reality before them.

'Gods preserve us,' Marcus murmured.

Julius exhaled slowly, his hand tightening on the hilt of his sword. He had been told about war, had read about it, listened to retired generals as they repeated their oft told stories of bravery and brilliant tactics, but this was…raw, an uncontrolled madness of suffering like nothing he had ever imagined. This was not an honourable battle in a war of equals, this was a slow, grinding death, a war of attrition that devoured both the victors and the vanquished alike.

The ship rocked gently as it approached the docks, and the crew moved into action, calling out to secure lines and prepare for disembarkation. But even as they did, the unease in the air was palpable. This was not the Rome they knew. This was not order… this was *chaos*.

Chapter Twenty

Lesbos

By the gods...' Marcus muttered beside him, 'I thought war was supposed to be glorious.' Julius said nothing. He had grown up hearing tales of conquest, of mighty generals carving their names into history with their swords, of Rome's legions marching in perfect formation, of honour, discipline and order. But here, in the ruins of Pyrrha, he saw none of those things.

A body lay sprawled in the gutter ahead of them, half-covered by a torn cloak. Julius forced himself to look. The man, Greek, judging by his clothing, had fallen face-first onto the stone, his tunic dark with blood. His right hand still clutched a rusted blade, but it had done him little good. The fight had been over before he had ever stood a chance.

'They resisted,' said Marcus, as if that explained everything. 'They must have known they had no hope, but they still fought.'

A sudden crash echoed from a nearby street and Marcus's hand went instinctively to the hilt of his gladius, but a moment later, a pair of Roman auxiliaries emerged from the smoke, dragging a screaming woman between them. Her dress was torn, her face streaked with grime, her words an incomprehensible mixture of Greek and Latin as she struggled against their grip.

Julius tensed. His instincts screamed at him to intervene, but Marcus caught his arm before he could take a step forward.

'Don't,' his friend warned under his breath. 'We have only been here a few heartbeats and know not the truth of the matter.'

The truth of it stung. Julius may have been a newly appointed Contubernalis, but he was still an untested officer. These men had fought and bled in the battle while he had only just set foot in a war zone. He forced himself to look away.

They continued through the streets, weaving between the wreckage of burned-out homes and abandoned market stalls. The cries of the wounded carried from a makeshift infirmary near the temple district, where medics laboured under torchlight to save what few men could still be saved.

Ahead, a Centurion stood atop a pile of rubble, his dented helmet tucked under one arm. His face was lined with sweat and dust, but he still carried himself with the authority of a man who had survived.

'Who are you?' he barked as Julius and Marcus approached.

'Gaius Julius Caesar, Contubernalis under Thermus,' Julius replied, steadying his voice.

The Centurion grunted.

'Never heard of you.'

'We arrived this evening with reinforcements from Bithynia. We were told to report to Commander Minucius.'

The Centurion spat into the dirt.

'Minucius is dead. Cut down in the first charge.' He turned his gaze back to the fires still burning along the waterfront. 'Doesn't matter anymore, the fighting's done. Scipio is now in charge so you should report to him.'

'Where will I find him?'

'His command post is near the centre. Look there.'

Julius nodded and turned away. The fires still raged, licking at the broken remains of temples and homes, the smoke thick and acrid. The cries of the wounded carried through the streets, Roman and Greek alike, some calling for their mothers, others begging the gods for mercy. Few would receive either.

A group of legionaries passed them, their eyes hollow, their faces streaked with blood and grime. One carried a severed hand still clutching the broken remains of a gladius. None of them spared Julius or Marcus a second glance. They had seen too much.

At last, the command post came into view, or what remained of it. A once-grand civic building, half its roof collapsed, its columns blackened with soot, now served as headquarters. The entrance was flanked by two battle-worn sentries, their pila planted in the ground, their faces as hard as marble. Julius stepped forward, straightening his shoulders.

'I am Contubernalis, Gaius Julius Caesar, here to report to Commander Scipio.'

The nearest guard barely spared him a glance.

'The commander is not to be disturbed.'

Julius exhaled sharply. They could push this, but there was little sense in antagonising exhausted men who had spent the day killing. Instead, he reached into the folds of his cloak and produced a rolled parchment bearing the insignia of Thermus.

'These are my orders,' he said, forcing authority into his tone. 'They are signed by Thermus himself. If Scipio wants to ignore them, that's his decision. But it won't be my head on the block when Thermus asks why his messenger was turned away.'

The second soldier shifted on his feet. He glanced at his companion, then jerked his chin toward the doors.

'Wait here.'

Julius said nothing as the younger man disappeared inside. He could feel Marcus vibrating with impatience beside him, but he held his ground. A confrontation wouldn't serve them here. A moment later, the soldier returned.

'The commander will see you.'

The first guard scowled but stepped aside.

Julius strode past them, Marcus at his side, and into the ruined building.

Inside, the devastation was no better. A table served as a makeshift war desk and a few surviving officers stood nearby, their faces gaunt with exhaustion. At the centre of it all stood Lucius Cornelius Scipio.

The man was younger than Julius had expected, barely older than thirty. His tunic was stained with blood, his own or another's, it was impossible to tell. His face was lined with soot, but his posture was straight, his presence commanding. He turned as they entered, his gaze sharp, assessing.

'You must be Caesar,' he said, his voice edged with weariness. 'We received reports that you were coming. I am led to believe you helped Thermus with Nicomedes and in return, he granted you a commission and passage here.'

Julius inclined his head.

'That's right. We seek to do our duty and help defeat the enemies of Rome.'

Scipio stared at Julius for a few moments before gesturing vaguely around him.

'Well, if you wanted to experience battle, you have certainly come to the right place. Welcome to war, Caesar, in all it's supposed bloody glory.'

An hour or so later, Julius and Marcus stepped into another half standing ruin, the headquarters of the first cohort having been assigned to it by Scipio. The smell hit them first, a thick, cloying stench of sweat and blood, made worse by the acrid smell of fire that still clung to the walls. The floor was covered in filth, discarded bandages stiff with dried pus, scraps of food swarming with flies, and dark stains that he knew, without needing to ask, were blood. Somewhere in the shadows, someone was coughing, a wet, rattling sound that sent a shiver down his spine.

The men inside barely reacted as he and Marcus entered. Some lay curled in their cloaks, faces turned to the wall, others sat hunched over, staring at nothing, their eyes hollow and rimmed with dark shadows. A few whispered in low voices, muttering prayers to gods who clearly hadn't been listening. These were the ones who had survived the assault on the docks, the ones lucky enough, or unlucky enough, to still be breathing.

A soldier near the centre of the room looked up as they approached. His face was lined with grime, his hair matted with sweat, and when he grinned, Julius saw half his teeth were missing.

'Well, would you look at this,' he rasped, his voice raw, probably from inhaling too much smoke. 'Fresh meat straight from the bathhouses of Rome. Are you lost, boys?'

A few of the others stared at the two young men, almost in resentment. Another, lying on his back with a rag pressed to a wound on his thigh, sneered without opening his eyes.

'No dirt under their nails,' he muttered. 'No blood on their boots. Pretty little things, smelling like olive oil and clean cloth.'

Julius ignored them, stepping carefully around a puddle of something dark and sticky, praying it was just spilled wine. He doubted it.

'Reinforcements, eh?' The first man spat onto the floor, missing Julius's boot by an inch. 'A bit fucking late for that. We took the docks, watched our comrades die for a spit of land, and now they send us Rome's whelps to keep watch over the ashes.'

Julius met his gaze, forcing his voice to remain steady.

'Scipio said you fought well,' he said. 'Your efforts did not go unnoticed.'

'No shit,' the man growled. 'But most of those we sailed with are in a fucking grave.'

The words hung in the air, heavy, undeniable. The only sounds were the distant crackle of burning timber outside and the groans of the wounded who hadn't been lucky enough to get a place in the medical tents.

Marcus found a space against the far wall and dropped his pack onto the dirt-caked floor. Julius rolled out his bed mat beside him. For years, he had imagined war, glory, honour, the clash of swords and the roar of victory. But here, surrounded by the filth, the stink, and the dead-eyed stares of men who had seen too much, the realisation settled over him like a lead weight.

This was real war, and it had nothing to do with glory.

The next morning, Julius and Marcus were woken by the shifting of bodies and the grumbling of tired men dragging themselves up from their bedrolls. A messenger found them before they had even finished lacing their boots.

'Domine, you've been summoned.'

They followed him through the shattered streets, stepping over splintered beams and the charred remains of carts and market stalls. Bodies, mostly Greek, had been dragged into rough piles, their flesh bloating in the morning heat, swarmed by flies. Roman auxiliaries worked nearby, digging massive graves, their faces blank, their movements mechanical.

The cohort's command post was little more than a half-collapsed warehouse near the docks, its roof partially caved in. Inside, a grizzled blood-soaked man sat bare-chested on a chair, drinking from a flagon of wine as a medicus bandaged a wound on his side. It was the Primus Pilus, the most senior Centurion in the legion… their new commander.

He was much older than Julius with a heavily scarred neck and the sloped shoulders of a man who had worn his armour for too many years. His face was dirty and unshaven, and his eyes, cold and grey, locked on to them the moment they entered.

Julius and Marcus saluted, fists to chests.

'I am Gaius Julius Caesar,' said Julius, 'posted to your cohort by Commander Scipio by the orders of General Thermus.'

The Centurion did not reply and lowered his gaze to a parchment in his free hand. The silence in the room stretched, broken only by the distant shouts of soldiers outside and the faint crackle of fires still burning in the ruins beyond. Finally, he looked up and stared at the new arrivals.

'This letter,' he said quietly, 'amongst others, was found amongst Minucius's things after he was killed. Apparently, it arrived several weeks ago. It says that you are a fugitive and Lucius Cornelius Sulla saw fit to send men across half of Italia to bring you to justice.' He paused and sat back. 'Is that true?'

Julius felt his stomach drop. He had always known this

moment could come, but not on Lesbos in the middle of the Aegean Sea. His throat tightened, but he forced himself to keep his face neutral, his breathing steady.

'It is true,' he said finally, realising it was pointless lying. The Primus Pilus didn't look away. He was watching Julius carefully, his expression unreadable, but there was something else beneath it. A quiet satisfaction, a cruel patience. He was *enjoying* this.

Julius stared back, awaiting the final decision on his fate. Whatever it was, he would face it with honour.

'The orders contain a great deal of information about the proscriptions,' continued the Centurion. 'Names of men marked for death, names of men already dead.'

Julius felt his pulse hammer in his throat as the Primus Pilus let the name linger, watching for a reaction, savouring the moment. Then, with a smirk tugging at the corner of his lips, he took a deep breath.

'However, it seems the gods are watching over you, Caesar. Or maybe,' he tapped the parchment again, 'you have very powerful friends in Rome.' He paused one last time, before finally revealing the words that made Julius gasp in shock.

'Sulla has taken your name from the lists, Caesar… you've been pardoned.'

Before Julius could comment, the officer changed the subject and allocated him his posting.

'First Cohort,' he said, turning towards a nearby scribe, 'under Centurion Rufio. You'll find them near the eastern quarter, where the fighting was heaviest.' He barely looked up as he continued. 'Report to him immediately. He'll sort out what to do with you.'

Julius frowned at the dismissive tone. A Contubernalis, particularly one with his lineage, should command men, not be 'sorted out' like a raw recruit. But before he could speak, the Primus Pilus fixed him with a hard stare.

'That will be all, Caesar. Unless you'd prefer different

163

arrangements?'

The warning in his voice was clear. Julius gave a curt nod and turned on his heel with Marcus following close behind.

Outside, they walked in silence for several moments, picking their way through the debris. The sounds of the aftermath surrounded them, hammers striking metal, wounded men groaning, officers shouting orders. Finally, Julius spoke, his voice tight with barely contained frustration.

'A Contubernalis serves on a general's staff, he helps organise campaigns, he could even lead men into battle. He doesn't report to a common Centurion like some fresh-faced recruit from the countryside.'

Marcus glanced at him, stepping over a fallen column.

'And how many battles have you led, exactly?'

'That's not the point.'

'It's exactly the point,' Marcus cut in. 'Look around you, Julius. These men have been fighting and dying here for months. They don't care about your rank or your name. They care about survival.'

Julius stopped walking, turning to face his friend.

'Do you think I don't understand that?'

'I think,' Marcus said carefully, 'that for once in your life, you're going to have to earn your position instead of claiming it by right.'

The words stung, but Julius couldn't deny their truth. He looked past Marcus to where a group of soldiers were carrying a dead comrade, the man's armour still caked with dried blood.

'Then perhaps it's time we learned how to do it,' he said, and gestured toward the eastern quarter. 'Let's find this Centurion Rufio?'

They resumed walking, the weight of their new reality settling over them. Somewhere ahead, a battle-hardened Centurion waited to judge their worth, and somewhere beyond that, the walls of Mytilene loomed, promising blood and death for those unprepared to face them.

'At least we're in the First Cohort,' Marcus offered. 'That's something, isn't it?'

Julius nodded grimly.

'It does,' he said. 'It means we'll be first in line when the killing starts again.'

They found Centurion Rufio in the makeshift training yard behind the cohort's quarters, watching a group of recruits struggle with their shields. His face was a map of old scars, and his arms bore the thick muscles of a man who had spent decades wielding a sword. When Julius and Marcus approached, he turned to look at them.

'So,' he said, his eyes settling on Julius, 'you are the new officer?' He spat into the dirt. 'Tell me, have you ever held a shield in battle formation? Ever felt the weight of it after four hours of combat?'

Julius met his gaze steadily.

'No, Centurio.'

'What about you?' Rufio turned to Marcus. 'Ever killed a man up close, felt his blood spray across your face as your blade opens his throat?'

Marcus swallowed hard but kept his voice steady.

'No, Centurio.'

Rufio finally turned to face them fully, his grey eyes sharp with assessment.

'In one month, the first cohort will lead the advance on Mytilene's walls and the Greeks aren't going to care about your rank or your family name. They'll just see Romans to kill.' He stepped closer, close enough that Julius could smell the sour wine on his breath. 'You have until then to learn what takes most men years. You'll train from dawn until your arms shake. You'll drill until your feet bleed. And maybe, just maybe, you'll survive the first hour.'

'We're ready to learn,' said Julius.

Rufio barked a laugh.

'Ready to learn? By the gods, you don't even know what that means.' He gestured to the training yard. 'Get your equipment from the quartermaster. His voice hardened. 'And leave your pride at the gate. Out here, you're nothing but fresh meat.'

Julius nodded, understanding the message clearly. Here, his name meant nothing. Here, only survival mattered.

'One more thing,' Rufio added as they turned to go. 'I've seen too many young nobles die because they thought war was a game. It's not. It's brutal, it's ugly, and it doesn't care about your dreams of glory.' He paused, his expression grave. 'One month. Make it count.'

The weight of his words settled over them like a physical thing as they walked toward the quartermaster's tent. War, real war, was waiting. And they had a month to prepare for it.

Chapter Twenty-One

Pyrrha

he quartermaster's tent stank of leather and iron. Rows of weapons and armour lined the walls, most of it stripped from the dead, cleaned, and readied for new owners. The quartermaster, a grizzled veteran with a missing ear, took one look at Julius's orders and grunted.

'Contubernalis, eh?' He disappeared into the back, returning with a bundle of kit. 'Not much left in the way of proper staff officer's gear, but this'll mark your station well enough.'

The military cloak was well-worn but serviceable, its deep blue wool marking him as part of the governor's staff rather than the crimson paludamentum reserved for commanders. The white tunic that came with it had seen better days, but the narrow purple clavi were intact, thin stripes that would identify him as an aristocrat attached to the governor's service even at a distance. A plain leather balteus completed the ensemble, designed to hang the gladius on his right side as befitted someone of his junior position, not yet earned the right to wear it on the left like seasoned officers.

'You'll need to provide your own fibula,' the quartermaster added, gesturing to where the cloak would be pinned at the shoulder. 'Most young nobles from good families bring their own, something with the family seal perhaps. Marks you out properly as a Julian.'

Marcus received simpler fare, a standard legionary's tunic, iron-reinforced leather armour, and a sword belt for the right side. Both men were given shields, not the ornate ones carried in parades, but battered scuta that bore the scars of real combat.

'Your predecessors won't need these anymore,' the quartermaster said, his voice matter-of-fact. 'Try not to join them too quickly.'

They found their assigned quarters in a partially collapsed building near the training ground. The room was small, the roof leaked, and the only furniture was a pair of straw pallets, but it was better than sleeping in the open.

They had barely set down their gear when a horn blasted across the compound. Outside, recruits were already gathering, a motley collection of volunteers, mercenaries, and conscripts. Some wore mismatched pieces of armour, others simple tunics. All looked as lost as Julius felt. Rufio stood before them, his scarred face hard in the morning light.

'Form ranks!' he bellowed. 'If you can't even stand in a straight line, you won't last five heartbeats in battle!'

The training ground became their world as Rufio worked them mercilessly, hour after hour, day after day.

'A legion isn't built in days,' Rufio had growled during their first week, 'it's forged over years. You lot get a month and at the moment I estimate all of you will die in the first few hours. Now let's start again.'

The progression was gruelling but methodical. The first week focused on basics, stance, shield work, formation keeping. Men who had never held a gladius learned to wield it effectively. Those who couldn't march in step became a unified force.

Week two brought combat drills. They learned to fight in pairs, in units, in full formation. They practiced until their arms trembled and their legs gave out, then practiced more. Marcus's previous training with Balbus showed, and he adapted quickly, his movements fluid and confident. Julius studied him, learned from him, driven by both pride and necessity.

'Your friend's a natural,' Rufio commented one evening, watching Marcus demonstrate shield techniques to newer recruits. 'You're not totally hopeless either.... for a nobleman.'

The third week tested their endurance. Full armour drills under the scorching sun and combat exercises that lasted hours. Men collapsed from exhaustion, only to be dragged back to their feet to start again.

Each day brought fresh reminders of what awaited them.

Patrols returned bearing their dead and wounded from other battles across the island. The surgeon's tent never emptied, and they learned to fight through fatigue, through fear, through the screams of dying men.

'This is your life now,' Rufio would say, pointing to the latest casualties. 'Learn or join them.'

Julius's body changed. His soft hands grew calloused, his muscles hardened, and the weight of shield and sword became familiar, almost comfortable. More importantly, his mind adapted. He learned to think tactically, to read terrain, to anticipate threats.

By the fourth week, they were soldiers. Not veterans, but no longer raw recruits. They could hold formation under pressure, execute complex manoeuvres, fight as a cohesive unit. Even Rufio's constant criticism took on a different tone, less disgust, more fine-tuning.

'You're still alive,' he noted during one particularly brutal training session. 'Maybe some of you will stay that way.'

The transformation was most evident in the quiet moments. Men who had been strangers now moved in instinctive coordination. They checked each other's equipment without being ordered, corrected each other's stances, shared water and food without thought.

Marcus thrived in this environment and his natural talent with weapons blossomed under Rufio's harsh tutelage. But Julius found his own path. What he lacked in raw martial skill, he made up for in tactical understanding. During mock battles, he could read the flow of combat, position men effectively, turn the tide through strategy rather than strength.

The final days of training focused on siege warfare. They practiced scaling walls, maintaining formation on narrow ramparts, fighting in the cramped conditions they would face on Mytilene's battlements.

Then came the last evening. A month of transformation lay behind them as they assembled in the training yard. Bodies that had been soft were now hard with muscle. Eyes that had been uncertain now held purpose. They were no longer merchants, farmers, or nobles, they were soldiers of Rome.

Rufio walked their ranks one final time, his grey eyes measuring what a month of relentless training had wrought. When he spoke, his voice carried the weight of experience, of battles survived and comrades lost.

'Tomorrow,' he said, his voice carrying across the yard, 'we advance on Mytilene's walls. The Greeks will be waiting with arrows, with spears, with burning oil and crushing stones. They'll try to kill you from above, and from the sides and from behind, and if you survive that, they'll meet you with swords when you breach the walls. They have had months to prepare, and they know every stone, every angle. You'll be fighting uphill, in their territory and will be exposed with little if any cover.' He paused. 'Many of us will die on those walls, but you're not the sheep you were a month ago. You know how to hold a shield wall, you know how to move as one unit, you know how to kill. But most of all, you are Romans, and believe me when I say, they will fear that fact.' He stepped closer to the front rank. 'When you're on those walls tomorrow, remember your training. Remember that your shield protects your brother and the men beside you are your family. Fight for them, die for them if you must, but do not shame them.'

Julius felt something stir in his chest. Around him, he could sense the other men standing straighter, their fatigue forgotten.

'The Greeks think we're barbarians,' Rufio continued. 'They think we're animals to be slaughtered. Tomorrow, show them what Roman 'animals' can do. Show them why Rome rules the world.' He looked along the ranks one final time. 'I've trained you as best I could. Now it's up to you to prove it wasn't wasted effort.' He stepped back, his voice dropping slightly. 'Now get some rest. We form up at dawn.' Then, almost quietly: 'Make me proud.'

The dismissal was clear and, as the men began to disperse, Julius caught a glimpse of something in Rufio's eyes, not quite concern, but perhaps the closest thing to it the old Centurion would allow himself to show. He knew that some of these men, perhaps many of them, would not see another sunset, but he had given them their best chance to survive. The rest would be up to them, and to whatever gods watched over soldiers in battle.

Dawn broke over Pyrrha with the promise of more death. Through the morning mist, Mytilene's walls were already visible on the horizon, barely eight miles distant, a grey smudge against the lightening sky. The city had dominated their view for weeks, but today, they would finally close that gap.

'Perfect weather for an ambush,' muttered Gallus, a grizzled veteran standing next to Marcus. 'Can't see a bloody thing in this mist.'

'That works both ways,' Marcus replied, checking his sword-belt for the third time. 'They can't see us either.'

'They don't need to see us,' said Lucius, another soldier who joined the same time as Marcus. 'They know exactly where we're going.'

The First Cohort formed up at the vanguard, their ranks tight and disciplined. Behind them, the rest of the legion spread out in a wide fan, ready to encircle the city once the ground was secured. The morning light caught on thousands of shield-bosses, each century a block of iron and determination in the growing light.

Julius watched as men made their final preparations. Some checked their equipment with methodical precision, others muttered prayers to Mars or Minerva, a few simply stared ahead at the distant walls.

'The Greeks won't surrender the approach easily,' shouted an Optio, loud enough for nearby soldiers to hear. 'They'll try to slow us, bleed us before we reach the walls. But remember your training. Remember what Rufio taught you.'

'Rufio taught us we're all going to die,' someone quipped from the ranks.

'Eventually,' Marcus shot back over his shoulder. 'But not today, eh?'

Behind their lines, the creak of wooden wheels grew louder as engineers prepared to move forward with their machines of war. The siege towers and rams sat on heavy carts, their wooden frames protected by fresh-cured hides. Rufio appeared among them, his scarred face hard in the growing light.

'Listen up,' he shouted. 'First Cohort has the honour of clearing the ground. That means we find the traps, we find the ambushes, we find every bloody Greek soldier between here and those walls.' He paused, his eyes sweeping the ranks. 'Keep the formation tight. Watch the olive groves, the broken walls, anywhere they might hide troops. If you see something, sound the alert. Don't try to be a hero.'

On their flanks, auxiliary cavalry moved into position. A Thracian captain trotted past, his curved sword gleaming.

'Try to keep up, Romans,' he called. 'We'll save some Greeks for you!'

'Save your breath for running away,' Marcus shouted back, earning a few laughs from the ranks.

Julius felt the tension ease slightly. This was good, soldiers trading insults, making dark jokes. It meant they weren't consumed by fear.

'Check your shields,' shouted his decurion. 'Make sure every strap is secure. I don't want anyone dropping their guard when the arrows start flying.'

A horn blast cut through the dawn air and the legion's eagle emerged from its leather cover, gold catching the first real light of day. Along the line, cohort standards rose, wolf, bull, and dragon marking each unit's position in the coming advance.

'Form up!' Rufio's voice carried along their ranks. 'Shields locked! First Century, ready!'

Julius took his position, feeling the press of shields to either side. This was what separated Romans from their enemies, not just courage or skill, but discipline, the ability to move and fight as one.

'Anyone want to place bets?' called a voice from the ranks. 'Ten denarii says we reach the walls before midday.'

'Save your coin,' Rufio snapped. 'You'll need it to pay the ferryman,' and as another horn echoed through the mist, they stepped off as one, their iron-shod boots striking the ground in perfect rhythm.

The cohort had covered perhaps half a mile when the first signs of resistance appeared. Movement flickered between the ruins ahead, shadows detaching from broken walls, glints of bronze catching the morning light. The mist was thinning now, revealing the extent of the Greeks' preparations.

Julius studied the ground ahead. What had appeared to be random debris now revealed itself as careful preparation. Fallen columns had been deliberately positioned, ditches had been dug during the night, and every piece of cover had been transformed into a defensive position.

Rufio's voice carried along the line.

'Tighten those ranks! They'll be coming soon.'

As if in answer, a horn blast echoed from somewhere in the ruins and the sound of drums began to build from the direction of the city walls, a slow, steady rhythm that spoke of coordination rather than chaos.

'Here it comes,' Marcus whispered, and as his grip on his shield tightened, the first arrows arced through the morning air, their dark shadows wheeling against the pale sky like birds of prey.

'Shields up,' roared one of the optios, but the first volley fell short, spattering harmlessly against the shield wall. The second came closer, iron heads ringing against bronze-rimmed scuta.

'Hold formation!' Rufio's voice cut through the din. 'Advance at pace!'

The Cohort increased speed, shields locked, their discipline unwavering. Behind them, the Roman auxiliary archers responded,

173

their arrows hissing overhead in controlled volleys. Several Greeks fell, but others simply shifted position, continuing their harassment.

'Keep moving!' Rufio ordered as the enemy arrows started to thud into the shields. 'Don't let them pin us down!'

To their left, horns blasted as Thracian cavalry engaged enemy skirmishers trying to work around their flank. The clash of steel and screams of wounded men carried clearly across the battlefield, while on the right, Numidian riders darted in and out of the ruins, their javelins finding targets among the defenders.

'They've got this whole approach mapped out,' Marcus shouted as an arrow scraped across his shield.

'Of course they do,' Julius shouted beside him. 'They've had months to prepare.'

As they reached the first barricade, a maze of overturned carts and debris, a team of engineers rushed forward, clearing paths with hooks and axes.

'Second Century, advance!' Rufio commanded. 'First Century, hold here and provide cover!'

Julius felt the rhythm of battle taking hold. This was what they had trained for, methodical, disciplined warfare. A group of Greeks charged from a hidden position, hoping to catch them while stationary, but they died on Roman spears, their bodies adding to the obstacles.

'Path clear!' shouted an engineer officer. 'Advance!'

They moved forward again, maintaining tight formation despite the broken ground. Ahead, more barriers waited, each position prepared to slow their advance, each requiring the same methodical clearance.

'Watch those buildings!' someone shouted as more Greeks loosed arrows from the upper floors of a partly collapsed structure.

The Roman artillery responded from behind, the Scorpio bolts punching through stone and wood, forcing the defenders back. But for every position cleared, another appeared ahead.

'They're falling back!' Marcus called out eventually, watching

Greeks abandon a barricade ahead of them.

'They're not running,' Julius replied grimly. 'They're regrouping at the next position.'

The morning air filled with the sound of battle, the crash of shields, the twang of bowstrings, the blare of horns signalling unit movements. Drums beat from the city walls, coordinating the defenders' responses.

Step by step, position by position, they pushed forward. The discipline of their advance was relentless. Greeks charged in desperate attacks, hoping to break their formation, but the shield wall held. Arrows continued to rain down, but the Roman advance continued.

Every yard gained was paid for in sweat and blood, but they gained it, nonetheless. This was how Rome conquered, not with single heroic charges, but with disciplined, inexorable progress.

Behind them, the rest of the legion followed in their wake, spreading out to secure the cleared ground. The siege engines waited, ready to move up once the approach was secured, but for now, there was only the next barrier, the next fight, the next step toward the walls of Mytilene.

The late afternoon sun cast long shadows across the churned ground before Mytilene's towering walls. Bodies lay scattered everywhere, mostly Greek, though Roman dead lay there too, their red cloaks darker with blood. The iron-bound gates had finally closed with a deep boom that echoed across the battlefield, sealing the surviving defenders inside their fortress.

'Dig in!' Rufio ordered, his voice hoarse from shouting commands all day. 'I want those defensive works finished before dark!'

Despite their exhaustion, the men of the First Cohort worked with practiced efficiency. Shovels bit into earth, creating a ditch that would make any counter-attack costly. In front of it, they drove sharpened stakes into the ground at an angle, not an impenetrable barrier, but one that would break up any organized assault.

'Just like training,' Marcus muttered, ramming another stake into position. His arms trembled with fatigue, his face streaked with dirt and dried blood. 'Though Rufio didn't mention how much harder it is after fighting all bloody day.'

Julius could barely lift his arms, but he worked alongside the rest. They had lost good soldiers today, he could see the bodies being carried back on makeshift stretchers, the wounded groaning as medics worked to save those they could. But they had achieved their objective. The ground before Mytilene was theirs.

As darkness approached, horns sounded from behind their position as relief forces moved up to take over the defensive line. The First Cohort gathered their equipment with weary determination, helping their wounded as they trudged back through the gathering gloom.

The support camp had sprung up quickly, ordered rows of leather tents, the cooking fires already burning. The smell of food drew them forward, though few had much appetite after the day's slaughter.

Julius and Marcus found their assigned space, a hastily erected tent big enough for ten men. They stripped off their blood-stained armour mechanically, their movements slow with exhaustion.

Julius sank onto his bedroll, too tired even to clean his sword properly. That would earn him a rebuke from Rufio tomorrow, but right now he couldn't bring himself to care. The sounds of the camp washed over him, men talking in low voices, the clank of equipment being maintained and the moans of the wounded from the surgeon's tent.

Marcus leaned against a tent pole, his usual wit quiet for once, as the reality of what they'd experienced slowly sank in. This had been nothing like training. Men they'd known, men they'd eaten with, joked with, trained besides, were dead. Gallus had taken an arrow through the throat during the third assault. Young Lucius, barely seventeen, had bled out after a Greek sword found the gap between his greaves and shield.

Outside, someone was singing, a low, mournful tune that spoke of home and peace and things far removed from this blood-soaked field.

'We did what we trained for,' Julius said finally, though whether he was reassuring Marcus or himself, he wasn't sure. 'We held the line. We took the ground.'

'We did but at what cost?'

'The cost it needed.' Julius found himself repeating Rufio's words from training. 'That's what war is.'

He lay back on his bedroll, his body feeling like lead. The events of the day played through his mind, the clash of shields, the screams of the dying, the metallic taste of fear in his mouth. His eyes grew heavy.

'You should eat something,' Marcus said, pulling himself to his feet with visible effort.

Julius tried to respond, but exhaustion was already claiming him and the last thing he heard was Marcus ducking out of the tent, heading toward the cooking fires.

The days blurred together in a haze of exhaustion and distant horror. The First Cohort rested, but there was no real peace to be found. The siege of Mytilene continued without them, its sounds a constant reminder of what awaited their return.

The thump of the onagers became as regular as a heartbeat, boom, pause, impact, each release sending another massive stone toward the city walls. The ballistae added their own rhythm, their sharp crack followed by screams when their bolts found targets. But it was the Greek fire that haunted them most.

'Gods, make it stop,' someone whispered one night as the screams of burning men carried across the darkened camp. No one answered. There was nothing to say.

Julius spent most of his time in the tent, lying on his bedroll, staring at the canvas above. The battle played over and over in his mind, every death he'd witnessed, every moment where fate had spared him while taking others. His hands would sometimes shake without warning, though he hid this when others were watching.

'You need to eat,' Marcus would say, bringing food that Julius barely tasted.

Rufio drove them to train despite their wounds, despite their exhaustion.

'Rest makes men soft,' he barked. 'And soft men die on those walls.'

They drilled with shields again, practiced sword work again, and ran through formation work… again. Their numbers were noticeably smaller now, with gaps in the ranks where familiar faces had been. The survivors moved with a different kind of determination, their training no longer about proving themselves but about survival.

The siege engines continued their work, day and night. Occasionally, sections of wall would collapse with a sound like thunder, but the Greeks fought for every stone, making the Romans pay in blood for each foot gained.

At night, the horizon would glow orange from the fires. Greek fire was a terrible weapon, it stuck to armour, burned through shields, consumed men alive and the victims' screams seemed to go on forever.

'That's why we use it,' an artillery officer explained dispassionately. 'It breaks their will to resist.'

Chapter Twenty-Two

Outside the Walls of Mytilene

A week later, the horn calls they'd been both dreading and anticipating finally came and the First Cohort assembled again, their armour repaired, their shields repainted, their weapons sharpened. But their eyes were different now, harder, haunted by what they'd seen and heard.

Rufio stood before them, his scarred face oddly calm in the morning light. The constant thunder of the siege engines provided a backdrop to his words, each impact a reminder of what was to come.

'You earned your rest,' he began, his voice carrying clearly across the assembled ranks. 'A few weeks ago, you were untested. Now?' He paused, looking along the lines. 'Now you're soldiers. Real soldiers. You proved that in the approach.'

The men stood straighter at his words. Coming from Rufio, this was high praise indeed.

'But what's coming next,' he said, shaking his head slowly, 'will make the approach look like a training exercise.'

He gestured toward the city walls, where another impact sent dust clouds billowing into the air.

'Those walls are going to fall. Maybe today, maybe tomorrow, but they'll fall. And when they do, we go in first.' His voice hardened. 'That's our honour and our burden.'

A heavy silence fell over the men, broken only by the continuing bombardment.

'I won't lie to you. Many of you, most of you, won't survive the breach. The Greeks know what happens to cities that resist Rome. They'll fight like cornered wolves, and the fighting will be close, brutal, and without mercy.' He began walking slowly along the ranks, meeting each man's eyes in turn. 'Once we go in, there's no pulling

back. No rest, no relief. We fight until the city falls or until we die. That's what it means to be the First Cohort. That's what it means
to be Roman.' Another impact shook the ground as somewhere in the city, a building collapsed. 'You knew what you were signing up for,' he continued, his voice growing quieter but no less intense. 'This is what Rome does. This is how it was built. With blood, with iron, and with men willing to die for something greater than themselves.'

He returned to his position before them, his face set like stone.

'Look to your brothers beside you and remember your training. Remember that you carry not just your own lives, but the honour of Rome itself.' He straightened, his hand resting on his sword hilt. 'That wall will fall, and when it does, we will be ready.'

The silence that followed was complete, even the siege engines seeming to pause in their relentless work. Every man there understood what Rufio wasn't saying, that for most of them, this would be their final battle, their last service to Rome. But not one stepped back. Not one looked away. They were soldiers now, and this was their duty.

The next impact shook the earth harder than before, and somewhere in the distance, a horn began to blow.

The approach to the front line felt like walking into another world. What had been a battlefield just days ago had been transformed into something from a nightmare. Julius barely recognized the ground they had fought so hard to take. Their own defensive works remained, ditches and palisades now reinforced by a week of continuous improvement, but everything beyond them had been reshaped by the relentless Roman bombardment.

Bodies lay everywhere. Some were half-buried in rubble, others sprawled where Greek fire had caught them. The latter were the worst, charred shapes that had once been men, frozen in their final agony. The once-proud towers were shattered, their stones blasted apart by the constant impact of onager fire. Through the thick smoke, Julius could see sections of wall where repeated hits had exposed the internal structure, like wounds in some giant beast.

'Gods below,' Marcus muttered beside him. 'This is what Rome does?'

'This is what resistance to Rome earns,' replied Julius. 'They could have surrendered. They chose this instead.'

The air was thick with smoke and the acrid stench of Greek fire. The constant bombardment had created its own weather, a haze of dust and debris that turned the morning sun into a pale disc overhead. Burning projectiles arced through this artificial twilight, their trailing flames drawing lines across the sky before smashing into their targets with devastating force. The impacts were constant now, a rhythm of destruction that shook the very ground.

They took position behind the forward palisade, joining other cohorts already in place. Men stood ready with shields and spears, their faces streaked with sweat and grime, watching the systematic destruction of Mytilene's defences. Julius could see the focus of the bombardment now, a section of wall that had been methodically pounded for days, each new hit sending cascades of stone tumbling down.

The highest hits struck just below the battlements, denying the Greeks any position to fight back. Lower strikes had steadily weakened the wall's face, while the heaviest stones struck again and again at the base.

A group of Greeks appeared briefly on a nearby section of wall, trying to repair some of the damage but a ballista bolt punched through their midst, sending bodies tumbling. Those who survived scrambled for cover as more missiles sought them out.

'Watch the wall!' someone shouted. *'It's starting to go!'*

Men began muttering prayers, to Mars, to Minerva, to any god who might listen. Julius felt his heart hammering against his ribs. The moment they had trained for, had dreaded, was approaching. Beside him, Marcus gripped his shield tighter, his knuckles white.

The onagers released another volley. Multiple stones struck the weakened section simultaneously. For a moment, nothing seemed to happen, then, with a sound like the gods themselves tearing the world apart, the wall began to collapse.

It began with whispers of stone - pebbles cascading, then chunks breaking free, until entire sections of wall surrendered to the bombardment. A low rumble turned into a thunderous roar as thousands of tons of ancient masonry crashed earthward. The ground trembled beneath their feet while vast clouds of dust billowed outward in choking waves and men instinctively raised their shields against the rain of debris, their faces turned away from the dying city.

When the dust began to clear, a massive breach gaped in Mytilene's defences like an open wound. The way in lay before them, a slope of broken stone leading up to a jagged opening in what had once seemed impregnable. Through the settling clouds, they could see movement inside, Greeks rushing to form defensive positions, civilians fleeing deeper into the streets.

The sound of horns filled the air, Roman signals calling the assault forces forward, and Greek horns raising the alarm throughout the city and, as drums began to beat from both sides, the final battle for Mytilene was about to begin.

'First Cohort!' roared Rufio, his voice cutting through the chaos. 'Ready yourselves!'

Julius looked at the breach, then at the men around him. Some were praying, others checking their equipment one final time. Many simply stared ahead, their faces set with grim determination. They all knew what came next. They had trained for it, prepared for it, dreaded it.

The horns sounded one last time, not the measured signals of normal combat, but a single, sustained blast that ripped through the air like a beast's roar. The Centurions and optios took up the call, their voices sharp with command and fury.

'*FORWARD!*'

Training dissolved into pure aggression as the First Cohort erupted from behind their temporary defences, not in disciplined lines but in a surge of controlled violence. Julius found himself running, shield raised, heart thundering in his chest. Around him, thousands more men charged, legionaries in their red cloaks, auxiliaries in their lighter armour and mercenaries in whatever protection they owned.

The ground shook with their advance but the Greeks were ready, and the first volley of arrows darkened the sky, rattling against shields like deadly rain. Men screamed as shafts found gaps in their armour and siege ladders clattered against the remaining walls, immediately becoming killing grounds as the defenders unleashed their fury.

But it was the breach that drew them like a lodestone. The First Cohort drove forward through the chaos, instinct and training carrying them toward that jagged gap in Mytilene's defences. The Greeks had quickly turned the collapsed rubble into a defensive position, every broken stone becoming cover for archers, every elevated position a platform for spear-throwers.

'*Keep moving!*' roared Rufio's voice over the din. 'Don't let them pin you down!'

Death came in every form imaginable. Arrows whistled through the smoke. Javelins plunged from above and boulders cascaded down the rubble slope, crushing men beneath them while others poured burning oil that sent armoured legionaries stumbling away in flames.

Yet still they advanced and for every man who fell, two more took his place. The air filled with screams, both of the dying and of men lost to battle-fury. Blood made the broken stones treacherous, smoke stung their eyes and the clash of steel on steel rang out as the first Romans reached the Greek defenders.

Julius found himself at the base of the breach, though he couldn't remember the final steps that brought him there. His shield was studded with arrow shafts and the world had narrowed to the rubble slope before him, the enemies above, and the press of men beside him.

The breach gaped above them like the mouth of some mythological beast, waiting to devour all who dared enter, a hell of broken stone and butchery. All formation was lost, all tactics forgotten. There was only the next enemy, the next swing, the next heartbeat of survival. The battle engulfed him completely, its ferocity overwhelming any capacity for contemplation or tactics, leaving only the primal drive to survive each brutal moment as it bled into the next.

Men fought pressed together so tightly they could barely swing their weapons, using shields as battering rams, daggers for close work, even hands and teeth when nothing else would serve. The Greeks fought with the fury of men defending their homes, the Romans with the relentless drive of an army that never accepted defeat.

A defender lunged at Julius with a broken spear. He deflected it instinctively, his sword finding the man's armpit. No time to watch him fall, another Greek was already swinging an axe at his head. Julius stumbled on the uneven ground, the axe missing him by inches as Marcus appeared from nowhere, his blade ending the threat.

The noise was overwhelming. Metal on metal, men screaming in multiple languages, the wet sound of blades finding flesh. Someone was calling to Apollo for mercy, someone else was reciting a prayer to Mars, most just roared wordlessly as they killed and died.

They gained ground one bloody step at a time and Julius found himself climbing over bodies both Roman and Greek. His arms burned with fatigue, but he kept swinging. There was no choice. Stop moving and die, stop killing and die.

The press of bodies carried him upward. His shield caught a sword blow that nearly drove him to his knees and he responded without thinking, his blade finding soft flesh beneath a chin.

Somehow, they were near the top where the rubble gave way to flat stone, the city street beyond the breach. A legionary ahead of Julius reached it first, his feet finding solid ground. The man raised his bloody sword and bellowed a victory cry that cut through the chaos.

'For Rome!'

A Greek spear took him in the throat, cutting off his triumph, but his cry had done something to the men behind him and the Romans surged forward with renewed fury, their collective will becoming an unstoppable force.

Julius found himself caught in the wave and they poured through the gap like water through a broken dam, spilling into the streets of Mytilene. The Greeks tried to hold them back, but the momentum was too great. The breach had been forced.

The narrow street twisted ahead, lined with two-story stone buildings. Wooden shutters slammed, terrified faces disappeared behind them and Julius knew this was where the real killing would begin.

Marcus appeared at his side, blood painting the side of his face.

'Watch the rooftops,' he shouted over the din and even as he spoke, an arrow thudded into the ground beside him.

The street was a maze of potential ambush. Every doorway could hide a defender, every window might conceal a man with a bow or a stone to drop. Julius's unit moved in a tight formation, shields overlapping, watching every angle.

A door burst open, and an older Greek man appeared, not with a weapon, but with a look of pure defiance. Behind him, Julius caught a glimpse of women and children and for the briefest of moments, the brutality paused. But Marcus didn't hesitate.

'Keep moving,' he shouted, shoving Julius forward, the moment of humanity dissolving in the urgent need to press the attack

Archers appeared on a second-story balcony and even more arrows rained down. A legionary to Julius's left took three in quick succession, his body jerking with each impact before crumpling. Another grabbed the man's fallen shield, using it to cover the unit.

The street ran red. Bodies of defenders and civilians alike lay broken among the rubble. Julius stepped over a child's body, its small form barely recognizable. The horror registered for just a moment before survival instinct pushed it away.

A Greek hoplite burst from a side alley, his massive round shield and long spear making him a deadly threat. Julius saw Marcus engage him, their weapons a blur of motion.

The hoplite was skilled, turning Marcus's first three strikes with practiced ease, but Julius saw an opening and while the hoplite focused on Marcus, Julius moved to his flank, his sword finding the gap between breastplate and greave and the hoplite went down with a strangled cry. Marcus nodded, there was no time for thanks.

'They're falling back,' he shouted, and Julius paused to stare up the hill, knowing the worst was yet to come. The Romans would pursue, room by room, building by building. No mercy, no quarter. This was total war.

The street ran like a river of blood. Behind them, the breach disgorged more legionaries, waves of red and bronze, metal and muscle. Julius knew without looking that his unit was leaving a trail of butchery. Entire families, defenders… anyone who stood in their path.

The slope of the street grew steeper, and Mytilene's acropolis loomed above, a promise of final resistance. Each step was a battle, each doorway a potential death trap.

Roman archers fired methodically into windows, into doorways. Bodies fell but no one stopped to check if they were combatants or civilians. Movement meant threat and threat meant death.

Julius's sword arm moved mechanically. Slice, thrust, block, repeat. Blood covered him so thoroughly he could no longer tell his own from his enemies'. Marcus fought beside him, equally transformed into a machine of destruction.

Burning buildings cast mad shadows and smoke choked the narrow street. Screams echoed, some of pain, some of terror, some simply animal sounds beyond human language but the first cohort moved like a single organism, consuming everything in its path.

A group of Greek warriors made a final stand on a narrow section of street, forming a tight circle, shields locked, but the Romans crashed into them like a wave. Spears first, then swords, then... everything else. Shields became battering rams, daggers found gaps in armour, hands grabbed and teeth bit. The Greeks died hard, but they died all the same.

The street ran red. Then darker than red, a colour beyond blood. Ahead, a massive wooden gate blocked the street, the final barrier before the acropolis. Greek defenders appeared on the walls above, raining down stones, spears, anything they could find. A legionary beside Julius took a stone to the helmet, crumpling instantly but another stepped into his place without hesitation.

Julius felt something breaking inside him. Not physical, something deeper. The constant violence had worn away whatever remained of his humanity. He was no longer a man, he was an instrument of Rome's will.

A Greek boy, no more than twelve, appeared in a doorway. For a moment, their eyes met, and Julius saw terror. The boy raised something, a kitchen knife. Pathetic. Useless. But Julius's sword moved before he could think, before he could feel… and the boy fell.

Marcus grabbed Julius's shoulder pushing him forward. No words of comfort, no judgment, just the need to continue.

Siege hooks appeared. Massive iron points driven by the collective strength of a dozen men, striking the wooden gate like a battering ram from hell. Men lined up to heave on the ropes with one arm, the other balancing their shields above them and within moments, the gate exploded outward.

The first cohort surged forward but inside, the Greek defenders had prepared a secondary barricade, furniture, broken carts, anything to slow the Roman advance. Behind it, stood a mix of warrior, some professional soldiers, some city militia, some simply men with whatever weapons they could find. They would die like all the rest.

Julius felt something like a laugh bubble up in his throat. Not a human sound. Something else.

A Greek commander appeared on a raised platform. He was shouting something, rallying his men, promising resistance, promising survival, but when a Roman ballista bolt took him in the chest, he simply vanished in a spray of red.

Julius climbed over bodies, some Roman, most Greek. It didn't matter anymore. Nothing mattered except the next step, the next strike, the advance.

The acropolis was close now. So close Julius could see the marble columns. The final sanctuary of Mytilene's leaders, but they would find no sanctuary today. The first cohort of Rome knew only one direction. Forward… forward… always forward!

Chapter Twenty-Three

Rome

The autumn sun cast long shadows through the vineyard as Aurelia and Cornelia walked arm in arm between the rows of ripening grapes. The vines were heavy with fruit, a reminder that time continued to pass, even when their world seemed frozen in uncertainty. Cornelia's fingers tightened slightly on Aurelia's arm.

'Still nothing?' she asked, though she already knew the answer. They had asked this question so many times over the past months that it had become almost ritualistic, a shared acknowledgment of their helplessness.

Aurelia shook her head, her expression carefully controlled. She had spent a lifetime mastering the art of hiding her emotions, but Cornelia had learned to read the subtle tensions in her mother-in-law's face.

'The merchant from Ephesus swears he saw him,' said Aurelia. 'But that was months ago, and since then...' She let the words trail off. Since then, there had been nothing but silence and rumours, each less reliable than the last.

They paused at the end of a row, looking out over the rolling hills toward Rome. The city sprawled beneath the afternoon haze, its temples and columns catching the light.

'We've sent hundreds of letters,' said Cornelia, her voice tight with frustration. 'To every port, every garrison, every merchant house from here to Bithynia. Someone must know something.'

'Knowledge is dangerous these days,' replied Aurelia. 'Perhaps those who know choose not to speak.' She turned to study her daughter-in-law's face. 'But there is other news. News that might change everything.'

Cornelia's breath caught.

'You mean the rumours about Sulla?'

'More than rumours now,' said Aurelia quietly. She glanced

around, though they were alone among the vines.

'My brother's wife's cousin serves in Sulla's household. She says he's grown increasingly ill and he speaks of retirement.'

The word hung between them, heavy with possibility. Sulla, the man who had driven Julius into exile, who had painted Rome's streets red with the blood of his enemies, was considering stepping down. The implications were staggering.

'Can we trust this information?' asked Cornelia.

'The signs are there for those who know how to read them,' said Aurelia. 'Sulla has begun arranging his affairs, meeting with his closest supporters. He speaks of writing his memoirs, of leaving a legacy.' Her lips curved in a slight, knowing smile. 'These are not the actions of a man who intends to rule much longer.'

A warm breeze rustled through the vines, carrying the sweet scent of ripening grapes. In the distance, a slave called to another, their voices carrying clearly across the terraced hillside. The women found a stone bench beneath an old olive tree, its gnarled trunk providing welcome shade from the afternoon sun.

'Tell me more,' said Cornelia, settling beside her mother-in-law. 'What else have you heard?'

Aurelia's eyes narrowed slightly as she gathered her thoughts.

'There are new factions forming. Men who once wouldn't dare whisper against Sulla now speak openly of what comes after. They gather in private homes, in the baths, in the temples, each trying to position themselves for the change they know is coming.'

'And what of Sulla's supporters?'

'Some remain loyal, of course. But others...' Aurelia's lip curled with disgust. 'Others are already seeking new patrons, new alliances. Like rats abandoning a sinking ship.'

Cornelia absorbed this, her mind working through the implications.

'And Gaius? If Sulla steps down, if the proscriptions end...'

'As you know, Gaius has already been pardoned,' said Aurelia, 'and perhaps he already knows this, but fears returning in case it is nought but a cruel trap. But if Sulla is indeed approaching the end, there is nothing stopping him coming home. Rome will still be dangerous for every ambitious man will see Sulla's retirement as an opportunity, and I have no doubt there will be blood in the streets again, though perhaps not as openly as before.'

They sat in silence for a moment, each lost in their own thoughts. A slave girl approached carrying a tray with wine and fruit, her head bowed respectfully. Aurelia waved her away, but not before Cornelia noticed how the girl's eyes darted between them, hungry for any scrap of information to share with the other household servants.

'Even the slaves listen now,' Aurelia murmured once the girl was out of earshot. 'Everyone senses the change coming.'

Cornelia leaned back, her fingers tracing patterns in the worn stone of the bench. 'Do you think he knows? Gaius, I mean. Do you think word has reached him about Sulla's condition?'

'If he's half the man I raised him to be, he's already planning his return,' said Aurelia. A hint of pride crept into her voice. 'My son has never been one to wait for opportunities to find him.'

'No,' agreed Cornelia, smiling despite her worry. 'He creates his own.'

The sun dipped lower, casting the vineyard in shades of gold and amber. From their position, they could see the first evening lamps being lit in the city below, tiny points of light appearing like stars fallen to earth.

'Whatever comes next,' said Aurelia, rising from the bench, 'we must be ready. Gaius will need allies when he returns, men of influence who remember his father's name with respect.' She straightened her stola, smoothing the fabric with practiced grace. 'I think it's time we hosted a dinner. Nothing too obvious, of course. Just a small gathering of...shall we say... *old friends.*'

Cornelia recognized the glint in her mother-in-law's eye. It was the same look Julius got when plotting his next move.

'Who did you have in mind?'

'Marcus Aurelius Cotta for one,' said Aurelia. 'He's been

distancing himself from Sulla's inner circle lately. And Quintus Lutatius Catulus... his daughter's wedding was quite the political gathering last month.' She smiled thinly. 'Amazing how much one can learn at such social occasions.'

They began walking back toward the villa, their steps measured and unhurried. To any observer, they were simply two noble women enjoying an evening stroll. But beneath their calm exterior, both women's minds were racing, calculating moves and countermoves in the great game of Roman politics.

'We'll need to be careful,' said Cornelia. 'If word gets back to Sulla that we're gathering his opponents...'

'My dear,' Aurelia cut in smoothly, 'we're simply hosting a dinner for family friends. What could be more natural than that?' Her voice hardened slightly. 'Besides, Sulla has larger concerns now than the social calendar of two lowly women.'

As they approached the villa, torches were being lit along the colonnade, casting long shadows across the courtyard. A messenger waited by the entrance, his expression eager. Both women quickened their pace slightly, hope rising unbidden. But it was just another commercial matter, a question about grain shipments that required Aurelia's attention.

Cornelia watched her mother-in-law deal with the messenger, admiring the way she dismissed him with a few precise words. Aurelia had taught her much about power in Rome - not the obvious power of swords and speeches in the Forum, but the subtle power of whispered words, carefully placed hints, and well-chosen dinner guests.

'Tomorrow then,' said Aurelia, turning back to Cornelia. 'We'll begin our preparations. Rome is changing, my dear, and we must ensure that when Gaius returns, he finds the ground prepared for him.'

Cornelia nodded, feeling the familiar mix of pride and fear that thoughts of her husband always brought. Somewhere in the East, Gaius was waiting, watching, planning. And when he finally returned to Rome, he would find that his mother and wife had been doing the same.

Across the city, Sulla's sickroom reeked of herbs and illness. Braziers burned constantly, filled with aromatic woods and resins that the physicians claimed would purify the air, but beneath the sweet smoke lingered the unmistakable stench of decay.

Sulla lay on his bed, his face waxy and yellow in the flickering lamplight, his once-powerful frame now wasted by disease. The physicians moved around him like cautious birds, each afraid to be the bearer of bad news. They whispered among themselves in Greek, the language of medicine, though their patient was too weak now to care what tongue they spoke in. Sulla's breath came in shallow gasps, his skin slick with fever despite the cool autumn air.

'More hellebore,' muttered the eldest physician, a Pergamene doctor who had treated kings. 'It will help balance the humors.'

A slave hurried forward with the preparation, but before it reached Sulla's lips, he turned his head away, his expression twisting with disgust.

'No more of your fucking potions,' he rasped. Even diminished by illness, his voice carried the edge of command that had once made Rome tremble.

The physicians exchanged glances. For weeks they had tried everything in their considerable knowledge. Bloodletting had left his arms mottled with bruises. Purgatives had wracked his body with spasms. Poultices of wild garlic and rue covered his swollen belly, and still the sickness advanced.

'Perhaps the liver of a wolf,' suggested another doctor, this one from Alexandria. 'Prepared with wine and cypress...'

'Perhaps you should all go fuck yourselves,' Sulla snarled, then doubled over as another wave of pain seized him. His skin, once tanned by years of campaigns, had taken on the sickly hue of dying leaves.

The youngest physician, a Roman trained in Greece, stepped

forward with fresh bandages. The bleeding had started again – not from their therapeutic cuts, but from within and when he pulled back the old dressings, the cloth was stained with dark, clotted blood.

'The corruption in the liver spreads,' he murmured in Greek. 'See how the whites of his eyes have yellowed? And the swelling in his belly grows worse.'

None of them needed to say what they were all thinking. The great Sulla, who had made Rome run red with the blood of his enemies, was being consumed from within by his own corrupted blood. A slave appeared at the door, his face carefully blank.

'The haruspex is here, Domine,' he announced. 'Shall I send him in?'

Sulla's laugh turned into a wet cough.

'Why not? Let him read my fate in sheep guts. It can't be worse than these butchers with their herbs and honey.'

The physicians withdrew to a corner, watching as the haruspex performed his divination. The man's hands trembled slightly as he examined the entrails, whether from genuine religious awe or simple fear of the dying dictator, none could say.

'The signs are... unclear, Domine,' the haruspex said finally, choosing his words with obvious care.

'Unclear?' Sulla's voice dripped with contempt. 'Or simply unwelcome?'

The haruspex blanched but said nothing. Sulla waved him away with a shaking hand, then turned his gaze to the gathered physicians.

'Well?' he demanded. 'What's your verdict, you learned men of medicine? How long before the worms feast on the great dictator?'

The doctors shifted uncomfortably. None dared meet his eyes until finally, the Pergamene spoke, his voice careful and measured.

'The illness is... serious, Domine. But with proper treatment…'

'Proper treatment?' Sulla tried to sit up, his face contorting with rage and pain. 'You've been 'treating' me for weeks, and I only get worse! Do you think I don't know what's happening to my own body?'

A fresh wave of pain doubled him over, and this time blood appeared at the corner of his mouth. The physicians moved forward automatically, but Sulla's glare stopped them in their tracks.

'Get out,' he whispered. 'All of you. Go tell my wife I'm resting. Go tell my supporters I'm recovering. Go spread whatever lies you think will keep Rome calm.' His voice dropped even lower. 'But don't think for a moment that you've fooled me.'

They fled like startled doves, their sandals whisking softly against the marble floors. Outside the sickroom, in the relative safety of the villa's corridor, they gathered in a tight knot.

'How long?' asked the Roman physician.

The Pergamene doctor shook his head.

'Weeks perhaps. A month at most. The corruption in his liver is too far advanced.'

'And who,' asked the Alexandrian, glancing nervously at the closed door, 'who will be the one to tell him?'

None of them spoke. They had all seen what happened to bearers of bad news in Sulla's Rome and even now, with death clearly approaching, none dared to be the one to speak the truth to the dying dictator.

'We will continue the treatments,' the Pergamene doctor said finally. 'We will do what we can to ease his pain, and we will pray to whatever gods might listen that when the end comes, it comes quickly.'

They dispersed quietly, each to their quarters to prepare fresh medicines that they knew would make no difference. Behind them, through the heavy wooden door, they could hear Sulla's laboured breathing, punctuated by occasional curses.

The mighty Sulla was dying, and all of Rome held its breath, waiting for the news that would shake the Republic to its foundations.

Chapter Twenty-Four

Mytilene

The acropolis loomed above them, its marble steps slick with blood. Bodies lay scattered across the approach while the screams of the dying mixed with the clash of steel on bronze. The air was thick with smoke and the copper stench of death, and through it all, the constant thunder of siege engines continued their relentless bombardment of the city's last stronghold.

From his position on top of one of the few buildings still standing, Marcus Minucius Thermus watched the battle unfold below him. The scene was like something from epic poetry - desperate defenders, relentless attackers, all played out against a backdrop of burning buildings and billowing smoke. His eyes narrowed as they fixed on a scene that made his breath catch - a Roman Centurion, separated from his unit, fighting alone against a circle of Greek defenders. It was Rufio.

The Centurion was already wounded, blood streaming from a gash in his side, his shield arm hanging useless. Yet still he fought, his gladius rising and falling as Greeks pressed in around him. Three bodies lay at his feet - defenders who had learned too late the cost of underestimating a wounded Roman. But more were coming. Always more.

'Someone should help him,' Thermus's aide muttered, but they both knew it was impossible. The space between the Roman lines and Rufio's position was a killing ground, swept by arrows and spears. No one could cross it and live.

Yet even as the thought formed, Thermus saw movement. A young officer broke from the Roman lines, ignoring the shouts of his commanders as he charged toward the Greeks with reckless abandon, his red cloak streaming behind him like a banner of blood.

Julius didn't think, there was no time for thought. He saw Rufio struggling alone and his body moved of its own accord. Everything narrowed to a singular purpose, a clarity of action that transcended fear or reason and the Greeks, focused on finishing the wounded Centurion, didn't see him coming until it was too late. His gladius took the first defender in the back, the blade punching through bronze armour with terrible force and the man fell without a sound.

The others turned, startled by this sudden attack from behind but Julius didn't give them time to recover. He fought like a man possessed, his sword a blur of motion, his shield smashing faces and breaking bones and the Greeks fell back, momentarily shocked by the fury of his assault.

'Caesar!' Rufio gasped, blood bubbling at his lips. 'Get... back...' but instead of retreating, Julius grabbed the Centurion, hoisting him over his shoulder in a single motion. The weight was enormous - Rufio in full armour was like carrying a bronze statue - but somehow, he stayed upright and turned back toward the Roman lines, stumbling under his burden.

The Greeks recovered quickly, reorganizing for the kill. Spears thrust at him from all sides, and he caught one on his shield, felt another slice across his thigh. The pain was distant, unimportant, all that mattered was movement, one foot in front of the other, again and again.

He slipped on the blood-slick marble, going down hard and Rufio rolled from his shoulder with a cry of pain. A Greek sword flashed down, but Julius caught it on his shield rim, deflecting it into the stone before kicking out hard and shattering the man's knee.

He struggled to his feet and fought without thought, without strategy, operating on pure instinct. His gladius found throats, groins, the gaps beneath arms. Men died and he barely noticed, his world narrowed to the space around Rufio's fallen form. A Greek officer charged him with a spear, but Julius stepped inside the thrust and drove his sword up under the man's chin, the blade emerging through the top of his helmet in a spray of bone, blood and brain. Blood ran into his eyes from a cut he didn't remember taking and his shield arm was numb from countless impacts, but still he fought, his body moving with the fluid grace of a man beyond exhaustion, beyond fear, beyond anything but the need to survive the next heartbeat.

From his tower, Thermus found himself leaning forward, transfixed by the scene below. The young Contubernalis fought with a savagery that bordered on madness, yet there was something almost beautiful in his movements, a deadly efficiency that spoke of natural talent honed by relentless training.

More Greeks fell back, perhaps sensing something unnatural in his fury. Some began to mutter prayers - not to their gods of war, but to darker powers that might protect them from this red-cloaked demon who seemed impossible to kill. It gave Julius the moment he needed, and he grabbed Rufio again, hauling him upright, dragging him toward safety. His muscles screamed in protest, but he didn't stop.

Arrows, both roman and Greek, began to fall around them like deadly rain. One took a Greek in the throat as he raised his sword to strike, another skittered off Julius's shoulder guard, the impact spinning him half around. A third found Rufio's leg, drawing a sharp cry of pain from the wounded Centurion.

'Leave me,' Rufio gasped, his face grey with blood loss. 'Save yourself, you mad fool.'

Julius didn't waste breath responding. The Roman lines were close now - he could hear familiar voices shouting encouragement. But the distance seemed impossible, each step an eternity of effort. His legs trembled with exhaustion and the world began to grey at the edges.

Through the fog of fatigue, he saw movement to his left - more Greeks, fresh warriors racing to cut them off and his heart sank. He couldn't fight them, not while supporting Rufio's weight. This, finally, was the end but as he started to form his last words to

Mars, a Roman voice cut through the chaos.

'Archers! *Loose!*' and a fresh volley of Roman arrows darkened the sky, forcing the Greeks to raise their shields. Another volley followed, then another, and the Greeks fell back, unable to press their attack under the relentless barrage.

Hands reached out from behind a makeshift barricade, pulling them to safety and Julius and Rufio collapsed together behind the shield wall as Roman artillery answered the Greek archers with devastating effect.

'You mad bastard,' Marcus muttered to one side, his voice thick with emotion. 'You absolute mad bastard.'

Julius couldn't respond. His body was shaking uncontrollably, delayed reaction setting in. Blood ran freely down his leg and his sword arm trembled so badly he could barely maintain his grip on the gladius. Medics swarmed around Rufio, working quickly to stem his bleeding.

'The arrow,' Rufio gasped as they examined him. 'In my leg...'

'Leave it,' the chief medic ordered. 'We'll deal with it later. For now, it's holding the blood in.'

Julius tried to stand but his legs wouldn't obey, and Marcus caught him as he swayed.

'Easy, brother,' he murmured. 'It's done. You did it.'

High above, Thermus stared down at the aftermath. He had seen countless battles, countless acts of bravery and stupidity. But this... this had been something else entirely. His eyes remained fixed on the young officer now being tended by medics behind the lines.

'Find out who that man is,' he said to his aide. 'When this is over, I want to speak with him personally.'

'Domine,' the aide replied hesitantly, 'I believe that was Gaius Julius Caesar.'

Thermus raised an eyebrow.

'The same one who secured Nicomedes' ships?'

'The same, Domine.'

Thermus nodded slowly, a slight smile touching his lips.

'Well then. It seems young Caesar is determined to make himself noticed.'

The battle raged on around them. The Greeks had retreated to their final positions around the temple, but their resistance was weakening. Everyone knew the city would fall, it was only a matter of time, and the Roman engineers were already bringing up the rams, preparing for the final assault.

But for those who had witnessed it, the day would be remembered not for the fall of Mytilene, but for something rarer, a moment of pure courage, when one man had defied death itself to save a comrade. They had seen something that would be spoken of in wine shops and barracks for years to come, a deed worthy of Rome's ancient heroes.

And in that moment, watching the young Contubernalis being helped away from the front line, Thermus knew he was seeing the birth of a legend. Whether that legend would serve Rome or destroy it remained to be seen.

Chapter Twenty-Five

Pyrrha

Weeks had passed since the fall of Mytilene, and the city bore its wounds like a slowly healing patient. Where siege engines had once hammered at the walls, workers now cleared debris. Where blood had stained the marble steps of the acropolis, rainwater had washed most traces away, though darker stains remained in the porous stone. The Romans had been merciful, by their standards and Thermus had agreed not to raze the city, though many buildings had already been destroyed in the fighting.

Administrators arrived daily from Rome, efficient men in clean togas, carrying wax tablets and scrolls, ready to impose Roman order on Greek chaos. They moved through the streets with the calm assurance of men who had seen this process before, the transition from resistance to occupation to grudging acceptance. It was how Rome always worked.

Prisoners laboured under the watchful eyes of legionaries, shifting rubble, rebuilding walls, draining flooded cellars. Those who worked well might earn Roman citizenship someday. Those who didn't would find themselves in the mines or worse. This too was the Roman way.

The First Cohort had been withdrawn from the city, camping on the plains outside the walls. They were soldiers of assault, not occupation, and fresh forces were already arriving to take their place. Soon they would depart, many of them heading back to Rome, others to new assignments across the Republic.

Julius made his way slowly through the camp, acknowledging the salutes and nods from men who now regarded him with a mixture of respect and wary admiration. Reports of his rescue of Rufio had spread through the ranks like wildfire, growing more outlandish with each retelling. By now, some claimed he had killed twenty Greeks single-handed, others swore they saw Mars himself guiding his sword arm.

The reality had been messier, bloodier, and far less glorious than the stories suggested, but Julius didn't correct them. He understood the value of such tales.

The hospital tent stretched before him, a long canvas structure marked with the symbol of the legion's medical corps. Inside, rows of pallets held the wounded, those too injured to march immediately, but not so badly hurt that they had been sent back to Rome on the slow-moving hospital ships. The air smelled of honey poultices, vinegar, and the underlying scent of men healing from wounds that would leave permanent reminders of Mytilene.

He paused at the entrance, suddenly uncertain. He had avoided this visit for days, though he couldn't have explained why. Perhaps it was the awkwardness that always came after such moments, the debt created that neither man could ever truly settle.

'Are you going in, Domine,' asked a gruff voice, 'or just admiring the view?'

Julius turned to find Marcus standing behind him. His friend had recovered quickly from his own minor wounds, though a fresh scar now marked his chin, and had been promoted to the role of Decurion, in charge of eight men within a century.

'I was just... considering,' Julius replied.

Marcus snorted.

'You've been 'considering' for three days. Go in. He's been asking about you.'

Julius nodded, steeling himself, and ducked through the tent flap. Inside, the wounded lay in various stages of recovery. Some slept fitfully while others stared at the tent ceiling with the vacant eyes of men still reliving the horrors they had witnessed. Medics moved between pallets, changing dressings and administering herbal infusions for pain.

Rufio was near the back, propped up on a makeshift bed, his heavily bandaged leg extended before him. The arrow had done considerable damage, but he had been lucky, no infection had set in. The Centurion was studying a wax tablet, making notes with a stylus. Even wounded and off duty, he was still working. Some habits never changed.

Julius approached, and Rufio looked up and for a moment, neither man spoke.

'Caesar,' Rufio said finally, setting the tablet aside.

'Centurion,' Julius replied, suddenly feeling like a raw recruit again. 'How's the leg?'

'Still attached,' Rufio grunted. 'The surgeon says I'll walk again, maybe even without a limp if the gods are kind.'

An awkward silence fell between them. Julius glanced around, looking for a stool, then simply lowered himself to sit on the ground near Rufio's pallet.

'You know you didn't need to risk yourself like that,' said Rufio after a moment, 'it was... it wasn't a sound tactical decision.'

Julius smiled faintly.

'No, it wasn't.'

'But...' Rufio continued, searching for the right words, 'I need to thank you. If you hadn't…'

'Don't,' Julius cut him off. 'Please. It's not necessary.'

Rufio fell silent, studying Julius with eyes that had seen too many battles, too many men die. The pause stretched between them, filled with the sounds of the tent, groans, whispered prayers, medics' quiet instructions.

'I didn't think much of you, you know,' Rufio said finally, changing tack. 'When you first arrived, I thought you were just another nobleman playing at war. Come to collect some glory before returning to Rome's comforts.'

Julius nodded.

'If I being am truthful with myself,' said Julius, 'you were probably right. I suppose that is exactly what I was.'

'No,' said Rufio. 'I've trained hundreds of men, led thousands into battle, watched good soldiers live and die.' He paused, his scarred hand tightening on the blanket. 'But I've rarely seen anyone fight like you did up there on that acropolis. It was like watching... I don't know... something from the old stories.'

Julius looked down, uncomfortable with the praise.

'It wasn't like that, I just reacted. There wasn't time to think.'

'That's exactly it,' said Rufio. 'Most men, thinking or not, would have left me there. It was the sensible choice, the right thing to do. But you...' He shook his head. 'You have instincts, Caesar, and possibly more courage than sense, which makes you either the best soldier I've ever trained or the most dangerous.'

Julius laughed, surprised by the Centurion's candour. He rose to his feet.

'I have to go,' he said. 'The legion is forming up. Thermus plans to address the men before we begin departures.' He hesitated, then extended his hand. 'Thank you, for training me and teaching me that war is not the glorious spectacle that the poets speak of. It is a dirty bloody mess that exists only for the glory of powerful men. Heal quickly, Centurion. Rome needs men like you.' He turned to leave, but Rufio's voice stopped him once more.

'Caesar,' he called, 'whatever comes next for you, in battle or in Rome, remember what you learned here. A man who fights like you did, with that sort of quick thinking and courage, that man could achieve greatness.'

Julius nodded, not trusting himself to speak before turning away to duck out of the tent into the bright sunshine, where the legion was already forming up in orderly ranks.

Banners snapped in the breeze, and the eagle standard gleamed gold against the blue sky as Julius found his place, slipping in beside Marcus. The First Cohort stood at perfect attention, their armour gleaming in the morning sun, shields polished to a mirror shine. Even after weeks of brutal fighting, Roman discipline held true.

The legion stretched across the plain like a great red serpent, over three thousand men in precise formation, standards raised high, the eagle of Rome prominent among them. Behind the fighting cohorts stood the auxiliaries, the support troops, the engineers who had built the siege engines, and the naval contingents who had blockaded the harbour. Together, they were a display of Rome's might that even the gods themselves might pause to admire.

A horn blast announced Thermus's arrival and the general rode in on a magnificent white stallion, his ceremonial armour polished to brilliance, his crimson cloak rippling in the breeze. The horse's hooves kicked up small clouds of dust as it pranced across the hardened ground, but Thermus sat straight-backed, every inch the Roman commander, his bearing that of a man who had led armies since before many of his soldiers were born.

He dismounted with practiced grace, handing the reins to a waiting servant. His boots struck the earth with authority as he climbed the wooden steps to the raised platform and from there, he surveyed his men, his eyes moving slowly across the assembled ranks.

The view before him was breathtaking. Six thousand men stood motionless as statues, a sea of Roman power. Spears and shields caught the morning light, and battle standards stirred gently in the wind. Behind them rose the walls of Mytilene, still scarred from the siege but many still standing, a testament to Roman mercy as much as Roman might. To one side the blue expanse of the Aegean stretched to the horizon, where Roman ships still patrolled, their sails bright against the sky.

When Thermus spoke, his voice carried clearly across the plain, trained by years of battlefield command to reach the farthest ranks.

'Men of Rome,' he began, 'look upon what you have achieved. Look upon those walls that defied us, those streets that ran with blood, the city that dared to stand against the might of the Republic. Look, and know that you have done what Rome asked of you.'

He paused, letting his words sink in.

'This victory belongs to all of you. To the sailors who blockaded the harbour, denying the enemy aid, to the engineers who built our engines of war, the quartermasters who kept you fed and armed and to every man who supported this siege, your service honours Rome.'

His voice grew stronger, filled with pride.

'But most of all, this victory belongs to you who carried steel into battle. You who climbed those walls knowing death waited above. You who fought street by street, house by house, never yielding, never breaking. Some of you will bear the scars of Mytilene forever. Others...' he paused, his voice softening slightly, 'others sleep now in Roman earth, having given their last full measure of devotion to the Republic.'

The silence was absolute and even the wind seemed to hold its breath.

'They died as Romans have always died, with honour, with courage, facing their enemy. They died so that Rome might live, might grow, might continue to bring order to a world of chaos. Their names will be remembered in the temples of their ancestors, their deeds recorded in the annals of our people.'

Thermus's voice swelled with emotion.

'But you who stand before me, you live. You live to fight again, to serve again, to bring glory to Rome again. Let no man say you were found wanting and let no man say you faltered in your duty. Instead, let the world know that when Rome called, you answered. When Rome needed warriors, you stepped forward and when Rome demanded victory, you delivered it!'

A ripple of pride passed through the ranks.

'Remember this day,' Thermus continued. 'Remember what you achieved here. Remember that you are the inheritors of a legacy that stretches back to Romulus himself, and know that as long as Rome has men like you, no power on earth can stand against us!'

The cheer that erupted from six thousand throats was like thunder. Spears struck shields, swords raised to the sky, and voices joining in a roar of triumph that seemed to shake the very heavens. It was the voice of Rome itself - proud, unconquerable, eternal.

Julius felt his own voice join the cry, felt the surge of pride and belonging that came with being part of something greater than himself. Beside him, Marcus's face shone with fierce joy. They were Romans, they were victors, they were immortal.

And in that moment, standing among his fellow soldiers as their voices reached toward heaven, Julius knew that he would never forget this day, this feeling, this perfect expression of what it meant to be Roman.

The cheers began to fade, men expecting the traditional dismissal, but Thermus remained at the podium, his presence commanding continued attention. A subtle shift in his posture told them there was more to come.

'Legions,' he continued, his voice carrying across the now-silent ranks, 'are built on three fundamental pillars: discipline, which you have shown in abundance, training, which turned you from men into soldiers, and loyalty, to Rome, to your officers, and most importantly, to each other.'

He paused, his eyes scanning the assembled troops.

'But there is one more quality, rarer than all others, that marks the greatest of soldiers, and that is bravery. Not the common courage that all soldiers must possess, but that extraordinary valour that makes mortal men into legends.'

The silence deepened.

'In every battle, there are moments of such courage. Most go unrecorded, witnessed only by the gods. But during the assault on the acropolis, I was privileged to witness one such act of extraordinary bravery myself.'

His gaze fixed on the First Cohort, and Julius felt his heart begin to hammer in his chest.

'I watched as a Centurion, separated from his unit, fought alone against overwhelming odds. Wounded, surrounded, his death was certain. No one could have reached him through that killing ground, no one should have tried.'

Thermus's voice grew stronger, filled with a fierce pride.

'But one man did. Ignoring all orders, all tactical sense and all concern for his own life, one man charged into that maelstrom of death. I watched as he cut through the enemy like an avenging god, fought his way to his fallen comrade, and then, burdened with a wounded man in full armour, fought his way back.'

The legion stood transfixed, many hearing the full story for the first time.

'When he fell, when the enemy closed in for the kill, he rose again. When arrows sought his life, he pressed on. When his strength should have failed, he found more. This was not just courage, this was the stuff of legend, the kind of valour that our ancestors would have recognized, that our poets would have sung of.'

Thermus stepped forward, his voice ringing with authority.

'Contubernalis Gaius Julius Caesar, step forward!'

Julius felt Marcus's hand briefly squeeze his shoulder before he moved. His steps were measured, deliberate, though his heart thundered in his chest until he stopped before the podium, saluting sharply.

'Your actions that day,' Thermus continued, 'saved not just a life, but reminded us all what it means to be Roman. You showed us that the blood of our ancestors, the blood of heroes, still flows in our veins.'

An aide approached, carrying something that gleamed in the sunlight.

'There is no higher honour that Rome can bestow upon a soldier than the Corona Civica , said the general. Awarded only to those who risk their lives to save a fellow citizen, it is a mark of valour that even consuls must bow before.'

Thermus took the crown - crafted from oak leaves in solid gold - and held it high for all to see.

'By the authority vested in me by the Senate and people of Rome, I present this crown to Gaius Julius Caesar, who has proven himself worthy of our highest traditions. Let all who see it know that here stands a true Roman, a man who embodies the virtues our Republic was built upon.' He placed the crown on Julius's head, then turned him to face the legion.

Remember this moment,' he roared 'Remember that such courage still exists. Remember that you serve in a legion where men will risk all to save their brothers. And remember that you are Romans, and this - *THIS* is what Romans can be!'

The roar that erupted from the legion dwarfed all previous cheers. It was not just approval - it was pride, inspiration, a recognition that they had witnessed something extraordinary. Spears hammered shields in rhythm, voices called Caesar's name, and the very earth seemed to tremble with their acclaim.

And through it all, Julius stood straight, the weight of the crown heavy on his brow but lighter than the weight of destiny he felt settling onto his shoulders. In that moment, before thousands of cheering legionaries, he felt something crystallize within him - a certainty, a purpose, an understanding of what he could become.

This was not just a reward for past actions. This was a beginning. For there on the plains of Mytilene, witnessed by gods and men alike, a legend was born. And Rome would never be the same.

Chapter Twenty-Six

Pyrrha

The Bay of Pyrrha heaved with ships, a forest of masts swaying against the cloudless blue sky. Warships and transports jostled for position along the crowded shoreline, their hulls creaking as they rose and fell with the gentle swell. The Legion's redeployment to Ephesus had begun.

From his vantage point on the headland, Julius watched as the cohorts marched down to the waiting vessels, their armour glinting in the bright morning sun, their standards held high above the ordered columns.

Somewhere among them, Marcus led a small squad, a decurion now, in charge of an eight-man contubernium. He had been reassigned to the third cohort which meant their paths would ultimately diverge, but he was happy with his assignment and was already committed to his new role.

The thought brought a small smile to Julius's lips. How far they had both come since those uncertain days in the goatherd's hut, fugitives with nothing but a vague plan and dwindling coin. Now Marcus had found his calling in Rome's legions, while Julius wore the oak-leaf crown that marked him as a hero of the Republic.

'Domine,' a voice called from behind.

Julius turned to find one of General Thermus's aides approaching, a young Optio who had somehow managed to keep his armour polished to a mirror sheen despite the dust and grime of deployment.

'The General requests your presence aboard his vessel,' the aide continued, gesturing toward the harbour. 'You'll be travelling to Ephesus with his command staff.'

Julius followed the aide's gesture to where a magnificent quinquereme sat anchored in deeper water. Unlike the utilitarian troop transports crowding the harbour, the Aquila was a ship built for both war and status. Three banks of oars extended from her sleek hull like the legs of some great waterborne insect. Her prow was fashioned into the shape of an eagle, its beak gleaming with bronze, its wings extending back along the hull in delicate carved relief. Two masts rose from her deck, their square-rigged sails furled for now but ready to catch the wind once they cleared the harbour.

'An honour,' Julius replied, conscious of his status as bearer of the Corona Civica. Since the award ceremony, he had learned that tradition dictated he wear it at all formal occasions, but the golden oak leaves were both a privilege and a burden, they marked him out, made him visible in ways that both helped and hindered him. 'When do we depart?'

'Within the hour,' the aide said. 'A boat awaits you at the main pier.'

As Julius gathered his few possessions and made his way down to the harbour, he couldn't help but reflect on how this summons represented an opportunity. To rise in Rome, a man needed more than courage on the battlefield; he needed connections, patrons, powerful friends. And few friends were more valuable than a governor with the ear of Rome's Senate.

The Aquila's deck buzzed with activity as final preparations for departure were made. Sailors scurried about, securing rigging and stowing supplies. Officers conferred over maps and charts spread across a table bolted to the deck. At the stern, the helmsman stood ready at the tiller, awaiting the command to guide the great vessel out of the harbour.

Julius was shown to a small but well-appointed cabin below decks. Unlike the crowded troop transports where men slept wherever they could find space, the old but well-maintained quinquereme, as command ship of the fleet, had been altered to provide private quarters for officers of rank. The cabin contained a narrow bunk fixed to the wall, a small writing desk secured to the floor, and hooks for hanging clothing and weapons.

Before long, the sound of commands from above, followed by the rhythmic splash of oars, signalled their departure and the Aquila moved majestically out of the harbour, her three banks of oars propelling her swiftly through the calm waters. As they cleared the headland, the sails were unfurled, billowing in the afternoon breeze, and the ship surged forward, leaving Mytilene and its memories behind.

On the second night at sea, as the sun dipped toward the horizon in a blaze of orange and crimson, a steward appeared at Julius's cabin door.

'Domine,' the man said with a respectful bow, 'General Thermus requests your presence at dinner. The officers gather in one hour.'

Julius nodded his acknowledgement, then turned to prepare himself once the steward had departed. He had anticipated this invitation, yet still felt a flutter of nervousness in his stomach. These were men of experience and power, veterans of campaigns across Rome's expanding domain. He was young, barely more than a boy in their eyes, despite the oak leaves he had earned in the crucible of war.

He dressed with care, donning his cleanest tunic and arranging his toga in the formal manner befitting a dinner with a provincial governor. The Corona Civica came last, settled carefully upon his brow, its weight still unfamiliar.

The officers' mess occupied the stern of the ship, a space that during battle would have housed marines and archers. Tonight, it had been transformed with military efficiency into a dining room suitable for a general. A long table dominated the centre of the room, its surface spread with maps that had been hastily cleared to make space for dinner. Oil lamps swung gently from hooks in the ceiling beams, their light gleaming off polished armour and military decorations.

Thermus sat at the head of the table, his weathered face animated as he gestured during conversation with a knot of senior officers. Beside him sat the fleet commander, Lucullus, his naval insignia distinctive against his dark blue cloak. Other officers filled the remaining seats, older, more seasoned men; Centurions with decades of service etched into their scarred face and staff officers who managed the thousand complex tasks that kept a legion functioning. All men who had climbed Rome's military ladder rung by brutal rung.

Julius paused at the entrance, waiting to be acknowledged. Thermus spotted him first, his conversation trailing off as he raised a hand in greeting.

'Ah, Caesar!' he called, voice carrying easily over the general murmur of conversation. 'Our hero of Mytilene! Come, join us.'

All eyes turned to Julius, some curious, others appraising, a few perhaps even slightly resentful. The Corona Civica was not awarded lightly, and its bearer commanded respect by ancient tradition. Even consuls were required to stand when such a decorated man entered a room, a courtesy that some prideful officers might resent extending to one so young.

'General Thermus,' Julius responded with a formal bow. 'Thank you for the invitation.'

'Nonsense,' Thermus waved away the formality. 'The man who saved Rufio deserves a place at my table.' He gestured to an empty seat halfway down the table's length. 'We were just discussing the naval blockade. Lucullus here believes our friend Mithridates is considering another attempt to challenge Rome's authority in the region.'

Julius took the offered seat, noting how the conversation had paused at his arrival. He was the newcomer here, the untested quantity despite his decoration.

'Caesar,' Lucullus said, leaning forward to get a better look at him. 'I understand this was your first real taste of combat. Quite the baptism by fire, wouldn't you say?'

'It was… educational, Domine,' Julius replied carefully, aware of the attention focused upon him. 'Though I suspect the lessons taught at Mytilene would be familiar to veterans such as yourself.'

A Centurion across the table barked a laugh.

'Diplomatic as well as brave! No wonder they say you're destined for the Senate.'

Servants appeared, bearing platters of food, simple fare by Roman standards, but luxurious for men at sea, fresh bread, olives, cheese, dried fruits, and wine that had not yet turned to vinegar. As the food was served, the initial tension eased, conversations resuming around the table.

'Tell me, Caesar,' Thermus said between bites, 'what do you make of our eastern situation? You've seen both sides now, Rome's power and the resistance to it.'

Julius felt the weight of the question. This was no idle dinner conversation; it was a test, a measuring of his political and strategic acumen.

216

'I believe,' he began, choosing his words with care, 'that Rome's greatest strength in the east is not our legions, formidable though they are, but the certainty we bring. Certainty of law, of commerce, of order.' He paused, gauging the reaction. Several of the older officers were listening intently now. 'The peoples of Asia have lived too long under the shadow of chaos, Mithridates, pirates, petty kings squabbling over territory. They resist us, yes, but what they truly resist is change, not the peace we ultimately deliver.'

Thermus nodded slowly, a hint of approval in his eyes.

'An interesting assessment. And how would you secure that peace, if you were in command?'

Another test, more direct this time. Julius took a sip of wine, using the moment to gather his thoughts.

'I would show them that resistance brings swift justice, as we did at Mytilene,' he said, 'but also that cooperation brings prosperity. Trade, infrastructure, stability, these are weapons as powerful as our swords, and far more enduring.'

'The words of a politician, not a soldier,' one of the older Tribunes commented, though his tone held more curiosity than criticism.

'Rome needs both, does it not?' Julius countered. 'The sword and the law, working in harmony.'

'Well said!' Lucullus raised his cup in salute. 'Though I wonder if our young Contubernalis has the stomach for the harsher necessities of campaign. Mytilene was one battle. Subduing a province requires years of vigilance, often brutal vigilance.'

'I've seen what resistance costs,' Julius said, his voice quieter now but no less intense. 'I've seen men burn alive in Greek fire, children crushed beneath falling stones, women...' He stopped, the memories of Mytilene's streets suddenly vivid. 'I understand the price of peace, Praefecte. I simply suggest we be strategic in how we extract payment.'

217

A thoughtful silence settled over the table, broken only by the creak of the ship and the distant calls of the night watch above. Julius wondered if he had overstepped, spoken too boldly for his rank and experience. Then Thermus laughed, a deep, genuine sound that seemed to release the tension in the room.

'By the gods, Lucullus, I think we've found a Roman who can both fight and think! A rare combination indeed.'

The other officers joined in the laughter, and Julius felt the atmosphere shift. He was still an outsider, still unproven in their eyes, but he had earned something tonight, if not respect, then at least interest.

As the dinner continued into the night, the wine flowed more freely, and with it, Julius felt a subtle transformation. Each time an officer nodded at his observations or laughed at his quick rejoinders, he felt a piece of his earlier caution fall away. This was not merely a table of superiors tolerating a young officer, these were his peers, men who spoke the same language of power, strategy, and ambition that had always whispered in his heart.

When the conversation turned to the governance of Rome's eastern provinces, Julius found himself leaning forward, no longer waiting for permission to speak.

'The Senate fails to understand the East,' he declared with newfound confidence. 'They see it as a collection of territories to be taxed, not as the future of Rome's prosperity.'

'Bold words from a junior,' one of the older officers remarked, eyebrows raised.

'Perhaps,' Julius replied, swirling the wine in his cup, 'but I've seen what others haven't. My father served in Bithynia, and through him, I learned that eastern kings respect strength paired with vision. Mithridates rose to power not just through brutality but by offering an alternative to Rome's often... shortsighted governance.'

He was conscious of overstepping, yet the words flowed with an ease that surprised even himself. The Corona Civica seemed to warm against his brow, as if lending weight to his pronouncements.

'And you believe you could do better?' Lucullus asked, his tone balanced between amusement and challenge.

'Given the opportunity?' Julius met his gaze directly. 'Yes. I believe I could.'

A momentary silence fell over the table. Julius had crossed an invisible line, from confident to presumptuous. Yet instead of rebuke, a chorus of chuckles rippled through the officers.

'I admire your confidence, Caesar,' said an older Centurion, raising his cup in mock salute. 'When I was your age, I thought I could command the entire eastern fleet with one hand while pleasuring Venus herself with the other!'

The table erupted in laughter, and Julius joined them, recognizing that they were both acknowledging and gently checking his growing boldness. They were humouring him, the decorated young officer with more courage than experience, but within their tolerance, he also sensed something else: recognition. Some part of them saw in him a reflection of their younger selves, ambitious and untempered by the full weight of command.

The evening continued, stories flowing as freely as the wine. Julius spoke less now but with no less assurance, carefully measuring when to assert and when to defer. By the time the dinner concluded, many of the officers clasped his arm with genuine warmth as they departed, a subtle shift from their earlier formal acknowledgments.

As the gathering dispersed, Thermus gestured for Julius to remain and when the last of the officers had left, the general poured two cups of wine.

'Walk with me,' he said, leading Julius up to the main deck.

The night was clear, stars scattered across the darkness like the campfires of some celestial army. The Aquila cut smoothly through calm waters, her oarsmen rowing with the steady rhythm of a disciplined legion. They stood at the rail, the soft spray occasionally misting their faces as they gazed out over the darkened sea.

'You made quite an impression tonight,' Thermus said finally.

'I hope a favourable one, General,' replied Julius.

Thermus turned to study him, his weathered face serious in the moonlight.

'You have a gift, Caesar. You speak well, you fight well, and men listen when you talk.' He paused, weighing his next words. 'But gifts can be squandered if not tempered with wisdom.'

Julius straightened, recognizing that beneath the conversation lay something important.

'I have no doubt,' Thermus continued, 'that you will one day be a great man in Rome. Your name, your mind, your courage, all mark you for distinction. But to reach those heights, you would do well to show more humility and respect to those you may come to rely on.'

'I meant no disrespect,' Julius began, but Thermus raised a hand to silence him.

'I know that. But others might see it differently. I've watched men of tremendous promise sabotage themselves through arrogance. The Senate is filled with aging men who would rather destroy a rising star than be outshone by it.' He gave Julius a pointed look. 'And unlike tonight's dinner, they won't simply chuckle at your presumption.'

Julius absorbed the rebuke silently, feeling its sting but recognizing its value. Thermus was offering more than criticism, he was offering guidance, the kind only given to those deemed worthy of investment.

'I know you can fight,' Thermus said, his voice softening slightly. 'Mytilene proved that beyond question. But command is something else altogether. It's knowing when to speak and when to listen, when to lead from the front and when to step back.' He turned to face Caesar. 'It's about earning the right to be heard, not demanding it.'

'I understand, General,' Julius said, and genuinely meant it.

'Good.' Thermus nodded, satisfied. 'Because when we return to Ephesus, I'm changing your role.'

Julius felt his pulse quicken.

'I'm moving you from administrative duties to military responsibilities,' Thermus continued. 'You'll be given command of detachments, some patrol responsibilities, genuine military duties. I want to see how you handle real leadership, not just heroics.'

Julius stared at the General. The promotion was everything he had hoped for, a chance to prove himself not just in battle but in command. Yet Thermus's words of caution hung between them, a reminder that the path to greatness was lined with pitfalls as well as opportunities.

'I won't disappoint you, Domine,' Julius said.

Thermus studied him for a long moment, then clapped him on the shoulder.

'See that you don't,' he said. 'Just remember that the greatest commanders know not only how to take power but how to wield it wisely,' and with that final piece of counsel, Thermus left him at the rail, alone with the night, the sea, and thoughts of the future that stretched before him like the vast, star-flecked sky above.

Chapter Twenty-Seven

Ephesus

The Roman fort of Castra Artemis stood on a low hill three miles inland from Ephesus, its rectangular perimeter commanding views of both the city and the surrounding countryside. Built in the classic Roman style, its walls formed a perfect rectangle, constructed of timber and packed earth topped with a wooden palisade, the ramparts wide enough for three men to walk abreast during patrols. At each corner rose a watchtower, manned day and night by sentries scanning the horizon for any sign of trouble.

Inside, the fort was laid out with the precision that characterised all Roman military establishments. Straight roads bisected the compound, dividing it into ordered sections. The principia, the headquarters building, occupied the centre, its stone-built walls setting it apart from the wooden barracks and storehouses that housed the garrison. The commander's quarters stood nearby, slightly elevated and built with a nod toward comfort that the common soldiers' barracks lacked.

Two full cohorts made their home here, supported by auxiliary cavalry from Thrace and Numidia. In times of peace, it was a base for maintaining Roman authority; in war, it could serve as a rallying point for the full legion scattered across the province.

For Julius Caesar, newly appointed as Tribunus Militum, the fort had become home. His promotion from administrative duties to proper military command had changed everything, now he was a genuine officer with men under his authority and shared responsibility for Rome's security in this volatile region.

Each morning began before dawn with the changing of the night watch. Julius would often observe this ritual from the ramparts, watching as the tired sentries were relieved and the fort slowly came to life with the sounds of men preparing for the day's duties. The responsibility sat well on his shoulders, as if he had been born to command men.

His daily duties varied. Some days were filled with overseeing the training exercises, and cavalry manoeuvres on the plain below the fort. Other days saw him reviewing patrol reports, tracking the movement of suspected bandits or rebels still loyal to Mithridates VI, the Pontic king whose shadow still loomed over Rome's eastern provinces despite his defeats.

The patrols were perhaps the most valuable experience. Thermus had ensured Julius accompanied different cohorts, learning the peculiarities of the territory and the challenges faced by men in the field. These excursions had been largely uneventful, enforcing Rome's peace meant showing the flag, reassuring loyal communities and reminding potential troublemakers of the consequences of defiance.

Julius had adapted quickly to life in the field. He rode for hours without complaint, slept on hard ground when necessary, and shared the rough fare of campaign rations with his men. Although the Corona Civica was safely stored in his newly acquired equipment chest, the fact that he was a bearer had already earned him the respect of the men and soon, his willingness to share hardships began to transform that respect into genuine loyalty.

Yet despite these successes, Julius felt a creeping frustration. The skirmishes he had participated in were minor, a few bandits scattered at the approach of Roman troops, a village headman refusing taxes until the sight of cavalry changed his mind. Nothing that tested his abilities or offered opportunities for distinction. Nothing like Mytilene.

So, when Thermus summoned him and ordered him to join the Third Cohort at their forward camp to address a growing bandit problem, Julius had embraced the mission eagerly. Reports indicated a well-organised group terrorising villages in the eastern part of the province, possibly with political motivations. Loyalists to Mithridates had been known to disguise their insurgency as common banditry, and the pattern of attacks suggested something more

223

coordinated than simple robbery.

The journey to the forward camp took two days, following the eastern road through rolling hills that gradually gave way to more rugged terrain. The camp itself was modest compared to Castra Artemis, a temporary fort established to extend Roman authority into the more remote regions of the province. Its walls were simple earthworks topped with wooden stakes, and the internal accommodation were little more than leather tents arranged in ordered rows.

The commander's quarters, which Julius was directed to upon arrival, consisted of a slightly larger tent divided into sections by hanging cloths. A camp bed occupied one corner, a folding table and a chair. Maps were pinned to a portable wooden board, marked with the locations of recent bandit activity. It was spare and functional, lacking even the modest comforts of the main fort, but it served its purpose.

Julius spent his first hours reviewing the situation with the camp prefect, a veteran Centurion named Gaius Hostilius. The bandits, Hostilius explained, struck isolated communities before disappearing into the hills. They seemed to know the territory intimately, suggesting local origins. Three attempts to track them had failed, with the bandits melting away before the Romans could bring them to battle.

'They're ghosts,' Hostilius had concluded with evident frustration. 'We find their camps still warm, but never the men themselves.'

After the briefing, Julius needed to stretch his legs after the long ride. He stepped out of the tent into the late afternoon sun, surveying the camp with a critical eye. Soldiers moved about their duties with the disciplined efficiency of a well-trained unit. Sentries stood at their posts, weapons ready and in the centre of the camp, a training session was underway, men practising close-quarter fighting techniques under the watchful eye of a grizzled Optio.

Julius began walking toward the practice ground, intending to observe, his mind already turning over strategies for dealing with the elusive bandits and was halfway across the parade ground when a voice called out, startling him from his thoughts.

'Gaius Julius Caesar! By all the gods, is that you?'

Julius turned toward the voice, a smile already forming as he recognised its owner. There, striding toward him with the confident gait of a man who had found his place in the world, was Marcus.

'Marcus!' Julius clasped his friend's forearm in greeting. 'I was wondering if I'd find you here.'

Marcus looked different from when Julius had last seen him. His face was tanned and weathered, his frame leaner but somehow more solid. The insignia of a decurion adorned his tunic, and a red commander's sash was tied at his waist. But his grin was the same as always.

'They told me a new officer had arrived to solve our little bandit problem,' Marcus said. 'I should have known it would be you. Trouble always seems to find you, or is it the other way around?'

'A bit of both, I suspect,' Julius replied, studying his friend. 'You look well. The military life suits you.'

Marcus glanced around to ensure no one was within earshot, then lowered his voice slightly.

'It does, strangely enough. I never thought I'd say it, but I've become rather good at ordering men about.' He gestured toward a cluster of tents at the edge of the camp. 'My contubernium is celebrating a successful patrol, a small victory, we captured a bandit scout. Join us for a drink? Like old times.'

Julius hesitated. As Tribunus Militum, he was expected to maintain the careful distance between officers and men that formed the backbone of Roman military discipline and sharing wine around a campfire with the ranks was generally frowned upon. Yet this was Marcus, his oldest friend, the man who had followed him into exile without question.

'I shouldn't,' he said, then smiled. 'But when have I ever done what I should?'

Marcus grinned.

'That's the Julius I remember. Come, they're good men. All Mytilene veterans, they'll welcome the hero of the acropolis.'

As dusk fell, they made their way to the edge of the camp where the centuries were housed. The Roman military system was built around the contubernium, a squad of eight men who shared a tent and fought as a unit with ten contubernia forming a century, commanded by a Centurion with an Optio as his second.

The tents were arranged in neat rows, with narrow streets running between them, the entire layout designed for efficiency and discipline. Marcus's tent was indistinguishable from the others, a standard leather shelter barely large enough for the eight pallets inside. But in front of it, a small fire burned, around which sat seven men in various states of relaxation. Their armour was stacked neatly nearby, their weapons within easy reach even in this moment of rest. They snapped to attention when they saw the officer approaching.

'At ease,' Julius said quickly, uncomfortable with the formality. 'I'm here as Marcus's guest, not as your officer.'

The men relaxed marginally, exchanging glances.

'Caesar,' one said, standing up and holding out his arm. 'We fought together at Mytilene. I was in the Second Century when you pulled Rufio out.'

Julius studied the man, recognition dawning.

'Titus Lanius,' he said. 'You held the left flank during the final push.'

The veteran's face broke into a surprised grin.

'You remember?'

'I remember every man who stood with us that day,' Julius replied, and it wasn't entirely untrue. The faces of those who had survived Mytilene were etched in his memory alongside those who had fallen.

That simple exchange broke the ice and Marcus motioned Julius to a place by the fire, as someone pressed a cup of wine into his hand. The night deepened around them as the rigid hierarchy of the legion temporarily dissolved into something older, more primal, warriors sharing stories of battle, honouring the dead, celebrating survival.

They ate a simple meal of stew thickened with barley and dried meat, far better than standard legionary rations. One of the men had apparently traded with a local village for fresh herbs and vegetables, a common practice on extended deployment.

As the wine flowed, the conversation grew louder, more animated. The men recounted moments from Mytilene, some harrowing, some darkly humorous, all bound together by the shared experience of battle. They spoke of comrades lost, using their names freely, keeping their memory alive in the firelight.

'To Gallus,' one man said, raising his cup. 'Mad bastard charged five Greeks with nothing but a broken spear.'

'To Lucius,' added another. 'Too young to die, too stubborn to run.'

Cup after cup was raised, name after name honoured, until it seemed they had toasted half the legion. Julius joined each salute, feeling again the weight of those days, the terror, the courage, the brotherhood forged in blood.

Gradually, as the night wore on, the men drifted away to their pallets until only Julius and Marcus remained by the dying fire.

'You've found a home here,' Julius observed, watching his friend's face in the flickering light.

Marcus stared into the embers.

'Perhaps. It's simpler than Rome. Clear orders, clear purpose.' He glanced up.

'And what about you? Does the great Julius Caesar plan to spend the rest of his life in frontier forts, hunting bandits?'

Julius took a long drink of wine, considering his words carefully.

'My pardon came through before Mytilene,' he said finally. 'Sulla has officially removed my name from the proscription lists and

227

Thermus has indicated he would not oppose my return to Rome if that's what I choose.'

'Is that what you want?' Marcus asked.

The fire crackled in the silence that followed, casting long shadows across their faces. When Julius spoke again, his voice was distant, as if already looking toward a horizon beyond this camp, beyond this province.

'Everything I've learned here, command, strategy, the loyalty of men, all of it is preparation. For what, I'm not entirely certain yet, but I know it all leads back to Rome.'

Marcus nodded, unsurprised.

'And me? What place does Marcus Antonius Gracchus have in this grand design?'

Julius looked at his friend, really looked at him. Marcus had changed in these months of military service. He carried himself with a new confidence, commanded respect not through family name but through proven ability. Perhaps Rome had more to offer him now than when they had fled as fugitives.

'The same place you've always had,' Julius said firmly. 'At my side, if you choose it. Or here, if that's where your path leads. Either way, you remain my oldest friend and the one man I trust without question.'

They sat in companionable silence for a time, each lost in his own thoughts about the future. Eventually, Julius rose, aware of the lateness of the hour.

'I should go,' he said. 'We have an early patrol tomorrow, and I'd prefer not to face bandits with a wine-clouded head.'

Marcus stood as well, swaying slightly as he found his balance.

'You're right,' he slurred, 'the bandits won't wait while we debate our futures. Tomorrow, we hunt.'

'Tomorrow, we hunt,' Julius agreed, and as Julius walked back toward the commander's tent, he felt the weight of decision pressing upon him. Rome called to him like a distant trumpet, promising opportunity, power, destiny. Yet here, in the provinces, he had found something valuable too, respect earned through action, not birth; authority tested in fire, not politics.

    The choice would wait. For now, there were bandits to find, a province to secure, a reputation to build. One step at a time, laying the foundation for whatever was to come. Rome had endured for centuries; and it would still be there when he was ready to claim his place in its story.

Chapter Twenty-Eight

The Fort at Ephesus

Dawn broke over the eastern hills, the forward camp stirring to life with the familiar sounds of a military unit preparing to move, the clink of armour being fastened, the low murmur of men checking equipment, the nickering of horses sensing the day's journey ahead.

Julius stood with the Centurions, reviewing the patrol route one final time. The map spread before them was crude by Roman standards, the terrain of the province still imperfectly charted despite years of occupation.

'We'll follow the river valley for the first day,' he said, tracing the path with his finger. 'Reports indicate the bandits have been striking villages along this route. On the second day, we'll split into three groups to cover more ground, then rendezvous here, ' he tapped a spot where two valleys converged, 'before nightfall.'

Gaius Hostilius, the most experienced Centurion, nodded his approval.

'They favour hit-and-run tactics. Quick strikes, then retreat into the hills. If we can catch them between our groups, we might finally bring them to battle.'

'Exactly my thinking,' Julius agreed. 'Remember, these aren't just common thieves. They target tax collectors, Roman merchants, anyone representing our authority. This is insurgency disguised as banditry.'

The Centurions nodded grimly. All had seen the pattern: the systematic way the bandits undermined Roman presence while sparing staunch locals, the propaganda they spread about Mithridates's eventual return, the careful selection of their targets. This was no random violence, it was the continuation of war by other means.

'Six centuries should be sufficient,' Julius continued. 'Light marching order, three days' rations. We move within the hour.'

The men dispersed to prepare their units, and Julius found himself momentarily alone. The weight of command settled over him like a familiar cloak. This was his first independent command, a small force, to be sure, but his to lead, his to succeed or fail with. The thought quickened his pulse but steadied his resolve.

As the patrol assembled, Julius noted with satisfaction the orderly formation, the quiet discipline of troops who had drilled together for months. His gaze fell on Marcus, who stood at the head of his contubernium, checking their equipment with practiced efficiency. Their eyes met briefly across the parade ground, and Marcus gave an almost imperceptible nod. No words were needed; they had faced greater challenges together.

'Centuries, advance!' commanded Julius, and like a great beast awakening, the patrol began to move.

The first day passed without incident. They marched steadily through the river valley, where scattered homesteads and small settlements dotted the fertile land. Farmers paused in their work to watch the Romans pass, their expressions guarded. This was frontier territory, where loyalty to Rome was often a matter of pragmatism rather than conviction.

They stopped at each settlement, questioning locals about unusual activity, strangers passing through, anything that might lead them to their quarry. Most claimed to know nothing, their faces blank with the practiced innocence of those caught between opposing powers. A few offered vague reports: men seen in the hills, unusual movements at night, distant sounds that might have been fighting.

As dusk approached, they established a temporary camp on high ground overlooking the valley. Sentries were posted, fires lit, and the centuries settled into the rhythm of soldiers on campaign. Julius walked the perimeter, checking defensive positions, speaking briefly with the men. It was a ritual of command he had learned from Rufio, be seen, be present, know your troops.

Later, as he sat with the Centurions reviewing the day's

progress, a sentry approached.

'Domine,' the man said with a salute, 'there's a villager at the edge of camp. Says he needs to speak with the commander. Says it's urgent.'

Julius exchanged glances with Hostilius, who shrugged slightly.

'Bring him here,' Julius ordered, and got to his feet.

The villager was a middle-aged man with the weathered look of a farmer. His clothes were simple but clean, his manner respectful but not servile. When he spoke, it was in accented but understandable Latin.

'My name is Hektor,' he said. 'I farm three miles east of here. Two nights ago, the men you seek attacked the village of Nysa, about fifteen miles upriver.' He pointed roughly northeast. 'It was bad, very bad. They killed the headman and many others who resisted.'

Julius leaned forward.

'How do you know this?'

'My sister's husband lives there,' the man replied. 'He came to warn us they might strike other villages. I thought... I thought the Romans should know.'

'Why tell us?' Hostilius asked, suspicion clear in his voice. 'Most locals avoid involvement.'

The farmer met his gaze steadily.

'My son serves in your auxiliaries, so I believe in Rome's peace, even if others do not.'

Julius studied the man, weighing his words. It could be a trap, of course, the bandits had proven cunning before. But the information aligned with their intelligence, and the man's demeanour suggested sincerity.

'Thank you, Hektor,' he said finally. 'We'll investigate your claims. You may go.'

After the farmer departed, Julius turned to his officers.

'Change of plans,' he said, 'we march for Nysa at first light.'

They smelled the village before they saw it, the acrid stench of burned timber and the sickly-sweet odour of death carrying on the morning breeze and as they crested the final hill, the devastation spread before them.

Nysa had been a modest settlement of perhaps thirty buildings. Now, half of them were charred ruins, their blackened timbers jutting against the sky like the ribs of slaughtered beasts. Bodies still lay where they had fallen, some outside the village as if caught fleeing, others in the central square where they had tried to make a stand. Carrion birds scattered at the Romans' approach, reluctantly abandoning their feast.

Julius halted the column, taking in the scene with a soldier's practiced assessment. This was no mere raid for supplies or coin, the destruction was too thorough, too deliberate. This was a message. If you defy the bandits and cooperate with Rome, you face annihilation.

In the village square, the village headman and five elders had been crucified on hastily constructed crosses, their bodies mutilated in ways that spoke of hours of torment before death had finally released them. Beneath them, painted on the stones in blood, was a crude message in Greek: 'Death to Rome's dogs.'

The wells had been fouled deliberately, dead animals thrown into the water to poison it. Grain stores had been burned rather than stolen, ensuring that even survivors would face starvation and children's simple toys lay scattered and broken in the dirt, small poignant reminders of lives shattered by calculated brutality.

A temple to Demeter at the village's edge had also been desecrated, the statue of the goddess dragged into the street and decapitated, a systematic assault not just on the people but on their beliefs, their identity, their very humanity.

'Centurions, to me,' Julius called, and the officers gathered quickly. 'Hostilius and Vibius, check for survivors and detail men to bury the dead. Septimus, you're with me. The rest of you, secure the perimeter.'

The Centurions dispersed to carry out their orders, and Julius dismounted, walking slowly into the silent village.

The devastation was more complete than it had first appeared. Houses that remained standing had been systematically looted, not for valuables alone but for anything that might sustain life, food, tools, even clothing. The attackers had been thorough in their cruelty, determined to ensure that surviving meant suffering.

In one home, they found a family lying in pools of dried blood, the children killed before their parents, positioned to ensure the adults had witnessed their deaths. In another, an elderly couple had been tied back-to-back and burned alive, their charred remains still bound together in a grotesque final embrace.

Each discovery hardened something in Julius's expression, each atrocity fed a cold fury that settled behind his eyes. This was not warfare; this was not even banditry. This was calculated terror, designed to break not just bodies but spirits.

Gradually, survivors began to emerge, from hidden cellars, from nearby woods where they had fled, from beneath the bodies of loved ones who had given their lives to protect them. Their eyes were hollow with shock, their movements slow and stunned.

A young woman approached them, carrying a baby wrapped in bloodstained cloth. The infant was unnaturally still, and when Julius looked closer, he saw that it had been dead for at least a day, yet the mother continued to cradle it, to whisper to it, unable to accept the truth.

An old woman approached Julius, her white hair matted with blood, her arm clearly broken but untreated.

'You came,' she said in Greek, her voice cracking with age and grief. 'Too late, but you came.'

Julius felt the accusation like a physical blow. She was right, Rome's protection had failed these people. His protection had failed them.

'We're here now,' he said in her language, surprising her. 'And we will make this right.'

For three days, Julius and his men remained in Nysa. They buried the dead with what honour they could provide, rebuilt essential structures, and treated the wounded with their limited medical supplies. Hunting parties were sent out to secure food, and clean water was carried from the river to replace the village's contaminated well.

The survivors watched the Romans with a mixture of gratitude and wary confusion. This was not the distant, tax-demanding Rome they knew, these were soldiers who laboured alongside them, who shared their rations, who treated their children's wounds with unexpected gentleness.

On the morning of the fourth day, as Julius oversaw the rebuilding of the village's small granary, a rider approached at speed, his horse lathered with the evidence of hard riding. It was Marcellus, one of the scouts Julius had sent into the surrounding hills.

'Domine!' the man called, dismounting in a cloud of dust. 'We've found them!'

Julius straightened, handing the hammer he'd been using to a nearby legionary.

'Where?'

'Ten miles northeast, in the foothills,' Marcellus reported, still catching his breath. 'A camp of about fifty men, well-established. They have sentries and wooden palisades. It is not just a temporary camp, Domine, this is a permanent base.'

Julius felt a surge of conflicting emotions. Here, finally, was the opportunity to strike at the heart of the insurgency, to eliminate the threat that had terrorised the region. Yet the villagers of Nysa still needed protection, still depended on the Romans for their survival. The work of rebuilding was far from complete, the new well was only half-dug, and the defensive perimeter they had begun to construct unfinished.

He looked around at the village, at the survivors who now watched him with a fragile hope that had not been there days before. Children who had been mute with shock were beginning to speak again. Men who had lost everything were working alongside Roman soldiers to rebuild homes. Women who had seen unspeakable horrors were finding the strength to care for the living rather than mourn the dead. They had begun to trust him, to believe in Rome's protection.

He looked over at Marcellus, whose discovery offered the chance to prevent this tragedy from repeating elsewhere. Other villages, other innocent lives, waited unaware in the shadow of the same threat. The bandits would strike again, that much was certain, and the only question was ,who would be their next victims? The decision crystallised in his mind with surprising clarity.

'Centurions!' he called, and within minutes, his officers had gathered.

'We've located the bandit camp,' he said. 'So, I'll need to divide our forces.' He paced before them, his mind already formulating a plan. 'I'll take three centuries to strike at the bandits directly, the rest will remain here to continue protection and rebuilding. Focus on completing the perimeter first, if we fail, they may attempt immediate reprisals.'

'Domine,' Hostilius began, a note of caution in his voice, 'splitting our force could be risky. These bandits have proven elusive and dangerous. Perhaps we should wait for reinforcements from the main camp?'

Two of the other Centurions nodded in agreement, but Julius shook his head.

'By the time reinforcements arrive, the bandits could have moved. This may be our only chance to end the threat permanently. The risk is necessary.'

He swept his gaze across the assembled officers, ensuring they understood the gravity of both missions.

'Vibius, Septimus, Antonius, your centuries will march with me. We leave in one hour.

Chapter Twenty-Nine

Nysa

Three centuries moved in tight formation across the barren landscape, their footfalls deliberately soft, their voices silent. Julius rode at their head, setting a pace that balanced speed with stealth.

By midday, they had left the valley floor behind, climbing steadily into the foothills that formed a natural fortress around the bandit camp. The terrain grew more challenging, narrow paths winding between steep slopes, sudden ravines cutting across their route, loose stones threatening to betray their presence with the clatter of an unwary step. The landscape was rocky and sparse, offering little cover but many places for ambush. Scrubby brush and the occasional twisted olive tree dotted the hillsides, survivors in a harsh land where water was precious and shade rare.

Julius ordered the column to halt frequently, allowing scouts to range ahead and ensure they weren't walking into an ambush.

'They're overconfident,' one of them reported, returning from a scouting mission as the sun began its descent. 'Their sentries are posted, but they're lazy. Drinking, some of them. I think they believe the mountains protect them.'

Julius nodded, unsurprised.

'What of their defences?'

'A wooden palisade surrounds the central area, but it's crude, a few splintered logs lashed together, not even sharpened properly.' He sketched a rough layout in the dirt. 'There's a single gate on the eastern approach. Perhaps twenty structures inside, a mix of permanent buildings and tents. The majority of their force appears to be present.'

Julius studied the improvised map, noting the positions of sentry posts, the terrain features, the possible lines of attack. Standard Roman doctrine called for a frontal assault in tight formation, the famous testudo, with interlocked shields creating an impenetrable wall of men and metal that would batter through the main entrance and crush all resistance through superior discipline and training.

But Julius had something else in mind.

As darkness fell, the column approached within a mile of the bandit camp. The glow of their fires was visible across the rocky terrain, and as the wind carried fragments of drunken laughter, Julius called the Centurions to him.

'We'll rest for two hours,' he instructed. 'Cold rations only, no fires. I want every man ready to move by midnight.'

The Centurions nodded, their faces shadowed in the fading light.

'And the plan of attack?' Septimus asked, his voice gruff with the bluntness of a career soldier.

Julius met their gazes steadily.

'We're not using the testudo.'

A momentary silence followed as the Centurions exchanging glances.

'The testudo would work, eventually,' Julius explained. 'But it would also alert them, give their leaders time to escape, perhaps cost us unnecessary casualties.' He knelt, drawing in the soft earth. 'Instead, we'll divide our force. Vibius, your century will circle to the north, using the ridge line for cover. Septimus, yours will take the southern approach through the ravine. Antonius, you'll be with me on a frontal assault.'

The Centurions studied the crude map with a mixture of surprise and professional interest. This was not how Romans typically fought. The legion's strength had always been in its unity, its ability to move and fight as a single overwhelming force.

'Night attack from multiple directions?' Septimus frowned. 'That's barbarian tactics. Risky.'

'Risky, yes,' Julius agreed. 'But they'll never expect it from Romans. Our discipline gives us an advantage even when adopting unconventional methods. And there's more.' He pointed to the camp's perimeter. 'I want fire arrows prepared, at least thirty per century. On my signal, we'll ignite their shelters, creating confusion before our main attack.'

Now genuine concern showed on the Centurions' weathered faces.

'If we burn the camp,' Antonius said carefully, 'we might lose valuable intelligence. Prisoners, documents...'

'I'm not interested in intelligence,' Julius replied, his voice taking on a hardness that surprised even himself. 'I want a message sent. The same message they sent at Nysa, but with Roman clarity. No survivors, no mercy.'

The Centurions fell silent, recognising the cold fury beneath his words. They had all seen the devastation at Nysa, had all helped bury the mutilated dead and though none would weep for the bandits, such total destruction was unusual even in Rome's punitive campaigns.

'You have your orders,' Julius concluded. 'Move your centuries into position. We attack at the third hour after midnight.'

The hours before the attack passed with agonising slowness. Julius and Antonius's century waited in a shallow depression near the eastern approach, the men lying still against the rocks, their breathing controlled, their weapons wrapped in cloth to prevent telltale reflections. The moon was a thin crescent, providing just enough light to move without risking discovery.

At the appointed hour, the first signal came, the soft call of an owl from the northern ridge, repeated moments later from the southern ravine. Vibius and Septimus were in position. Julius gave a nod to Antonius, who passed the command in whispers down the line.

Moments later, Julius raised his hand, then dropped it sharply and the signal passed through the darkness with invisible swiftness. Suddenly the night was split by dozens of flaming arcs as fire arrows soared over the palisades to land among the tents and wooden structures within.

For a breathless moment, nothing happened. Then, as the first structures caught, shouts of alarm rose from the camp. Men stumbled from tents, confused and half-dressed, calling to comrades, searching for weapons.

Julius gave the second signal and from three directions, Romans surged forward in coordinated waves. Unlike the tight formations of traditional legion tactics, they moved in smaller, more flexible groups of eight men, the contubernia that lived, trained, and fought together. Each contubernium had a specific target, a building, a tent cluster, a section of the palisade.

The bandits, already disoriented by the spreading fires, now found themselves under attack from all sides. The disciplined contubernia crashed into their disorganised groups like wolves among sheep.

Julius fought with cold efficiency, his gladius an extension of his will. There was none of the frenzied heroism of Mytilene here, only the calculated application of lethal skill. He parried a wild swing, stepped inside his opponent's guard, and drove his blade up beneath the rib cage. Without pausing, he withdrew and turned to the next threat, his movements fluid and economical.

On the far edge of the camp, Marcus led his contubernium in a systematic clearing of the larger structures. They moved from building to building, room to room, leaving no corner unchecked, no shadow unexplored. Those who surrendered were dealt with as efficiently as those who fought, a quick thrust, a severed throat, bodies left where they fell.

The battle, if it could be called such, lasted less than an hour, the outcome never in doubt. Caught unprepared, surrounded, confused by the fires and the multi-directional assault, the bandits stood no chance against Roman discipline. Some fought bravely, others fled into the darkness only to run into waiting blades… a few begged for mercy that never came.

By the time the eastern sky began to lighten, it was over. The camp was a charnel house, the ground soaked with blood, the air already beginning to smell of death and burning. Bodies lay everywhere, sprawled in doorways, crumpled beside extinguished fires, piled where final stands had been attempted and broken.

Julius walked through the devastation, his armour splattered with blood, his gladius finally still in his hand. Around him, Romans moved methodically, checking for survivors, ensuring their grim work was complete. There was no celebration, no triumphant shouts or victory cries, only the quiet, terrible efficiency of professional soldiers completing their task.

Across the smoking ruins, Julius saw Marcus directing his men to search the remaining structures. Their eyes met briefly across the carnage, and a moment of silent understanding passed between them. This had been necessary. This had been just. But there was no glory in it, no honour to be found in the slaughter of inferior foes, only the satisfaction of a duty fulfilled.

Marcus gave a small nod, perhaps of respect before turning back to his men. The sun crested the eastern hills, illuminating the scene in harsh clarity, the blackened remains of tents and buildings, the still forms that had once been men. A single standard still stood in the centre of the devastation, not a Roman eagle, but a crude banner bearing the emblem of Mithridates. Julius watched as a legionary tore it down, trampling it into the bloody earth.

By midmorning, the centuries had regathered at the assembly point east of the destroyed camp and Julius gave his final orders with the same calm precision that had characterised the entire operation.

'We return to Nysa immediately,' he said. 'Take no trophies, no souvenirs. Leave everything as it is.'

'Domine,' Vibius asked, 'should we not bury them? The smell will reach for miles once the sun's been on them a day.'

'That's the point, Centurion,' Julius replied. 'I want everyone within fifty miles to know what happened here. I want them to smell it, to see it, to understand exactly what becomes of those who murder Roman allies.'

Vibius nodded but raised no further objections. The centuries
formed up, and with one last look at the carrion birds already circling overhead, Julius gave the order to march.

The message had been sent, written in fire and blood, in a language even Rome's most determined enemies would understand.

Chapter Thirty

Ephesus

A full year had passed since the slaughter of the bandits, and the countryside around Ephesus had settled into an uneasy peace. Villages once terrorized now flourished under Roman protection, their markets bustling with trade, their fields yielding harvests without fear of raids. For the people of the province, peace meant prosperity. For Rome, it meant taxes flowing smoothly once more.

Julius Caesar had remained in the east, his position as Contubernalis unchanged in title but transformed in substance. What had begun as a courtesy appointment had become something more, a position of genuine authority earned not through family connections but through demonstrated ability. The survivors of Nysa had not forgotten the Roman officer who had avenged their dead, and word of his ruthless efficiency had spread throughout the province, both reassuring allies and deterring potential enemies.

Within the legion, he had earned a different kind of respect. Officers appreciated his tactical mind, his willingness to embrace unconventional solutions when traditional methods proved inadequate. Common soldiers valued his fairness, his attention to their needs, and the strange, unshakable confidence that seemed to radiate from him like heat from a brazier. He never asked men to take risks he wouldn't face himself, never demanded sacrifices he wasn't willing to make, and in the rough meritocracy of military life, such qualities mattered more than a distinguished family name.

Even Thermus, initially sceptical of the young nobleman playing at war, now called upon Caesar regularly for patrols requiring both military skill and political finesse. The eastern provinces were a complex patchwork of loyalties, Roman allies, Greek city-states, client kingdoms, and populations still harbouring sympathies for

Mithridates. Navigating this terrain required more than a strong sword arm. It required judgment, a quality Caesar had demonstrated repeatedly.

The morning sun was already high when the messenger found Julius overseeing cavalry drills on the dusty plain outside their forward camp. The horses kicked up clouds that hung like bronze mist in the sunlight, and shouts of instruction echoed through the air punctuated by the thunder of hooves as the riders practiced the complex manoeuvres that gave Roman cavalry its edge.

'Caesar,' the messenger called, approaching with the brisk efficiency of a military courier. 'General Thermus requests your presence at Castra Artemis immediately.'

Julius wiped sweat from his brow with the back of his hand, squinting against the bright sunlight.

'Did he say why?'

'No, Domine. Only that you are to travel to Ephesus without delay.'

Julius nodded, already calculating the journey. Two days' hard ride from their position, less if he pushed. He turned, searching the training ground for a familiar face, and found Marcus walking toward him.

'I assume duty calls?' Marcus asked, watching the messenger walk away.

'Thermus has summoned me to Ephesus,' Julius replied. 'No explanation given.'

Marcus raised an eyebrow.

'Perhaps he's finally realized Rome would function better with you running it.'

Julius laughed, though both men knew the jest carried an undercurrent of seriousness. Julius had never made a secret of his ambitions, and his achievements in the east had only strengthened his conviction that greater things awaited.

'Watch yourself while I'm gone,' he said, turning his horse away, 'these hills still hide enemies.'

An hour later, Julius rode eastward, accompanied by a small escort of four legionaries. The road to Ephesus was relatively safe these days, but a Contubernalis traveling alone would be an inviting target for any remnants of the insurgency seeking revenge.

They rode hard, stopping only when necessary to rest the horses, and reached the outskirts of Ephesus as the sun was setting on the second day. The city sprawled before them, its white marble buildings catching the last golden rays of daylight. The great Temple of Artemis dominated the skyline, its massive columns visible for miles, while the bustling port beyond teemed with ships from every corner of the Mediterranean.

Ephesus was a city of contradictions. Greek in culture and history, it now served as the administrative heart of Rome's province of Asia. Streets that had once echoed with the philosophies of Heraclitus now rang with the commands of Roman officers. Temples dedicated to Artemis and Athena stood alongside shrines to Roman gods, and in the marketplace, Latin mingled with Greek as merchants haggled over goods from across the known world.

Julius had spent enough time in the city to navigate its crowded streets with ease. The fort, Castra Artemis, stood on high ground overlooking both the city and the harbour, its walls a statement of Roman permanence in this foreign land. The sentries recognized him immediately, snapping to attention as he approached.

'Julius Caesar to see General Thermus,' he announced, dismounting at the main gate.

The guard nodded respectfully.

'The General is expecting you, Domine. You're to go directly to his quarters.'

Thermus's quarters reflected the man himself, austere, practical, with few concessions to comfort beyond what his rank required. Maps covered one wall, detailed charts of the province showing roads, settlements, and terrain. A simple desk dominated the centre of the room, its surface spread with documents bearing the seals of Rome and various client kingdoms.

Thermus himself stood by the window, gazing out over the city as dusk settled over it. When Julius entered, he turned, and Julius was struck by how the year had aged him. New lines marked his face, and silver now threaded through his close-cropped hair. The burden of command was etched into his features, the responsibility of maintaining Rome's hold on a province surrounded by potential enemies.

'Caesar,' he said, gesturing toward a chair, 'you made good time. Wine?'

Julius accepted the wooden cup offered to him, noting that the vintage was better than standard military issue. Whatever this meeting was about, Thermus considered it significant enough to break out his private reserves.

'You've done well this past year,' Thermus began, settling into his own chair. 'Better than I expected, if I'm being honest. Your handling of the bandit situation was... effective, if unconventional.'

Julius inclined his head, accepting the mixed compliment. The destruction of the bandit camp had sparked heated debate among the officer corps. Some had criticized the total annihilation as excessive, while others had praised its decisive impact on the insurgency.

'Every report I've received speaks highly of your tactical judgment,' Thermus continued. 'Even that old war dog Hostilius, who typically reserves his praise for men who've been fighting since before you were born.' He took a sip of wine, studying Julius over the rim of his cup. 'And yet I sense that your talents are being wasted here.'

Julius set his wine down carefully, keeping his expression neutral despite the sudden quickening of his pulse.

'Domine?'

'You're not just a good soldier, Caesar, you also have the makings of a natural politician, and I firmly believe your future lies back in Rome, in the Senate. Thermus smiled faintly. 'Don't look so surprised. You wear your ambition openly enough.'

'I've never concealed my intentions to return to Rome eventually,' Julius admitted.

'Eventually' may be sooner than you anticipated.' Thermus reached for a sealed document on his desk, passing it to Julius. 'This arrived three days ago. Read it.'

The parchment bore the seal of the Senate, the wax still intact. Julius broke it carefully, unrolling the document to reveal elegant Latin script. As he read, he felt a strange lightness in his chest, as if something long compressed was finally expanding.

Thermus watched him, a hint of amusement in his eyes.

'From your expression, I gather the news is welcome.'

Julius looked up from the document.

'Sulla is dead,' he said, still processing the implications. 'I can return to Rome.'

As the last light of day slipped through the narrow window of his quarters, Julius lay on his bunk, his mind too restless for sleep. The document from Rome rested on a small table nearby, its message both liberation and challenge. The man who had driven him from Rome, who had threatened everything he held dear, was now nothing more than ashes in a funeral urn.

He should have felt triumph, perhaps even joy. Instead, he felt something more complex, a strange ambivalence that kept him staring at the ceiling beams long after the fort had fallen silent.

In the stillness of the night, he allowed himself a rare moment of pure honesty. He had grown to love this life, the clarity of military command, the unambiguous nature of success and failure, the instant response to bold decisions. There was a simplicity here that Rome, with its tangled web of politics and alliances, could never offer.

Here, a man was measured by his actions, not his ancestry. Here, he had earned respect through blood and judgment, not through family connections or political manoeuvring. The Corona Civica that had marked him as a hero of Rome had opened doors, but it was his decisions in the field that had cemented his growing reputation.

He shifted on the narrow cot, his thoughts turning to Marcus. His friend had found his place in the legion, had discovered strengths he never knew he possessed. Would Marcus follow him back to Rome? Or had the army claimed him for good?

Yet even as he recognized what he would be leaving behind, Julius knew where his destiny lay. Rome called him, not just as a place of birth and family, but as the arena where true power was won and wielded. His father had been praetor, a man of consequence but not of greatness, but Julius had always known he was meant for more.

And now, with Sulla gone, the opportunity was there. The proscriptions would end, and men would cautiously reclaim their positions, rebuild their fortunes, recapture their influence. The game would begin anew, with different players but the same ruthless rules. He needed to be there, to establish himself while the power structures were still fluid.

Then there was Cornelia. He had married her for political alliance, for the connection to the Populares faction, but something deeper had grown between them in the brief time they had together. She deserved more than a husband in distant exile, she deserved the man she had married, the man who had defied Sulla rather than repudiate her.

He sighed, turning onto his side. His father had dreamed of a son who would raise the Julian name to new heights, who would command respect in the forum and the battlefield alike and now he opportunity to fulfil that dream, if he had the courage to seize it.

His thoughts circled, restless and unsettled. The practical Roman in him methodically listed the advantages and disadvantages of each path, weighing opportunities against risks with cool precision. But beneath that calculation ran a deeper current, the inexorable pull of ambition, the knowledge that his name was meant for greater things than commanding patrols in a distant province.

Julius closed his eyes, willing his mind to stillness. Tomorrow he would inform Thermus of his decision, would begin preparations for the journey home. Marcus would need to be told, arrangements made, and responsibilities transferred. It would take time, perhaps weeks, but the path was clear. He was going home. To Rome. To Cornelia. To the future that awaited him.

Chapter Thirty-One

Ephesus

Dawn filtered through the narrow window, casting a pale rectangle across Julius's face. He woke instantly, a soldier's habit, his mind clearing even as his body rose from the cot. The restlessness of the night had settled into resolution.

After a quick meal in the fort's dining hall, he made his way through the morning bustle to Thermus's quarters. Officers hurried past with maps and dispatches, couriers arrived breathless with news from distant outposts, and behind it all, the steady rhythm of soldiers drilling in the courtyard below. This world of ordered chaos had become familiar, comforting even, but it was no longer his world.

The sentry outside Thermus's door recognized him immediately.

'The General is inside, Dominc. He's expecting you.'

Of course he was. Thermus had always possessed an uncanny ability to anticipate decisions before they were made.

Julius found the general standing over his map table, moving small wooden markers that represented cohorts and auxiliary units. The province might be pacified, but maintaining that peace required constant vigilance and strategic deployment of limited forces.

'Caesar,' Thermus said without looking up, 'I wondered when you'd make your decision.'

Julius smiled faintly.

'Is it that obvious?'

Thermus glanced up, his weathered face creasing into something almost like affection.

'You have many qualities, Caesar, but a talent for concealing your ambitions isn't among them.' He gestured to a chair. 'Sit. Tell me what you've decided, though I suspect I already know.'

Julius settled into the seat, his posture straight, formal. This was not a casual conversation between friends, but a meeting between a commander and his subordinate, perhaps the last such meeting they would have.

'I need to return to Rome,' he said simply. 'With Sulla gone, the path is open for me to reclaim my place there. My wife has waited long enough, my mother grows older, and the family's affairs require attention.'

'And Rome itself calls to you,' Thermus added, his tone knowing. 'The Forum, the Senate, power.'

Julius met his gaze directly. There was no point in false modesty, not with this man who had seen through him from the beginning.

'Yes,' he admitted. 'Rome calls to me.'

Thermus studied him for a long moment, then nodded, as if confirming something to himself.

'You've learned much in your time here, Caesar. Not just about military matters, but about leadership, about men, about the realities of Rome's power beyond her walls.' He leaned back in his chair. 'Those lessons will serve you well in the arena you're entering.'

'The Senate is a different battlefield altogether,' Julius acknowledged.

'But a battlefield nonetheless,' Thermus replied. 'With different weapons, different tactics, but the same objective, victory.' He paused, choosing his next words carefully. 'You have the makings of a great leader, Caesar. I've seen it in how you command men, in how you think beyond conventional approaches, in your willingness to take bold action when necessary.'

Julius inclined his head, accepting the compliment. From Thermus, such words were rare and therefore precious.

'Rome needs men like you,' Thermus continued, 'though she may not always appreciate what she needs. The Republic faces challenges, within her borders and beyond them. The social wars may be over, but their causes remain unresolved. Mithridates still lurks in the East, pirates control the seas, and the balance between the Senate, the equites, and the people grows more precarious each year.'

'You paint a bleak picture, General.'

'I paint a realistic one,' Thermus corrected. 'And into this reality, you will step, with your name, your ambition, and the lessons learned here.' He smiled slightly. 'It will be interesting to watch your rise.'

'You assume I will rise,' Julius said.

'I do,' Thermus replied simply. 'Because men like you, men of vision, of intelligence, of boldness, always do. The only question is how high, and at what cost.' He straightened, his tone shifting back to the practical. 'When do you wish to depart?'

'I need to return to the forward camp first,' Julius said. 'There are things I must settle there.'

'Of course,' Thermus nodded. 'Marcus Antonius Gracchus.'

Julius raised an eyebrow, surprised that Thermus would single out his friend.

'Among others, yes.'

'Your friendship with him has been noted,' Thermus said. 'He too is a solid young man, with potential for further advancement but as he did not come through the normal route and has not taken the sacramentum he, is also able to leave, if he should so wish. But consider carefully what you advise him, Caesar. Not every man is suited for Roman politics. Some find their true place in service, away from the intrigues of the capital.'

Julius nodded, understanding the implied caution. Marcus had thrived in the structured environment of the legion. Would he flourish or flounder in the cutthroat world of Roman power politics?

'I'll speak with him,' Julius promised.

'Good.' Thermus rose, signalling the end of their meeting. 'You have my permission to depart when your affairs are in order. I'll have letters prepared, commendations for your service. They may prove useful in Rome.'

Julius stood, recognizing the practical value of such documents. A military reputation, properly leveraged, could open many doors in Rome.

'Thank you, General. For everything.'

Thermus extended his arm, and Julius clasped it in the Roman gesture of respect between equals. For a moment, something like regret flickered across the general's face.

'May the gods favour your journey, Gaius Julius Caesar. I suspect Rome will never be quite the same once you return to her.'

As Julius left the fort, the morning sun now high above Ephesus, his mind was already turning to the journey ahead. First, to the forward camp, to Marcus, and the men who had served him so well. Then, home to Rome, to opportunity, to destiny.

The thought quickened his pulse as he strode toward the stables. The die was cast. His future awaited.

The journey back took less time than the ride to Ephesus. The landscape flashed by in a blur of dust and scrubby vegetation, the familiar terrain of what had become, against all expectations, a second home.

He arrived just as the afternoon drill was ending, legionaries marching back to camp in orderly formation, dust rising from their sandaled feet. The sentries snapped to attention as he passed through the gates, word of his return spreading quickly through the ranks. Men nodded in respect, some calling greetings, but Julius barely registered them. His thoughts were elsewhere. After handing his horse to a groom, he summoned a young messenger.

'Find Decurion Antonius and tell him to meet me at the eastern overlook. He'll know the place.'

The boy nodded and darted away, threading through the rows of tents that made up the camp's ordered geometry.

Julius made his way out of the eastern gate and up the winding path that led to a rocky outcrop overlooking the valley. It was a place he and Marcus had discovered months ago during a patrol, a natural vantage point that offered views across the rolling desert terrain. They had returned here many times since, sometimes to
discuss tactics, sometimes simply to share wine and conversation away from the constant demands of the camp.

The rocks still held the day's heat as Julius settled onto a familiar perch, his back against a weather-worn boulder. Below, the desert stretched to the horizon, its harsh contours softened by the approaching sunset. The sky was already beginning to change, deep blue giving way to streaks of orange and gold.

He heard Marcus's approach before he saw him, the familiar rhythm of his friend's stride on the rocky path. There was no need for formality here, no salutes or titles, just the easy companionship forged through years of shared danger and trust.

Marcus appeared around the bend, silhouetted against the darkening sky. He was dressed simply in a standard military tunic, his armour and insignia left behind in camp.

'Your messenger found me at the worst possible moment,' he said by way of greeting. 'I was about to win a small fortune at dice.'

Julius smiled.

'The gods must have intervened to save you from your own vices.'

'My vices have served me well enough so far,' said Marcus settling onto a rock opposite, reaching for the wineskin that Julius had brought. He took a long pull, then wiped his mouth with the back of his hand. 'So, you're back from Ephesus sooner than expected. I assume you didn't insult the general or set fire to his maps?'

'Not this time,' Julius replied. The easy banter felt like a delaying tactic, a way to postpone the real conversation that lay ahead.

They sat in companionable silence for a moment, watching as the sun sank lower, its light painting the desert in shades of amber and bronze. A distant eagle circled on thermals, hunting the small creatures that emerged in the cooling air.

'Do you remember that summer at my father's villa?' Julius asked suddenly. 'The one where you convinced me that we should hunt boar without guides?'

Marcus laughed, the sound echoing off the rocks.

'How could I forget? You nearly got yourself gored, and I nearly got myself thrashed by your father.'

'He was more impressed than angry, as I recall.,' replied Julius. 'He said we showed initiative, if not sense.'

'Your father was always kinder to me than I deserved,' Marcus said, his tone softening. 'I think he knew my own father's temper would have broken bones rather than spirits.'

The memory hung between them, one of countless shared experiences that had forged their bond long before they had become men, before Rome's politics had forced them into exile, before war had taught them its harsh lessons.

'And then there was that time in the baths, when you decided to correct a senator's pronunciation of Greek,' Julius continued.

'In my defence, he was butchering the language so badly even the slaves were wincing,' Marcus protested. 'How was I to know he was related to half the Senate?'

'You couldn't have. Just as I couldn't have known that standing by Cornelia would lead us here.' Julius gestured to the camp below, now lit by cooking fires as night approached.

The mood shifted subtly, both men sensing the conversation turning toward its true purpose.

'So,' Marcus said finally, his voice deliberately casual, 'Did Thermus summoned you to Ephesus to discuss the weather? Or is there something else you wish to tell me.'

Julius met his friend's gaze directly.

'Sulla is dead.'

The words hung in the cooling air. Marcus's expression didn't change, but something flickered in his eyes, understanding, perhaps, or resignation.

'Ah,' he said quietly. 'So, the path back is clear.'

'Yes.'

'And you're going.' It wasn't a question.

'I am,' Julius confirmed. 'I've already spoken with Thermus. He's granted me leave to return to Rome.'

Marcus nodded slowly, then turned to look out over the darkening landscape. The sun was almost gone now, just a sliver of gold on the distant horizon.

'I've known this day would come,' he said. 'Ever since we left Rome, I knew it was temporary. That one day, you would go back. That Rome was in your blood in a way it never was in mine.'

'It doesn't have to be just me,' Julius said. 'Thermus mentioned that you've distinguished yourself well. He implied that if you wanted to return as well…'

'Is that what you want?' Marcus interrupted. 'For me to follow you back? To walk those marble halls again, to bow and scrape before men whose only accomplishment was being born to the right family?'

'I want you to have the choice,' Julius said carefully. 'The same choice that I have.'

Marcus laughed, but there was no humour in it.

'Is it really a choice for you, Julius? Has it ever been? Since we were boys, I've watched you stare at the city as if it belonged to you, as if you were just waiting for the moment to claim it.' He shook his head. 'No, my friend. You're returning to Rome because that's what you've always been meant to do. The only surprise is that it took this long.'

The last light faded from the sky, leaving them in the deepening twilight. Below, the campfires burned brighter, pinpricks of warmth in the gathering darkness.

'So, what will you do?' asked Julius.

Marcus was silent for a long moment. When he spoke, his voice was quieter, more reflective than Julius had heard it in years.

'I've found something here, Julius. Something I never had in Rome.' He gestured vaguely toward the camp. 'These men... they follow me because of what I can do, not who my grandfather was. They respect me because I've earned it, not because I wear the right clothes or know the right people.' He took another drink from the wineskin. 'In Rome, I was always "that friend of the Julian boy" or "the troublemaker from the Subura." Here, I'm Decurion Antonius. Here, I matter.'

Julius felt a tightness in his chest, a complex mixture of pride for his friend and sorrow at what his words meant.

'Our friendship doesn't end because our paths diverge,' he said.

'No,' Marcus agreed. 'But it changes. It has to.' He looked directly at Julius. 'You're going back to become whatever great thing the gods have planned for you. Consul, probably, knowing you. And I'm staying here to be what I was meant to be, a soldier.' He smiled, a genuine smile that reached his eyes. 'We both found our calling, Julius. Just not in the same place.'

The night had fully descended now, the stars emerging in the vast desert sky, cold and distant. Julius studied his oldest friend's face in the faint light, seeing in it a certainty he had never noticed before.

'I thought our paths would always run together,' he admitted.

'So did I,' Marcus replied. 'But perhaps this is better. You, reshaping Rome from within. Me, defending her out here at the edges. Different battles, but the same war.' He raised the wineskin. 'To Rome.'

Julius took it, completing the toast.

'To Rome.'

They sat in silence as the night deepened around them, two friends at a crossroads, each understanding that this moment marked an ending and a beginning. Their boyhood was finally, irrevocably over and the men they had become would follow different stars, drawn by different destinies.

'When do you leave?' Marcus asked finally.

'Within the week,' Julius replied. 'There are arrangements to make, responsibilities to transfer.'

Marcus nodded.

'I'll help you prepare. And I'll see you off properly, with enough wine to ensure you remember us fondly.' He smiled, though his eyes remained serious. 'Just promise me one thing, Julius.'

'Anything.'

'When you rule Rome, and we both know you will someday, remember what you learned here. Remember the men who fought beside you, who bled for Rome far from her marble columns, far from their loved ones. Remember that Rome is built on their sacrifices, not just on speeches in the Senate.'

Julius reached out, clasping his friend's forearm.

'I will remember,' he promised. 'And I will find a way to honour what you've chosen here.'

Finally, they headed back down to the fort, laughing at some distant memory, but as they laughed, they both knew they were finally saying goodbye. The friendship forged in childhood had weathered persecution, exile, and war, and now would endure separation. Different roads, but the same stars to guide them.

Chapter Thirty-Two

Rome

The Julii villa on the outskirts of Rome hummed with anticipation. Servants hurried through its marble halls, arranging fresh flowers, polishing silver serving trays, and laying out the finest linens that had been stored away during the long years of their master's absence. The atrium sparkled in the afternoon light, the impluvium freshly cleaned, its waters reflecting the blue sky above. Garlands of laurel and myrtle adorned the doorways, their fragrance mingling with the scent of roasting meats and baking bread from the kitchen.

Cornelia stood in the centre of it all, directing the preparations with calm authority. The years of separation had only enhanced her beauty, adding a quiet dignity to her elegant features. Her dark hair was arranged in the latest fashion, adorned with pearl pins that had been a gift from her late father. Her stola, dyed the deep blue that only wealthy Roman women could afford, swept the marble floors as she moved from room to room, ensuring everything was perfect.

'More wine from the cellar,' she instructed an older servant. 'The Falernian, not the Greek. And make sure the couches are arranged properly, the Consul will expect the place of honour.'

Aurelia observed quietly, her eyes taking in every detail. She had maintained the family's dignity during her son's absence, had kept their name relevant in Rome's social circles despite Sulla's shadow. Now, with Gaius's return, the family would reclaim its rightful place among Rome's elite. She had invited carefully, senators who had opposed Sulla, wealthy equites whose support would be valuable, a few key military men whose alliance with a promising young Julian might prove fruitful.

'He should have been here by now,' she murmured, glancing toward the entrance for the hundredth time that afternoon.

'The roads from Ostia are crowded,' Cornelia replied. 'And he may have stopped at the temple to make offerings.' She adjusted a fold in her stola. 'After so long away, he'll want to thank the gods for his safe return.'

The sound of arriving guests interrupted their conversation. The first visitors were already at the door, greeted by slaves who took their cloaks and offered cups of honeyed wine. These were the second-tier guests, arriving early to secure the best positions and perhaps have a private word with the family before the crowd gathered.

By the time the sun began to set, the villa was filled with the sound of conversation and laughter. Oil lamps were lit, casting a warm glow over the assembled guests. Among them were several senators in their purple-bordered togas, their expressions carefully composed to reveal nothing of the political calculations going on behind their eyes. Wealthy merchants circulated, seeking connections that might benefit their businesses and military officers in their dress uniforms stood in clusters, exchanging war stories and eyeing the political men with barely concealed disdain.

'Have you heard about Pompey's latest campaign?' one senator asked another, keeping his voice low. 'They say he's demanded another triumph, though half the victories were won by his subordinates.'

'Typical Pompey,' the other replied. 'Always ensuring the glory falls on him alone.'

Nearby, a group of women huddled in elegant conspiracy, their voices hushed but their eyes sharp.

'I heard the Julian boy distinguished himself in the East,' one whispered. 'Earned some military honour that even Sulla's supporters couldn't deny.'

'My husband says he's one to watch,' another replied. 'The Julii have always known how to choose the winning side eventually.'

Throughout it all, Aurelia and Cornelia maintained their composure, greeting guests, ensuring wine cups remained full, orchestrating the complex dance of Roman social politics. But their eyes continually drifted to the entrance, waiting for the one guest who mattered above all others.

The sudden hush that fell over the gathering was the first sign. Conversations paused mid-sentence, heads turned toward the atrium, and a ripple of anticipation passed through the crowd. Then came the sound of footsteps on marble, firm and measured, and a figure appeared in the doorway.

Gaius Julius Caesar stood at the threshold of his ancestral home, tall and straight, his bearing transformed by years of military service. The sea voyage from Asia had tanned his skin to a deep bronze, and the physical demands of campaign life had hardened his body, eliminating any trace of the soft aristocrat who had fled Rome years before. He wore a simple white tunic with the narrow purple stripes of his rank, and a red military cloak was draped over one shoulder, a deliberate choice that reminded everyone present of his service to Rome.

Yet despite the commanding presence, something seemed slightly off-key. His eyes scanned the room with a soldier's attentiveness, but there was a reservation in his manner, a subtle distance that even the most casual observer might notice. This was not the triumphant return of a hero, but something more complex, more measured.

For a moment, he simply stood there, taking in the familiar space that had haunted his dreams throughout exile. Then his gaze found Cornelia, and something in his expression softened, a private message passing between them across the crowded room.

Aurelia was the first to move, crossing the space with dignified steps that belied the emotion evident in her eyes.

'My son,' she said, her voice steady despite the slight tremor in her hands as she reached for him. 'Welcome home.'

Julius embraced her, the formal Roman greeting replaced by a moment of genuine warmth. When they separated, both had composed their features again, aware of the watching eyes.

'Mother,' he said. 'You've kept our house well in my absence.'

'As was my duty,' she replied. 'Now it returns to your hands, stronger than when you left it.'

Cornelia approached next, her eyes never leaving her husband's face. The years of separation seemed to vanish as Julius took her hands in his, raising them to his lips in a gesture that honoured both her position as his wife and the private bond between them.

'You are even more beautiful than I remembered,' he said, his voice low enough that only she could hear.

'And you have returned to us at last,' she replied, equally quiet. She studied his face with the perceptiveness of a woman who knew her husband well, noting the faint shadows beneath his eyes, the slight tension in his jaw.

The formality of the moment was broken by a shout from the back of the crowd.

'By all the gods, Julius! Are you going to greet your wife properly or stand there like a statue?'

Laughter rippled through the gathering, releasing the tension. Julius smiled and stepped closer to Cornelia, placing a chaste kiss on her cheek.

The gathering surged forward then, guests pressing close to offer welcomes, to clasp arms, to ensure that the returning Julius remembered old friendships and past favours. He navigated the crush with practiced ease, naming each person correctly, recalling connections and family ties with a memory that impressed even those who had known him well.

But as the evening progressed, both Aurelia and Cornelia noticed the same thing, Gaius was going through the motions perfectly, saying all the right words, making all the correct gestures, but something was absent. The fire that had always burned within him, the barely contained ambition that had defined him since boyhood, seemed muted, as if covered by a thin layer of ash.

Servants brought more wine, and the volume of conversation rose as the initial formality gave way to genuine celebration. Julius moved through the crowd with careful attention, spending time with each important guest, ensuring no one felt neglected. He answered questions about the East with diplomatic precision, neither boasting nor diminishing his role there. When asked about Sulla, he expressed appropriate respect for the dead dictator while allowing his listeners to draw their own conclusions about his personal feelings.

It was a masterful performance, Aurelia thought as she watched from the edge of the gathering. Her son had left Rome a rash young man; he had returned a polished politician, capable of navigating the treacherous waters of Roman society with confidence and skill. But something was troubling him, something he was concealing beneath that careful exterior.

As the evening progressed, the gathering moved to the triclinium for the formal dinner. Couches were arranged in the traditional U-shape, with places of honour assigned according to strict Roman protocol. Julius reclined at the central position, with Quintus Lutatius Catulus, a senior senator who had maintained connections to the Julian family through the difficult years, at his right hand.

Slaves brought the first courses, eggs prepared with garum sauce, oysters from the bay of Naples, olives soaked in herbs and oil. Wine flowed freely, the best vintages from the Julian cellars, preserved for just such an occasion.

As the main dishes arrived, roasted boar, peacock arranged with its feathers displayed, sow's udder prepared with complex spices, Catulus rose, lifting his wine cup high.

'Friends,' he called, his voice cutting through the din of conversation. 'Honoured guests. I ask for silence.'

The room quieted, all eyes turning to the elderly senator. His toga, edged with the broad purple stripe of high office, gleamed in the lamplight.

'We gather tonight to welcome home one of Rome's sons, returned to us after years serving the Republic in distant lands.'

Catulus's voice, trained through decades in the Senate, carried to every corner. 'Gaius Julius Caesar has honoured his family's name, upheld Roman virtues in foreign soil, and proven that the blood of ancient houses still runs strong.'

Murmurs of agreement rippled through the gathering. Catulus turned to Julius, who had risen to stand beside him.

'We have heard rumours, Julius, of your accomplishments in the East. Of battles fought, of honour earned.' He paused, his eyes twinkling with the knowledge of a well-prepared dramatic moment. 'But rumours are but pale shadows of truth, so, I ask, on behalf of all gathered here: Are you going to show us that which you won with blood and Julii courage?'

A hush fell over the room. Julius hesitated, caught between Roman modesty and something else, not reluctance to boast, but a deeper, more private hesitation, as if the battlefield memories brought with them shadows he was not eager to revisit. He glanced at Cornelia, who gave him a slight nod of encouragement.

'I had thought to wait for a more appropriate moment,' he said, his voice carrying the slight reluctance of a man unused to boasting of his own deeds.

'There is no more appropriate moment than this,' Catulus insisted. 'Among friends, among supporters who stood by your family when others wavered.'

The political calculation was clear to everyone in the room. By displaying his military honours now, Julius would be making a statement, that he had returned not as a pardoned exile but as a Roman of achievement, ready to claim his place in the hierarchy of power.

Julius nodded and turned to where his travel chest had been placed against the wall. He approached it, knelt, and unfastened the iron clasps. The room was silent as he reached inside, past folded clothing and leather scroll cases, to withdraw something wrapped in soft cloth.

When he turned back to the gathering, his expression had changed. This was no longer the charming dinner host but the soldier who had faced death in Rome's service. With deliberate movements, he unwrapped the cloth to reveal the Corona Civica in all its glory.

The oak-leaf crown, crafted in solid gold, gleamed in the lamplight. Gasps rose from several guests, particularly the military men who understood the rarity and significance of such an honour.

'The Corona Civica,' Catulus announced, his voice reverent. 'The highest military decoration Rome can bestow upon her sons.'

Julius held the crown carefully, his eyes momentarily distant, perhaps seeing again the blood-soaked steps of Mytilene's acropolis.

'Tell us,' urged a military tribune from the back of the room. 'How did you earn it?'

'I did only what any Roman would do,' said Julius looking up. 'A comrade had fallen. I could not leave him to die.' He looked around at the expectant faces, understanding that the full tale could not be avoided, so, with measured words, he recounted the battle of Mytilene, the desperate assault on the acropolis, the moment when Rufio had been surrounded and cut off from the main force.

He told the story plainly, without embellishment or false modesty, letting the facts speak for themselves, but those listening heard what he did not say, that he had shown courage beyond what Rome expected even of her bravest sons, that he had risked everything not for glory but for loyalty, that he had faced death and emerged victorious.

When he finished, silence held the room for a long moment. Then Catulus stepped forward and, with deliberate ceremony, took the crown from Julius's hands and placed it upon his head.

'Wear it with pride, Gaius Julius Caesar,' the senator said. 'Rome honours her heroes, and you have proven yourself worthy of her highest esteem.'

The gathering erupted in applause, wine cups raised in salute. And Julius stood before them, the golden oak leaves resting on his dark hair, accepting their praise with grace, but without the hint of triumph that might have been expected. Even in this moment of honour, there was a reservation in his manner, as if part of his mind remained elsewhere.

The feast continued long into the night, the mood shifting from formal welcome to genuine celebration. Music played, dancers performed, and as the wine continued to flow, the strict boundaries of Roman society relaxed slightly. Men who had been cautious in their initial greeting now pressed closer to Julius, eager to establish connections with this newly revealed hero. Women spoke more openly with Cornelia, commending her patience during the long separation, praising her loyalty to a husband who had chosen principle over safety.

It was nearly dawn when the last guests departed, carried home in litters by slaves who had spent the night waiting patiently outside the villa's walls and as the door closed behind them, Aurelia reached up to touch her son's face, a gesture she would never have permitted herself in front of others.

'You have done well,' she said simply. 'Your father would be proud.'

Julius took her hand, the Corona Civica still resting on his brow.

'I hope so,' he replied. 'Everything I've done has been to honour his memory, to raise our family's name as he would have wished.'

Cornelia moved closer, her presence a reminder of the private reunion that still awaited.

'You seem troubled,' she said softly, her perceptive eyes searching his face. 'Is it Rome? Is it being home after so long away?'

Julius looked from his mother to his wife, the two women who had maintained his household, protected his interests, and kept faith during his long absence. In their faces, he saw not just love and loyalty but intelligence and understanding. These were not merely the women of his family; they were his most trusted advisors, as politically astute as any senator.

'It should be joy I feel,' he admitted. 'A triumphant return, the beginning of everything we've planned and hoped for.' He paused, struggling to articulate the shapeless unease that had shadowed his homecoming. 'But something troubles me, and I know not what.'

Aurelia's eyes narrowed slightly. She had always been able to read her son better than anyone.

'The battlefield changes men,' she said. 'Even the strongest. Give yourself time, Gaius. Rome has waited this long; it can wait a little while longer.'

He nodded, grateful for her understanding. The reasons behind his disquiet remained elusive, too complex to name or confront in this moment of exhaustion after so much intensity.

'Tomorrow is soon enough to think of the future,' Cornelia said, sliding her arm through his. 'Tonight, rest. Be home. Be with me.'

Julius felt the tension in his shoulders ease slightly at her touch. Whatever shadows had followed him from the East, whatever uncertainty awaited in Rome's political arena, those concerns could wait for the morning light.

'You are wise, as always,' he said, removing the golden crown and placing it carefully on a side table. The symbol of his achievements could rest there until he was ready to wear it again, until he had reconciled the soldier he had become with the politician he must now be.

Aurelia embraced them both before retiring to her own chambers, leaving husband and wife alone for the first time in years.

'Come,' Cornelia said simply, taking her husband's hand.

As they walked arm in arm toward their bedchamber, Julius pushed the nameless disquiet to the back of his mind. This night belonged to reunion, to remembering what had been and imagining what could be. Whatever troubled him, memories of battle, the absence of Marcus, the uncertain political landscape of post-Sulla Rome, he would face it tomorrow, with the clarity of daylight and the strength that had carried him through exile and war.

For now, it was enough to be home, to feel Cornelia's arm entwined with his, to know that whatever challenges lay ahead, he would not face them alone.

Chapter Thirty-Three

Rome

The rhythm of civilian life returned slowly, like the feeling in a numbed limb. After years of military routine, the precise schedule of watches, drills, and patrols, Julius found himself adrift in the more fluid patterns of Roman domestic existence. He rose at dawn out of habit, but there were no formations to inspect, no reports to review, no decisions that might mean life or death before the day was done.

Instead, there were account books.

Julius sat at the desk in his study, a room that still felt like it belonged to his father despite the years that had passed. Scrolls and wax tablets covered the polished surface, each recording the family's modest financial affairs in neat columns of income and expenditure. The morning light streamed through the narrow window, illuminating the dust motes that danced in the air.

He frowned at the figures before him. The Julian estates, never vast to begin with, had been managed carefully by Aurelia during his absence. There had been no catastrophic losses, no ruinous mismanagement. But neither had there been growth. The properties yielded enough to maintain the family's dignified position among Rome's aristocracy, but little more.

'Three farms in Latium,' he murmured, running a finger down the list. 'Rents from tenements in the Subura. The vineyard near Cumae.' The income was steady but unspectacular.

In Rome, wealth translated directly into influence. The great families, the Metelli, the Claudii, the Cornelii, owned vast estates across Italy and the provinces. Their wealth allowed them to field armies of clients, to stage lavish games, to bribe officials when necessary, but the Julii, despite their ancient lineage, had never achieved such financial power.

Julius set aside the accounts with a sigh. He would need to find other paths to influence.

Each morning, after reviewing the household affairs, Julius would don his toga and make his way down to the heart of Rome. The Forum Romanum pulsed with the city's political life, a grand stage where careers were made and broken, where laws were born and old enemies reconciled or destroyed.

He moved through the space with careful attention, observing the shifting alliances, the patterns of patronage, the subtle indications of power for though Sulla was dead, his shadow still stretched across Roman politics.

Julius would pause near the Rostra, listening as advocates argued cases before the praetors. He studied their techniques, noting which appeals stirred the crowd, which logical constructions swayed the judges. At the Senate House, he observed which men entered together, which avoided each other's eyes, which sought private conversations in the shade of the columns.

'Tactics,' he murmured to himself one afternoon, watching as a prominent senator deftly extracted himself from an unwanted conversation with a provincial petitioner. 'Always tactics.'

He was careful to maintain his public dignity, to speak respectfully of Sulla's memory when the occasion demanded, to navigate the complex web of post-dictatorship politics without becoming entangled in its most dangerous strands. The Corona Civica earned him respect from military men, but he was conscious of the eyes that followed him, watching for signs of excessive ambition or Populares sympathies.

At home in the evenings, Julius would share his observations with Cornelia and Aurelia as they reclined in the atrium, the day's heat giving way to cooler night air.

'Pompey grows stronger each day,' he noted. 'His veterans are devoted to him personally, not to Rome. The Senate fears him but cannot control him.'

'And Crassus?' Aurelia asked, her political instincts sharp as ever.

'Buying influence wherever it can be found,' Julius replied. 'Land, slaves, businesses. They say he owns half the rental properties in Rome now.'

Cornelia listened carefully, her quick mind fitting these pieces into the larger puzzle of Roman power dynamics.

'The optimates still control the senior magistracies,' she observed. 'But they are divided among themselves. Catulus leads one faction, Lucullus another.'

Julius nodded, appreciating her insight. His wife had grown even more politically astute during his absence, maintaining the family's connections while navigating the complex feminine side of Roman politics.

'And where do the Julii stand in all this?' Aurelia asked.

The question hung in the air, unanswered. It was the essential problem, how to position himself in this landscape, how to advance without antagonizing powerful enemies, how to build influence from his modest foundation.

As weeks stretched into months, Julius felt a growing restlessness. The management of family affairs, while necessary, provided none of the challenge or satisfaction he had found in military command. The accounts balanced, but just barely. The income provided comfort but no means for expansion, no resources for the kind of political campaigns that elevated men to higher office.

There were moments, alone in his study or walking the quieter paths of his estate, when he considered returning to military service. There he had found purpose, clarity, the respect of men whose opinion actually mattered. The army offered a more straightforward path to distinction than the tangled thicket of Roman politics.

But such thoughts always led to the same conclusion: his destiny lay in Rome. This was where power resided, where decisions were mad. This was where his family name carried weight, where his heritage traced back to Rome's founding myths and this was where Cornelia waited each evening, her intelligent conversation and warm embrace reminding him of what he had missed during the long years of separation.

No, his future was here, not on some distant frontier. Somehow, he needed to find his way in this arena, to master its rules as thoroughly as he had mastered military tactics in Asia.

Decision made, Julius began to cultivate relationships strategically. He renewed old family connections, paid formal visits to influential senators, hosted modest but elegant dinners for carefully selected guests. The Julian name opened doors, and his natural charm and quick intelligence did the rest. He was careful not to align himself too openly with any faction, presenting himself instead as a thoughtful patriot concerned only with Rome's wellbeing.

Slowly, as summer gave way to autumn and autumn to winter, a plan began to take shape in Julius's mind. The traditional Cursus Honorum, the sequence of political offices leading ultimately to the consulship, remained the established path to power. But in the chaos following Sulla's death, alternative routes had emerged. Pompey had risen through military command rather than civilian office while Crassus had leveraged his enormous wealth to build a network of clients and debtors loyal to him alone.

Julius had neither Pompey's legions nor Crassus's fortune. But he had other assets: his name, his intellect, his growing reputation as an orator, and his understanding of both the aristocracy and the common people of Rome.

'The people,' he murmured one evening, standing before the family shrine where his ancestors watched in silent approval. 'Sulla weakened the tribunate, but he couldn't destroy the people's power entirely. There lies my path.'

The tribunate of the plebs had traditionally been the office through which the common people of Rome exercised their political will. Sulla had stripped the tribunes of much of their authority, but even he hadn't dared abolish the position entirely. Now, with the dictator gone, there were stirrings among the Populares to restore the tribunes' full powers.

As the winter solstice approached and Romans prepared for the Saturnalia celebrations, Julius found himself staring into the flames of the household hearth, the flickering light casting shadows across his face. For the first time since his return, he felt the stirring of genuine purpose, the familiar heat of ambition rekindling in his chest.

Rome was changing. The Republic that Sulla had tried to freeze in place was already evolving under new pressures, new personalities, new realities. There were spaces opening in this shifting landscape, opportunities for a man with the vision to see them and the courage to seize them.

He would need allies, and he would need resources. He would also need to step carefully among the factional minefields of post-Sullan politics. But the path was becoming clearer with each passing day.

Julius Caesar smiled into the fire, his mind already racing ahead, plotting moves and countermoves in the great game of Roman power. The soldier was fading, the politician emerging, and somewhere in that transformation, he was finding himself again.

Julius returned to the villa just as dusk was falling, his mind settled after days of private deliberation. The late afternoon shadows stretched across the atrium as he entered, finding the house unusually still. Most of the household slaves had completed their daily tasks and withdrawn to their quarters, leaving only the soft sounds of distant kitchen preparations to break the silence.

He found Cornelia and Aurelia in the small garden at the rear of the villa, a private space enclosed by vine-covered walls where the women of the household could enjoy fresh air away from public eyes. They sat on a stone bench beneath a fig tree, their conversation halting as he approached.

'Gaius,' Cornelia said, rising to greet him. Her eyes searched his face with the careful attention of a woman who had learned to read her husband's moods. 'You've been at the Forum all day?'

'For part of it,' he replied. 'The rest I spent walking and thinking.'

Aurelia remained seated, her hands folded in her lap, but her sharp gaze missed nothing.

'And what conclusions have you reached during these thoughtful walks?'

Julius gestured for Cornelia to return to her seat, then positioned himself before both women. The formality of his stance told them this was not casual conversation but something more significant.

'We need to speak plainly about our situation,' he began. 'I've been home nearly six months now, and I've spent that time observing, learning, calculating. It's time to act.'

Cornelia tensed visibly.

'You're not returning to the legions,' she said, her voice caught between question and statement.

'No,' Julius reassured her quickly. 'My place is in Rome, as it always has been. But our position here is precarious.' He began to pace, the energy that had been building within him for weeks finally finding release.

'Our family's finances are adequate for maintaining our current status, but little more. The accounts balance, but there is no surplus for the kind of expenditure that advances a political career in Rome today.' He turned to face them. 'Without substantial wealth, we cannot compete with men like Crassus in building a network of clients. Without military command, we cannot follow Pompey's path to power.'

Aurelia nodded, having made these same calculations herself during her son's absence.

'And despite Sulla's death,' he continued, 'many in government remain loyal to his vision of Rome, a vision that has little place for men with our family connections. The Optimates control most high offices, and they still view anyone associated with Marius or the Populares with suspicion.'

'We are aware of these obstacles, Julius,' Aurelia said. 'What is your proposed solution?'

Julius stopped pacing, his expression resolute.

'To make a difference, I need to enter the halls of power, I need to make a name for myself, a name that cannot be ignored, regardless of political faction. I need to be noticed, to demonstrate abilities that even our opponents must acknowledge.'

Cornelia leaned forward.

'And how do you intend to accomplish this?'

'Through the courts,' Julius replied. 'As a voluntary prosecutor.'

The women exchanged glances, understanding immediately. In Rome's legal system, criminal prosecutions were not conducted by state officials but by private citizens who volunteered to bring cases against alleged wrongdoers. Any free male citizen could volunteer to prosecute, but the courts typically assigned cases to the most talented, most persuasive candidates, men whose oratory could sway both judges and the public.

A successful prosecutor gained not only public acclaim but also the gratitude of those who had been wronged, political capital that could be leveraged into higher office. But it was a risky path, one that created powerful enemies with each conviction secured.

'You would make yourself the enemy of whoever you prosecute,' Aurelia observed. 'And their entire network of friends and allies.'

'Yes,' Julius acknowledged. 'But I would also make myself known throughout Rome as a man of principle, a defender of justice, a voice too compelling to ignore.'

Cornelia studied her husband.

'Your speaking skills are already remarkable, Julius.

'But I could be better,' he replied. 'Much better. And to reach that level, the level that can topple even the most well-protected criminal, I need to study with the very best.'

He drew a breath before continuing.

'To that end, I've decided to travel to Rhodes and study oratory under Apollonius Molon.'

The statement landed heavily in the quiet garden. Apollonius was perhaps the greatest living teacher of rhetoric, a master who had trained many of Rome's finest orators, including Cicero himself. His school on Rhodes attracted ambitious young men from across the Roman world, all seeking to perfect the art of persuasion that was so central to political advancement.

'Rhodes?' Aurelia's voice was carefully controlled. 'You've only just returned from years abroad, and now you speak of leaving again?'

'For a year at most,' Julius said firmly. 'A single year to develop the skills that will serve me for a lifetime in Rome.' He turned to Cornelia, whose eyes reflected a complex mixture of understanding and sadness. 'I know what I'm asking. Another separation, more time alone. But this is not exile, not military service in dangerous lands. This is an investment in our future.'

'You've just come home to us,' Cornelia said softly. 'The house has barely grown accustomed to your presence again.'

Julius knelt before her, taking her hands in his.

'And it pains me to leave so soon. But consider the alternative: years spent struggling for minor recognition in Rome, fighting against the barriers erected by Sulla's supporters, watching opportunities pass to men with greater resources or fewer political liabilities.'

He glanced at Aurelia. 'Or I could take a military commission again, serve under someone else's command in some distant province. Is that what either of you wants?'

Aurelia's lips thinned, but she didn't answer immediately. She understood political calculation better than most men in Rome, and she could see the logic in her son's plan.

'Rhodes is not so far,' Julius continued. 'Regular ships make the crossing. We would be able to correspond. And when I return, I will come with the skill to make our family name resonate throughout the Forum, to take on cases that will establish me as a force in Roman politics.' He rose, once again addressing both women. 'This is not an impulsive decision. I've thought carefully about our options, about the paths available to us. This is the surest route to advancement with the resources we have.'

Cornelia looked at her mother-in-law, a silent communication passing between them. These two women had maintained the Julian household through years of uncertainty, had navigated the treacherous waters of Roman society during Sulla's dictatorship. They knew when to bend and when to stand firm.

'A year,' Cornelia said finally. 'No longer. And you must write regularly.'

'And select your first case carefully upon your return,' Aurelia added. 'The right prosecution could establish your reputation immediately. The wrong one could destroy it before it begins.'

Julius felt the tension ease from his shoulders. They understood. Of course they did. These were not ordinary Roman women content with weaving and household management; these were his most trusted advisors, as politically astute as any senator.

'I've already begun making inquiries about passage,' he said. 'A merchant vessel leaves Ostia for Alexandria in three weeks, with planned stops at Rhodes.'

'So soon?' Cornelia's composure slipped slightly.

'The academic term begins with the spring equinox,' Julius explained. 'I must arrive in time to secure a place in Apollonius's sessions.'

The practicalities were discussed as twilight deepened around them, arrangements for the household during his absence, management of the family's affairs, the correspondence that would need to be maintained. Through it all, Julius watched his wife and mother, grateful for their understanding, their support, their shared vision of what the Julian name could become.

Later that night, as he and Cornelia lay in the quiet darkness of their bedchamber, she finally asked the question that had been lingering unspoken between them.

'Are you certain this is not simply restlessness, Gaius? A man accustomed to action suddenly confined to household accounts and formal visits?'

He considered the question seriously, respecting her insight too much to dismiss it.

'There is some truth in that,' he admitted. 'I've found it difficult to adjust to civilian life. But this decision comes from something deeper, the knowledge that our opportunities in Rome are limited unless I can distinguish myself dramatically.'

He turned to face her, though in the darkness he could see only the outline of her features. 'I believe in my ability to move men with words, Cornelia. I've seen it in the military. But to compete with the very best, to take on the cases that will truly matter, I need the training that only Apollonius can provide.'

She was silent for a moment, her hand finding his in the darkness.

'Then go,' she said at last. 'Learn what you must learn. Perfect this weapon you believe in so strongly, and then return to us, to the future we've always planned.'

He drew her closer, feeling the warmth of her body against his, storing the sensation in memory to sustain him through the coming separation.

'One year,' he promised. 'And then I return to claim what Rome has always owed the Julian name.'

Chapter Thirty-Four

Off the Coast of Rhodes

The Aegean stretched in every direction, an endless expanse of blue beneath an equally boundless sky. From his position at the ship's rail, Julius watched as sunlight danced across the surface of the water, transforming ordinary waves into flashes of gold and silver. The breeze carried the scent of salt and distant lands, a constant reminder that he was once again between worlds, leaving Rome behind while his future awaited elsewhere.

The merchant vessel, Aphrodite, had departed Ostia ten days earlier, a sturdy craft built for reliable commerce rather than speed or luxury. Its hold was packed with Italian wines, fine pottery, and bales of dyed textiles bound for eastern markets, while its deck accommodated two dozen passengers making the journey to various ports across the Mediterranean.

Most of his fellow travellers were young men from wealthy families, bound for Athens or Rhodes to complete their education, a traditional finishing touch for ambitious Romans of good birth. They were soft-handed and smooth-faced, many leaving Italy for the first time, their conversation revolving around poetry, philosophy, and the grand cultural experiences that awaited them in the Greek world.

Amongst them, Julius had found an unexpected companion in Quintus Aquillius, a young man close to his own age but from a wealthier equestrian family. Unlike many of the others, Quintus possessed a genuine intellectual curiosity rather than merely following fashion. Their conversations had quickly progressed from polite small talk to substantive discussions of rhetoric, history, and the political shifts occurring in Rome.

'It's almost unfair, isn't it?' Quintus said, joining Julius at the rail. 'That Greek should be so much more suited to philosophical discourse than our practical Latin.'

Julius smiled.

'Each language has its strengths. Latin commands. Greek persuades.'

'And which do you prefer?' Quintus asked, genuinely interested.

'Both have their place,' Julius replied. 'A wise man knows when to use either.'

This kind of conversation had become their daily routine as the ship made its steady progress eastward. Each morning, they would gather with three or four other students on the aft deck, away from the bustle of the sailors, to discuss whatever topic had captured their interest. Sometimes they debated formal questions of rhetoric or philosophy; other times, they simply shared their hopes for their studies abroad.

Julius had deliberately revealed little about his past. He made no mention of his military service and to these young men, he presented himself simply as another student bound for Rhodes, perhaps a bit older, a bit more reserved than the others, but nothing more.

It was easier this way. His experiences in Asia Minor had set him apart from these sheltered young aristocrats in ways they could never understand. What did they know of battle, of life-or-death decisions, of the weight of command? Their education had come from books and tutors; his had come from blood and steel as well as scrolls.

As the days passed and the Italian coastline faded into memory, Julius found himself relaxing into the rhythm of shipboard life. There was a simplicity to it, a clear delineation of responsibilities and expectations that reminded him, in some ways, of military routine. Each day unfolded with predictable patterns, the changing of watches, the serving of meals, the careful adjustments of sail and course as the captain navigated by sun, stars, and the familiar contours of coastlines.

On this particular afternoon, their discussion group had been debating the merits of different rhetorical styles, with Quintus advocating for the ornate Asiatic approach while Julius defended the more restrained Attic tradition. The conversation had drawn in two other students, and they had passed a pleasant hour arguing the finer points of cadence, metaphor, and emotional appeal.

'You argue like a man who has actually spoken in public,' one of the younger students observed, looking at Julius with newfound respect.

Julius was about to respond when he noticed a change in the atmosphere on deck. The sailors, normally focused on their tasks with the steady concentration of professionals, had stopped what they were doing. They were looking out across the water, their postures suddenly tense.

Following their gaze, Julius saw a ship on the horizon, moving towards them at considerable speed. It was still distant enough that its details were unclear, but something about it raised the hairs on the back of his neck, a soldier's instinct for approaching danger.

'What is it?' Quintus asked, noticing the sudden shift in Julius's attention.

'Another vessel,' Julius replied, his eyes never leaving the approaching ship. 'Moving quickly.'

By now, other passengers had noticed the commotion among the crew and began to gather at the rail, pointing and speculating about the distant ship. Some suggested it might be another merchant vessel, perhaps carrying news from Rome. Others wondered if it could be a naval patrol.

But Julius knew better. The approaching ship's profile was unmistakable to anyone who had spent time in these waters, the low hull, the abundance of oars in addition to its sail, the aggressive speed with which it cut through the waves. This was no merchant vessel or Roman patrol.

The captain appeared on deck, his weathered face grim as he assessed the situation. He conferred briefly with his first mate, both men gesturing toward the approaching vessel, their expressions growing more concerned with each passing moment.

'Why are they coming so close?' one of the students asked, his voice betraying a nervousness he was trying to hide.

'Perhaps they're in distress,' another suggested hopefully. 'Needing assistance?'

Julius remained silent, calculating distances and times in his head. The vessel was moving much faster than their heavily laden merchant ship could hope to match and there would be no outrunning them, no clever manoeuvre that could create an escape. The captain knew this too; Julius could see it in his resigned expression as he ordered the crew to make what preparations they could.

'What's happening?' Quintus asked Julius, sensing his friend's tension. 'You know something.'

Before Julius could respond, the captain approached their group, his eyes moving across the assembled passengers before settling on Julius. There was a moment of recognition there, a soldier's awareness of another man who had seen combat.

'You've been in the military,' he said. It wasn't a question.

Julius nodded once.

'Mytilene. Under Thermus.'

The captain exhaled slowly.

'Then you know what that is.' He jerked his chin toward the approaching vessel.

'Yes,' Julius confirmed. 'Pirates.'

The word sent a ripple of alarm through the assembled passengers. Some paled visibly, while others began talking all at once, their voices rising in panic.

'Pirates? Here? Surely not!'

'But we're in Roman waters!'

'My father will pay any ransom. They must be told!'

283

The captain raised his hands for silence.

'Listen carefully,' he said, his voice cutting through the growing hysteria. 'That ship is faster and better armed than we are. They have three times as many men, all of them killers. If they catch us, and they will, our only chance is to surrender without resistance.'

'Surrender?' one of the younger men protested. 'But we're Romans!'

'And they're pirates,' the captain replied flatly. 'They don't care about your citizenship or your family name. They care about whether you're worth more alive or dead.'

Julius understood the brutal calculation. Pirates in these waters operated as a business. Wealthy captives could be ransomed for substantial sums; those who resisted were typically killed as a warning to others. The Aphrodite was not a fighting ship, and apart from himself, and perhaps one or two of the crew, its passengers had no combat experience.

'What should we do?' Quintus asked, turning to Julius rather than the captain.

Julius considered for a moment.

'Hide anything valuable but not everything,' he said at last. 'Keep some jewellery, some coins visible, enough to show you're worth ransoming, but not enough to make killing you for immediate profit tempting.'

The practical advice seemed to steady the group somewhat. They began securing their possessions, preparing for what was to come. Julius himself had little of value beyond a modest sum for his living expenses in Rhodes.

As the pirate ship drew nearer, its details became clearer. It was a liburna, a type of vessel favoured by pirates for its speed and manoeuvrability. The deck bristled with armed men, their weapons catching the sunlight as they prepared to board. No colours flew from its mast, but painted on its prow was the crude image of a sea serpent, a common emblem among Cilician pirates.

The crew of the Aphrodite made what preparations they could, securing hatches and rigging, but there was no attempt to arm themselves or resist the coming attack. They were merchantmen, not warriors, and their captain had made the only decision that offered some hope of survival.

Julius watched the approaching vessel with a soldier's eye, noting the discipline of its crew, the practiced efficiency with which they positioned themselves for boarding. These were not random brigands but a well-organized force, part of the pirate networks that had grown increasingly bold in recent years, taking advantage of Rome's internal conflicts to expand their operations across the Mediterranean.

The distance between the ships closed rapidly. From the pirate vessel came a warning shot, a flaming arrow that arced high over the Aphrodite before plunging into the sea beyond, a traditional signal demanding surrender.

The captain ordered the sails lowered in response, the universal sign of submission, and the merchant vessel began to slow, wallowing in the gentle swells as its momentum died.

'Steady now,' the captain told his passengers, who had gathered in a tight cluster near the main mast. 'No sudden movements, no resistance. They want ransom, not corpses.'

Julius stood slightly apart from the others, his posture deliberately non-threatening but still dignified. He had faced death before, had made peace with its possibility on the blood-soaked steps of Mytilene. This was different, surrender rather than combat, but the core principle remained the same: stay calm, stay focused... survive.

The pirate ship glided alongside the Aphrodite with practiced precision. Grappling hooks sailed across the gap between vessels, biting into the merchant ship's rail with iron teeth and the pirates pulled the lines taut, drawing the ships together until they touched with a jarring thud.

And then they came, pouring over the rails like a wave of human predators. They were a mixed group, Greeks, Syrians, renegade Romans, men from every corner of the Mediterranean united only by their choice of profession. They carried short swords and daggers, dressed in a hodgepodge of styles but moving with the coordination of men accustomed to fighting together.

Their leader stepped forward once the ship was secured, a tall man with a salt-stained beard and arms corded with muscle. His eyes swept the assembled passengers, assessing their worth with the cold calculation of a man who traded in human lives.

'Romans,' he said, his Latin accented but clear. 'How fortunate for us. How unfortunate for you.'

No one responded. The passengers stood frozen, some trembling visibly, others maintaining a fragile composure that threatened to shatter at any moment.

The pirate captain smiled, revealing teeth stained by years of harsh living.

'Don't worry,' he said, almost conversationally. 'If your families value you, you'll be home soon enough. If not...' He shrugged, leaving the sentence unfinished, the threat hanging in the salt-tinged air.

Julius watched, his expression carefully neutral, as the pirates began to search the ship and its passengers, confiscating visible valuables and looking for hidden caches of coins or jewellery. He knew what came next, the captives would be transferred to the pirate vessel, the merchant ship likely scuttled or set adrift, and then would begin the long process of negotiating ransoms.

It had happened this way countless times across the Mediterranean in recent years, a constant tax on Roman commerce that the Republic, distracted by civil conflicts and foreign wars, had failed to address effectively. Ships disappeared, crews vanished, and wealthy travellers found themselves captives in hidden coves along the Cilician coast.

As a pirate approached him, Julius offered no resistance. He allowed himself to be searched, surrendered the modest purse at his belt, and kept his gaze steady. The man paused, studying Julius more closely than he had the other passengers.

'You're different,' the pirate said in rough Greek. 'A soldier?'

Julius neither confirmed nor denied, maintaining his neutral expression.

The pirate grunted, then moved on to the next captive. But Julius had seen the flicker of recognition in his eyes, the awareness that not all these soft-handed Romans were the same. It was a small thing, but in the dangerous days ahead, such distinctions might matter.

As the pirates completed their initial search, their captain gave the order to transfer the captives to the pirate vessel. One by one, the passengers were forced across the narrow gap between ships, stumbling onto the deck of their new prison. Julius went calmly, helping Quintus and some of the younger students who seemed paralyzed with fear.

'What's going to happen to us?' Quintus whispered as they stood on the pirate deck, watching more captives being brought across.

Julius looked out across the endless blue expanse of the Mediterranean, the route to Rhodes now interrupted by this unexpected detour into captivity.

'We wait,' he said simply. 'We observe. We survive.'

The pirate vessel began to pull away from the Fortuna which the pirates had decided to set adrift rather than sink, perhaps as a message to other ships in these waters, perhaps simply because burning or scuttling it would take too much time. The merchant captain and his crew had been taken captive along with the passengers, their fate now tied to the same uncertain process of ransom and negotiation.

As the ships separated, Julius watched his plans receding with the abandoned vessel. Rhodes, Apollonius Molon, the careful strategy he had devised for his return to Rome, all now replaced by this new reality, this unexpected chapter that fate had thrust upon him.

But as the wind filled the pirate ship's sail and it began to slice through the waves toward whatever hidden base its captain had chosen, Julius felt something unexpected stir within him, not just concern or resignation, but a flicker of the same cool tactical awareness that had served him well at Mytilene. This was not the end of his journey, merely a diversion.

And like every challenge he had faced before, he would find a way to turn it to his advantage.

Chapter Thirty-Five

The Aegean Sea

he pirate vessel cut through the water with predatory grace, its oars rising and falling in perfect rhythm, driving the ship eastward through the Aegean. Three days had passed since the capture of the Fortuna, three days in which Julius and his fellow captives had begun to adjust to their new reality.

The pirates had bound their prisoners' hands with rough hemp rope, tight enough to prevent escape but loose enough to avoid damaging the valuable merchandise they represented. The captives were kept on the main deck, exposed to sun and occasional sea spray, but sheltered at night beneath makeshift awnings of sailcloth. Water was provided in sufficient quantities, and simple food, hard bread, dried fish, olives, was distributed twice daily. It was clear that these pirates understood the economics of their trade; dead hostages brought no ransom.

From his position against the port railing, Julius observed the operation with professional detachment. The pirate crew worked with the discipline of men who had performed these tasks countless times before. Watches changed at regular intervals, lookouts scanned the horizon continuously for potential threats, and even the distribution of food and water followed an established routine. This was no rabble of desperate men but an organized enterprise, almost military in its precision.

The captain, a Cilician named Heracleo, maintained strict authority. Orders were given once and executed immediately. Discipline was enforced with the occasional lash for those who failed in their duties, but such punishments were relatively rare. These men worked together effectively because they knew their roles and the rewards that awaited them.

'They're taking us to Pharmakonisi,' whispered Quintus, who had managed to understand fragments of the pirates' conversations despite his limited Greek. 'Apparently they have a base there.'

Julius nodded slightly. Pharmakonisi, a small, low-lying island near the coast of Asia Minor, had become one of several outposts used by Mediterranean pirates. Unlike the dramatic fortress-like strongholds of Cilicia far to the southeast, Roman naval patrols often overlooked such minor islands, focusing instead on the more notorious pirate havens, which allowed these secondary bases to persist despite periodic campaigns against piracy.

'How long before we arrive?' asked one of the younger students, a pale youth whose initial panic had given way to dull resignation.

'Tomorrow, if the wind holds,' Julius replied. He had been keeping track of their course and speed, calculating their position by the stars at night and the sun's path during the day, a skill learned during his military service.

A few spaces away, a cluster of captives had drawn closer together, their whispers becoming more animated. Julius caught fragments of their conversation,

'...could rush them at night,' '...take a weapon when they're not looking,' '...better to die fighting than...'

He felt a chill of concern. These pampered young aristocrats, raised on tales of Roman heroism and Greek epics, were beginning to nurture dangerous fantasies of resistance. He moved closer to them, his face composed but his eyes intent.

'Whatever you're planning,' he said quietly, 'abandon it now.' They looked up, startled and defensive. 'We can't just surrender without a fight,' protested a senator's son named Publius. 'We're Romans!'

'Being Roman doesn't make you immortal,' Julius countered. 'These men outnumber us three to one. They're armed. They're experienced fighters and you have probably never held a sword outside of a training ground.'

'So, we just accept captivity?' another demanded. 'Wait meekly for ransom like chattel?'

Julius met his gaze steadily.

'Yes. Because that's how we survive.' He glanced meaningfully toward Heracleo, who was observing them from the helm. 'These men don't want to kill us. It's bad business. But if we force their hand, they will make examples of us. I've seen the bodies of pirates' victims, men who resisted and it's not a death you want to experience.'

This was not entirely true, he had never personally witnessed such victims, but the statement had the desired effect. The would-be rebels fell silent, the fire of their resistance dampened by the cold water of reality.

'What should we do, then?' asked Publius

'Observe, learn and endure,' Julius replied. 'Notice how they operate, their routines, their weaknesses, not for escape, but for understanding. Knowledge is never wasted and who knows when it may become useful.'

The group dispersed, chastened by his words but perhaps also reassured by his calm authority. Julius returned to his position by the rail, continuing his methodical assessment of their captors.

Heracleo caught his eye from across the deck and gave a barely perceptible nod, acknowledgment, perhaps even approval, of Julius's intervention. The pirate captain had likely seen similar foolhardy resistance attempts before, and they never ended well for the captives.

As the day wore on, the Aegean's blue expanse remained their constant companion, occasionally broken by the distant silhouette of another vessel, merchants giving the pirate ship a wide berth once they recognized its profile, or fellow pirates exchanging signals before continuing on their predatory patrols. This sea, once dominated by Roman galleys, had become a hunting ground for men like Heracleo, their power growing in direct proportion to Rome's internal distractions.

That night, as most of the captives huddled together beneath the sailcloth awnings seeking warmth against the cooling sea breeze, Julius remained awake, watching the stars trace their familiar paths across the night sky. His thoughts drifted to Rome, to Cornelia, to the carefully constructed plans that had been interrupted by this unexpected diversion. How long before word reached them that he had been captured? How would they raise the substantial ransom that would surely be demanded?

These concerns circled in his mind, practical problems requiring practical solutions, but beneath them lay a deeper current of thought, a recognition that fate had thrust him into yet another test, another opportunity to demonstrate the qualities that separated him from ordinary men. He had endured the deprivations of exile, survived Sulla's proscriptions and had distinguished himself at Mytilene. This, too, was merely an obstacle to be overcome.

By dawn of the fourth day, the island of Pharmakonisi had appeared on the horizon, a low-lying silhouette barely visible above the sea line. As the morning progressed, the features of the landscape became more distinct: a relatively flat terrain with scattered rocky outcroppings, small coves and inlets providing natural harbours, and modest settlements that from a distance appeared like any fishing community.

'There,' Quintus murmured, pointing toward the larger of the island's natural harbours. 'Pharmakonisi.'

The pirate stronghold was unlike the dramatic fortress of Coracesium in Cilicia. Here, the pirates had established a base that blended into the landscape, utilizing the island's natural features rather than imposing massive fortifications. The harbour was sheltered by a curved peninsula, creating a protected anchorage that was difficult to assault but didn't immediately betray its purpose to passing ships.

As they approached, signal flags were raised along watchtowers strategically positioned to overlook the surrounding waters, not warnings but greetings, acknowledging the return of one of their own. The pirate crew became more animated, calling to each other in their mixture of languages, pointing out landmarks to shipmates, their postures relaxing as they neared home.

'Jupiter's balls,' whispered one of the younger captives. 'It looks so... ordinary.'

'That's the point,' Julius corrected. 'Their strength lies in appearing unremarkable.'

Their ship glided toward an open berth, oarsmen responding to short, sharp commands from the helmsman. Dockhands stood ready with ropes, securing the vessel as it nudged against the weathered wooden pier. A small crowd had gathered, curious about the new arrivals, and Julius could see another group of captives being marched toward a collection of stone buildings, presumably from ships that had arrived earlier.

Heracleo assembled his prisoners on the deck, looking them over one final time before they disembarked.

'You will be taken to the holding pens,' he announced in his accented Latin. 'Food and water will be provided. A scribe will record your names and families for ransom negotiations.' His gaze swept across them, lingering briefly on Julius. 'Behave, and you will be treated fairly. Resist, and...' He left the threat unspoken, but its meaning was clear enough.

One by one, they were herded off the ship onto the pier, their bound hands making the descent awkward. Julius steadied Quintus when he stumbled, earning a grateful nod from his friend and another evaluating look from Heracleo.

The path to the settlement wound through some nearby low hills and guards positioned at intervals watched the procession of captives with bored expressions. This was routine for them, almost a monthly occurrence in a community built on kidnapping and ransom. The captives walked in silence, save for the occasional murmur between companions.

As they progressed, Julius took in the full scope of the Pharmakonisi operation. The natural harbour below was perfect for the pirates' needs, deep enough for their ships yet inconspicuous enough to avoid drawing undue attention. The island's terrain offered multiple escape routes should a Roman fleet appear, and the settlement itself blended seamlessly with other Aegean communities, housing perhaps a hundred pirates and traders willing to deal in stolen goods.

The 'holding pens' proved to be a series of stone structures near the centre of the island, their thick walls and small, barred windows making their purpose clear despite their outwardly ordinary appearance.

The captives were divided by worth, the wealthier Romans, including Julius and his companions directed to a relatively clean chamber with straw pallets for sleeping and a central courtyard for exercise. Merchant sailors and less valuable prisoners were housed in more crowded, less comfortable quarters nearby.

Inside their new prison, a pirate with the bearing of a former legionary untied their hands.

'You'll be here until ransoms are arranged,' he informed them, speaking soldier's Latin. 'Behave, and you'll be treated well. Food twice daily, water available in the courtyard and the latrine is through that door.' He pointed to a narrow opening in one corner. 'Don't cause any trouble.' With that, he departed, the heavy wooden door closing behind him with a definitive thud.

Julius's fellow captives immediately scattered through the space, claiming sleeping spots or exploring the limited confines of their prison. The chamber held perhaps thirty men in total, including captives from other ships. Some had clearly been there for weeks, their beards grown out, their expressions resigned rather than frightened.

Quintus joined Julius near one wall, lowering his voice.

'What happens now?'

'Now,' Julius replied, 'we wait. They'll contact our families, negotiate ransoms and arrange exchanges. It could take weeks, possibly months.'

'Months?' The despair in Quintus's voice was evident.

'The process isn't quick,' Julius confirmed. 'But it's established. These men have turned kidnapping into a business, with procedures, standards, expected outcomes.' He glanced around the chamber. 'They don't want us dead, they want denarii, and plenty of them.'

A thin man with the appearance of a Greek merchant approached them, offering a clay cup of water.

'New arrivals, yes? I am Demetrios of Syracuse.' His Latin was fluent but heavily accented. 'Three weeks I have been here, waiting for my brother to arrange payment.'

'Has there been word of your ransom?' Julius asked.

'Negotiations progress.' Demetrios shrugged. 'The pirates are reasonable in their demands, surprisingly so. They know what each man is worth and do not ask the impossible.'

This aligned with what Julius had observed thus far. The pirates operated with a pragmatism that bordered on professionalism. Excessive demands would only delay payment; realistic ransoms kept the money flowing and the prisoners cycling through their system.

295

As the day progressed, Julius methodically explored their prison, noting exits, guard rotations, the construction of the walls and windows. Not because he planned escape, that would be suicidal on an island controlled by pirates, but because understanding one's environment was the first rule of survival in any captivity.

The courtyard offered fresh air and a limited view of the settlement beyond. Guards watched from a raised platform, bows within easy reach but rarely pointed at the prisoners. In the distance, Julius could see ships coming and going from the harbour, the constant motion of a community dedicated to preying on Mediterranean shipping.

That evening, as the captives received their meal, simple but adequate portions of bean stew and bread, Julius sat slightly apart, observing both his fellow prisoners and their captors. The routines were being established, the patterns that would define their lives until ransoms were paid and freedom restored.

Nearby, Publius and his erstwhile rebels had abandoned all thoughts of resistance, instead trading stories of their families' wealth and influence, each trying to outdo the others in describing the speed with which their ransoms would be paid. Their earlier bravado had been replaced by the more practical concern of returning home as quickly as possible.

Quintus settled beside Julius, breaking his bread thoughtfully.

'You seem almost comfortable here,' he observed. 'As if this is not the first time you've been in such a situation.'

Julius allowed himself a small smile.

'Not comfortable.' He said, accepting, 'there's a difference.' He took a sip of water. 'We cannot change our circumstances at present, so we adapt to them and wait.'

'For rescue?' Quintus asked, lowering his voice further.

'For opportunity,' Julius corrected. 'But not the kind those fools were contemplating on the ship. Our opportunity comes when the ransoms are paid, when we return to our lives and remember what we've learned here.'

'And what have we learned?' Quintus's question was genuine, seeking understanding rather than challenging.

'That Rome has abandoned control of its own waters,' replied Julius quietly. 'That while senators debate and consuls manoeuvre for advantage, men like Heracleo grow more powerful each day. That our Republic's weakness has created space for others' strength.' He turned to Quintus, his expression hardening slightly. 'These are lessons worth remembering when we return to Rome, when we take our places in public life.'

Quintus nodded slowly, perhaps seeing his companion in a new light. This was not merely another student bound for Rhodes, but a man with deeper purpose, with ambitions that extended far beyond the study of rhetoric.

As darkness fell over Pharmakonisi, torches were lit along the settlement's paths and guards called to one another as watches changed. In the holding pen, prisoners settled onto their straw pallets, some praying to gods they had neglected until necessity reminded them of divine power, others simply staring at the ceiling, calculating the days until freedom might come.

Julius lay awake longer than most, his mind working through probabilities and plans. His path to Rhodes had been interrupted, but the destination remained unchanged. This detour, this captivity, was merely another experience to be absorbed, another challenge to be overcome. And perhaps, in ways he could not yet fully articulate, another step on the journey that would lead him back to Rome, back to power, back to the destiny that had always seemed to hover just beyond his reach.

Chapter Thirty-Six

Pharmakonisi

Life in captivity quickly established its own rhythms. The pirates maintained a surprisingly organized operation, with clear routines for feeding, exercise, and the complex business of arranging ransoms. Each morning began with a simple meal followed by access to the central courtyard where prisoners could walk, converse, or simply feel the sun on their faces after the damp chill of the stone chambers.

While most captives withdrew into themselves, counting the days until their release and avoiding interaction with their captors, Julius took a different approach. From the first day, he began to engage with the guards, asking questions about their patrols, commenting on their weapons, initiating conversations in the mixture of Greek, Latin, and Cilician dialects that comprised the pirates' common tongue.

Initially, the guards responded with suspicion and curt answers. But Julius persisted, his manner neither obsequious nor confrontational, simply conversational, as if they were fellow travellers at a roadside inn rather than captors and captive. Gradually, their wariness began to ease.

'You speak Greek well for a Roman,' one guard commented on the third day, accepting a draught of water from the same jug Julius was using.

'A Roman of education should master the language of Homer,' Julius replied with an easy smile. 'How else can we appreciate what we've conquered?'

The guard laughed, surprising himself with the reaction.
'Conquered but not understood, perhaps.'

By the end of the first week, Julius had established himself as an unusual prisoner, one who observed but did not flinch, who engaged but did not grovel, who carried himself with the quiet confidence of a man temporarily inconvenienced rather than fundamentally diminished by his captivity.

His fellow captives noticed the change in how he was treated. The guards would nod to him in the morning, occasionally share bits of news about ships arriving or departing, even ask his opinion on minor disputes among the prisoners.

'How do you do it?' Quintus asked one evening, as they sat against the courtyard wall watching the sun set over the distant sea. 'They treat you almost as an equal.'

Julius considered the question.

'Men respond to what they perceive,' he said finally. 'If you act as a cowering victim, they treat you as one. If you carry yourself with dignity, they may not free you, but they recognize something familiar, the same pride they would feel in your position.'

Quintus shook his head in wonder.

'Only you could find a way to command respect from pirates holding you for ransom.'

On the tenth day of their captivity, a significant development occurred. Heracleo himself entered the holding area, accompanied by a thin Greek scribe carrying wax tablets. The pirate captain's gaze swept the chamber before settling on Julius.

'Caesar,' he called, gesturing for him to approach. 'News of your family.'

Julius rose smoothly, aware of the eyes of both captives and guards upon him. He crossed to where Heracleo stood, neither rushing nor dawdling, his posture straight but not rigid.

'Your ransom has been set,' Heracleo announced, as the scribe consulted his tablets. 'Twenty talents of silver. A fair price for a man of your family's standing.'

Julius's eyebrows rose fractionally. Twenty talents was substantial but far from excessive, roughly equivalent to what a wealthy equestrian might pay for a prestigious home in Rome. It suggested the pirates had significantly underestimated his family's resources and his personal importance.

'Twenty talents?' Julius repeated, his tone making it a question rather than an acknowledgment.

Heracleo frowned slightly.

'It is a fair price. Your family can afford it.'

'I'm insulted,' Julius said, his voice suddenly cold.

The pirate captain blinked, momentarily taken aback. 'Insulted?'

'Twenty talents? For a Julius? For a descendant of Venus herself?' Julius drew himself up, his expression one of aristocratic disdain. 'You might as well announce to all of Rome that you consider me barely worth ransoming at all.'

A dangerous silence fell over the courtyard. The other captives froze, certain they were about to witness Julius's punishment for such audacity. The guards' hands moved to their weapons, anticipating Heracleo's order.

But the order didn't come. Instead, the pirate captain studied Julius with narrowed eyes, searching for the motive behind this unexpected reaction.

'What would you suggest?' he asked finally, curiosity overcoming anger.

'Fifty talents, at minimum,' Julius replied without hesitation. 'My family would consider anything less an insult to our dignity, a suggestion that we cannot afford a proper ransom for one of our own. They might even suspect you had harmed me and were attempting to conceal it by asking for less.'

The absurdity of a prisoner demanding a higher ransom for himself hung in the air for a long moment. Then, unexpectedly, Heracleo laughed, a genuine bark of amusement that broke the tension.

'By Poseidon's trident,' he said, 'I've taken hundreds of Romans, and not one has ever complained that his price was too low.' He gestured to the scribe. 'Make it fifty talents. Let us not insult the descendant of Venus.'

The scribe made the adjustment on his tablet, his expression carefully neutral despite the unprecedented nature of the exchange he had just witnessed.

Heracleo turned to leave, then paused, looking back at Julius with a mixture of amusement and respect.

'You are an unusual Roman, Caesar. Most of your countrymen speak of their importance only until they are captured. Then they become very humble indeed.'

'I am not most Romans,' Julius replied simply.

The pirate captain nodded.

'So I see.' Then he was gone, the heavy door closing behind him with a definitive thud. The other captives stared at Julius in stunned disbelief.

'Are you insane?' Publius whispered. 'Fifty talents? Can your family even raise such a sum?'

'That's not the point,' Julius answered, his composure unruffled. 'The point is that the Romans in this prison are now worth more to them alive than they were an hour ago. Our treatment will improve accordingly.'

Quintus studied his friend with growing admiration.

'You turned a negotiation for your freedom into a tool to ensure better conditions for all of us.'

Julius shrugged.

'The pirates understand value. By increasing mine, I increase the importance of maintaining my wellbeing, and by extension, yours.' He didn't add the other calculation that had driven his demand, that the higher the ransom, the more significant his capture would appear in Rome. News of a fifty-talent demand would attract attention, would become a story told in the Forum and whispered in senatorial corridors.

In the days that followed, the subtle shift in how the pirates regarded Julius became more pronounced. The guards granted him additional freedoms within the confines of the compound, allowing him to move between the courtyard and the main chamber at will, rather than only during designated periods. When he requested access to the small shrine to Neptune that the pirates maintained near the holding pens, permission was granted without hesitation.

Julius used this increased mobility to observe more of the pirates' operations. He noticed the training regimen that the newer recruits underwent each morning in an adjacent courtyard, a mixture of sword drills, boarding techniques, and the specific skills required for their predatory profession. From his vantage point, he could see the flaws in their approach, the inefficiencies in their movements, the gaps in their defensive positions that a disciplined Roman force could exploit.

One morning, as a group of young pirates practiced with wooden swords, their instructor barking commands in a mixture of Greek and Cilician, Julius found himself commenting aloud.

'Wrong. His grip is wrong.'

The nearest guard glanced at him.

'What?'

Julius nodded toward a burly young pirate whose wild swings were technically impressive but tactically useless.

'His grip. Two fingers over the crossguard would give him more control, less chance of the sword being knocked from his hand.'

The guard studied the training session with new attention, then grunted in reluctant agreement.

'Perhaps. But he's strong enough that it hardly matters.'

'Strength without technique is just wasted energy,' Julius observed. 'In a real fight, against a disciplined opponent, he'd be dead within seconds.'

Word of his comments reached the training master, and the next day, as Julius watched from his usual position, the instructor approached the boundary of the courtyard.

'I hear you have opinions on our training, Roman.' he called in accented Latin.

Julius met his gaze calmly.

'Merely observations.'

'Share them,' the man challenged. 'If you dare.'

Julius glanced at the guard beside him, who shrugged and gestured for him to approach the boundary. Drawing closer, but remaining on his side of the dividing line, Julius pointed to two young pirates who were sparring.

'The taller one leaves his right side exposed each time he attacks. A simple feint would draw his strike, opening him to a killing blow.' He shifted his attention to another pair. 'Those two waste energy with elaborate movements. In close quarters, on the rolling deck of a ship, such flourishes would get them killed.'

The training master's eyes narrowed, but he didn't disagree.

'And how would you correct these flaws, Roman?'

Without hesitation, Julius began to outline the basics of Roman legionary training, the emphasis on simplicity, efficiency, the coordination of movement with breath, the importance of stance and balance. As he spoke, using his own body to demonstrate certain positions without actually crossing into the training yard, the pirates paused in their practice to watch and listen.

This impromptu instruction became a daily occurrence. Julius would observe the morning training, offer critique and suggestion, and the training master, a former mercenary named Syrax, would incorporate elements of this advice into his teaching. The young pirates, initially resentful of a Roman captive presuming to instruct them, gradually began to appreciate the practical value of his observations. Julius's fellow captives were equally fascinated by this development.

'You're teaching them to be more effective killers,' one of the merchants observed, his tone caught between admiration and accusation.

'I'm passing the time in a way that interests me,' Julius replied with a slight shrug. 'What they do with the knowledge is their concern.'

But there was more to it than mere diversion. Each day that Julius advised the pirates was another day they saw him not merely as a hostage but as a man of knowledge and skill. Each correction he offered reinforced the impression that he was someone of substance, someone to be reckoned with beyond the simple arithmetic of ransom value.

The situation came to a head on a clear morning nearly thirty days into their captivity. Heracleo himself had come to observe the training, standing watching as Syrax put the young pirates through increasingly complex drills, many of which now incorporated Julius's suggestions. The improvement in their form and efficiency was noticeable even to the untrained eye, and as the session concluded, Heracleo crossed to where Julius stood at the boundary.

'My men tell me you've been quite the instructor these past weeks,' he said, studying Julius with renewed interest. 'Sharing the secrets of Roman military training with those who prey on Roman shipping. Some might call that treasonous.'

'If I were showing them how to defeat a Roman legion, perhaps,' Julius replied. 'But teaching basic sword technique is hardly revealing state secrets.'

Heracleo made a sound that might have been amusement.

'Still, it puzzles me. Why help men who hold you captive? Men who are, by any definition, your enemies?'

The other captives had gathered nearby, drawn by the unusual spectacle of the pirate captain conversing directly with a prisoner. Even the young pirates, finished with their training, lingered at the edge of the courtyard, curious about the exchange.

Julius met Heracleo's gaze directly, his expression confident, almost dismissive.

'I'm not concerned about helping them,' he said, 'as they will never have the opportunity to use these skills against Rome.'

A murmur ran through the assembled pirates. Heracleo's eyebrows rose slightly.

'And why is that?' he asked, his tone deceptively light.

Julius's response was delivered with the calm certainty of a man stating an obvious fact.

'Because when I am released, I will return with a fleet, hunt down every pirate in these waters, and crucify them all.'

The silence that followed was absolute, leaving only the echo of Julius's words hanging in the still air.

Then, starting with a single chuckle from somewhere in the back, laughter began to spread through the gathered pirates. It built quickly, from nervous titters to full-throated roars of amusement. Even Heracleo joined in, his weathered face creasing with genuine mirth.

'Crucify us all?' he repeated, wiping a tear from his eye. 'You? A single Roman captive with no fleet, no army, no authority?'

The pirates' laughter redoubled. Some slapped their thighs, others leaned on their companions for support as they howled at the absurdity of the threat. A few mimicked Julius's serious expression before dissolving into fresh peals of mirth.

Julius did not join in their laughter. He stood motionless, his gaze steady, his expression unchanged. There was no anger in his eyes, no embarrassment at being the object of their derision, only the same calm certainty with which he had delivered his promise.

Heracleo's laughter gradually subsided as he noticed Julius's unwavering demeanour. His eyes narrowed slightly, reassessing the man before him.

'You're serious,' he said, his voice dropping so that only those closest could hear. It wasn't a question but a realization.

'I am,' Julius replied simply.

For a moment, the two men regarded each other in silence, while around them the pirates' amusement continued unabated. Something passed between them in that moment, a recognition, perhaps, that beneath the roles of captor and captive, they were both men who understood power, who knew the difference between empty threats and genuine intent.

Heracleo broke the gaze first, turning to his men with a final chuckle.

'Come, let our Roman friend return to his dreams of

vengeance. We have ships to prepare and more realistic Romans to capture!'

The pirates dispersed, still laughing and repeating Julius's threat to one another, embellishing it with their own mocking additions.

As the courtyard cleared, Quintus approached Julius, his expression a mixture of awe and concern.

'You cannot possibly mean what you said,' he whispered. 'It was just... bravado, surely? To maintain dignity in captivity?'

Julius watched the retreating figure of Heracleo, his eyes calculating, his mind already turning over possibilities and plans.

'When we return to Miletus,' he said quietly, 'remember this day. Remember their laughter.'

Quintus studied his friend's profile, seeing something there that the pirates, in their amusement, had missed, the cold flame of absolute conviction, the unwavering certainty of a man who did not make promises he did not intend to keep. And in that moment, he understood that he was witnessing not just the dignity of a Roman aristocrat in captivity, but something far more significant: the emergence of a man who viewed the world, and his place in it, on a scale that ordinary men could barely comprehend.

Eight days later, a small vessel arrived from Miletus carrying the ransoms and as the pirates counted the silver, Julius and his fellow captives prepared for their release, gathering their meagre possessions and readying themselves for the journey back to civilization. Before they departed, Heracleo approached Julius one final time.

'It seems your family values you as highly as you claimed,' he said, gesturing to the chests of silver being carried into the pirates' stronghold. 'You were right to demand the higher ransom.'

'I usually am right,' Julius replied without a trace of humour.

Heracleo studied him for a moment, then extended his hand in an unexpectedly formal gesture.

'Safe journey, Roman. Perhaps we'll meet again someday,

under different circumstances.'

    Julius took the offered hand, his grip firm.

    'Yes,' he said. 'We will.'

Chapter Thirty-Seven

Miletus

The ship that carried Julius and his fellow captives from Pharmakonisi approached the harbour of Miletus as the afternoon sun gilded the city's white marble buildings. The ancient Greek metropolis rose from the coastline in terraces of stone and tile, its temples and colonnades gleaming in the golden light. Once one of the greatest cities of the Ionian Greeks, Miletus remained a hub of commerce and culture despite the growing shadow of Roman dominance over the region.

Julius stood at the ship's rail, his eyes fixed on the approaching city. Unlike his companions, who radiated relief and exhaustion after their ordeal, his expression betrayed neither jubilation at their freedom nor lingering fear from their captivity. Instead, his features were set in lines of focused calculation, as if the city before them represented not the end of an ordeal but the beginning of something else entirely.

'We're free,' Quintus murmured, joining him at the railing. 'By Jupiter's grace, we're actually free.'

'From the pirates, yes,' Julius replied, his gaze still fixed on the harbour. 'But freedom is merely the first step.'

Quintus studied his friend's profile with growing concern.

'Surely you're not still thinking about what you said to Heracleo? About returning with a fleet?'

Julius turned to him, and the cold certainty in his eyes made Quintus take an involuntary step back.

'I do not make idle threats, Quintus.'

Before his companion could respond, a shout from the helmsman announced their approach to the harbour. The captain, a dour Greek who had transported the ransom money to Pharmakonisi and was now returning with the freed captives, called for them to prepare for docking.

The harbour of Miletus teemed with activity. Trading vessels from across the Mediterranean jostled for position alongside local fishing boats and the occasional Roman military craft. Dockworkers swarmed the wharves, loading and unloading cargo beneath the watchful eyes of merchants and customs officials.

As their ship nudged against the dock, Julius noted the efficiency of the harbour operations, the number and types of vessels present, the organization of the warehouses that lined the waterfront. Where others saw merely the chaos of commerce, he saw resources, possibilities, the raw materials from which vengeance could be crafted.

The freed captives disembarked with varying degrees of enthusiasm. Some fell to their knees and kissed the solid ground, others rushed toward the city gates, eager to distance themselves from anything remotely connected to the sea that had betrayed them to pirates. A few, less certain of their welcome or resources in Miletus, lingered on the dock, eyeing the unfamiliar city with apprehension.

'What will you do now?' Quintus asked as they stood on the weathered planks of the pier. 'Return to Rome? Continue to Rhodes?'

Julius shook his head.

'Neither. Not yet.'

Without further explanation, he strode purposefully toward the harbour master's office, a solid stone building that overlooked the docks. Quintus hesitated, then hurried after him, curiosity overcoming his exhaustion.

The harbour master, a corpulent Greek with the harried expression of a man perpetually juggling too many responsibilities, barely glanced up as they entered his office.

'If you're looking for passage to Rhodes or Athens, try pier three,' he said in accented Latin, correctly identifying them as Romans by their dress. 'The Artemis sails with the morning tide.'

'I'm not seeking passage,' Julius replied. 'I need information about available ships. Warships, specifically.'

That got the harbour master's attention. He looked up, taking in Julius's bearing and the quality of his clothing despite its travel-worn state.

'Warships?' he repeated. 'Those are the province of the Roman governor or the city's defence council. I merely oversee commercial traffic.'

'Then I'll need to speak with this defence council,' Julius said. 'Immediately.'

The harbour master's expression shifted from dismissive to wary.

'And who exactly should I say is making this request?'

'Gaius Julius Caesar, of the Julian family of Rome. Recently ransomed from Cilician pirates, and now intent on delivering Roman justice to those same men.' The words were delivered not as a boast but as a simple statement of fact.

The harbour master's eyebrows rose. Word of Julius's capture and the unusual ransom demand had clearly reached Miletus before them.

'Wait here,' he said, rising from his desk with surprising agility for a man of his girth. 'I'll send a messenger to Anticrates. He sits on the council and oversees the city's defences.'

As the harbour master waddled out, Quintus turned to Julius with undisguised astonishment.

'You're really going through with this,' he said. 'You're actually going to try to raise a fleet to attack the pirates.'

'Not try,' Julius corrected. 'I am going to raise a fleet, and I am going to destroy those pirates.'

'But how? With what resources? With what authority?'

Julius's expression hardened slightly.

'Rome's authority extends wherever Romans are threatened. As for resources...' He glanced out the window toward the bustling harbour. 'Miletus is wealthy, and its leaders understand the pirate threat better than most. They'll help, if only to protect their own commerce.'

'And if they refuse?'

'They won't.'

The conviction in his voice was absolute, and Quintus found himself unable to argue further. There was something in Julius's demeanour, a certainty that transcended ordinary confidence, that made opposition feel not just futile but somehow misguided.

They waited in silence as the afternoon shadows lengthened across the harbour. Finally, the door opened to admit a tall, austere Greek with the bearing of a military man despite his advanced age. Silver hair crowned a face marked by the lines of experience rather than mere age, and his eyes, quick and assessing, took in both men before settling on Julius.

'I am Anticrates, commander of Miletus's defensive forces,' he announced. 'Demetrios tells me you're seeking warships for a private vendetta against pirates. Is this true?'

Julius met his gaze with equal directness.

'Not a vendetta. Justice. The pirates who held me and my companions have preyed on shipping in these waters for too long. Rome has failed in its duty to protect these seas, and I intend to correct that failure.'

Anticrates studied him for a moment.

'Bold words from a single Roman with no official position. What makes you think Miletus would commit its limited naval resources to your personal crusade?'

'Because it serves Miletus's interests as well as Rome's,' Julius replied without hesitation. 'Every ship these pirates take is a blow to your commerce. Every merchant they capture is a loss to your treasury. You've tried to fight them before, I assume?'

Anticrates nodded cautiously.

'And failed, because they scatter before a large force and regroup once you've withdrawn,' Julius continued, building his case with the precision of a practiced advocate. 'But I know where they are based now.

I know their numbers, their routines, their weaknesses. With a small but well-armed fleet, we can strike before they realize the threat.'

'And what do you offer in return for our assistance?' Anticrates asked.

'The gratitude of Rome,' Julius said. 'And the elimination of a threat that costs Miletus more in lost commerce each year than the expense of a few warships for a single expedition.'

Anticrates considered this, his weathered fingers tapping thoughtfully against the hilt of the ceremonial sword at his hip.

'The council will need to discuss this,' he said finally. 'But I am... intrigued by your proposal. Return tomorrow at midday. We will have an answer for you.'

With a curt nod to both men, he departed, leaving Julius and Quintus alone once more.

'That went better than I expected,' Quintus admitted.

'It went exactly as I expected,' Julius replied. 'Miletus has suffered from piracy for generations. They want these raiders eliminated as much as Rome does, but they lack the will to commit to a proper campaign. A surgical strike, with limited risk and the possibility of Roman favour? That they can support.'

They left the harbour master's office as the sun dipped toward the western horizon, bathing the city in the warm glow of approaching evening. Quintus suggested finding accommodations for the night, but Julius had other plans.

'There's someone else I need to see first,' he said, turning not toward the city centre but toward the wealthier district where Roman officials and wealthy expatriates maintained their residences.

'Who?' Quintus asked, struggling to keep pace with Julius's determined stride.

'Publius Servilius Vatia.'

Quintus stumbled in surprise.

'The proconsul's legate? How do you even know him?'

'I don't,' Julius admitted. 'But he knows of my family, and he has a particular interest in piracy.'

The home of Publius Servilius Vatia, a high-ranking officer serving under the Roman governor of Asia, was modest by the standards of wealthy Romans but imposing in the context of Miletus. A two-story structure with a colonnaded entrance, it combined Roman architectural preferences with concessions to the local climate. Guards stood at the gate, their weathered faces marking them as veterans rather than ceremonial figures.

Julius approached with the confidence of a man who expected to be admitted, not turned away.

'Tell your master I bring information about the Cilician pirates that will interest him greatly,' he said.

The guard departed, returning minutes later with a changed demeanour.

'The legate will see you,' he announced, gesturing for them to follow.

Inside, the house was furnished with the restrained elegance of a Roman who appreciated Greek aesthetics without fully embracing them. Vatia himself proved to be a man of similar character, Roman to his core, but with the pragmatic adaptability that successful provincial administration required. In his fifties, with the muscled build of a career soldier maintained despite his current administrative role, he regarded his unexpected visitors with undisguised curiosity.

'Gaius Julius Caesar,' he said, testing the name. 'Of the Julii Caesares. Nephew of Marius's wife, if I recall correctly.'

Julius inclined his head in acknowledgment.

'You have an excellent memory, Legate.'

'I make it my business to know Rome's families,' Vatia replied. 'Especially those with connections to men like Marius.' There was no hostility in his tone, merely a professional awareness of political realities. 'My guard tells me you have information about pirates?'

'More than information,' Julius said. 'I have recently spent thirty-eight days as their captive on Pharmakonisi. I know their numbers, their routines, their defences. And I intend to lead an expedition to destroy them.'

Vatia's eyebrows rose.

'Bold ambition for a man so recently their prisoner.'

'Fortune favours the bold,' Julius replied. 'And Rome needs men willing to take action against this scourge.'

For the next hour, Julius outlined what he had observed during his captivity, the layout of the pirates' base, their patterns of patrol and response, the weaknesses in their defences and the number of fighting men they could field. He spoke with the clear, precise detail of a military report, not the emotional account of a former captive. Vatia listened with growing interest, occasionally interjecting questions that revealed his own extensive knowledge of pirate operations in the region.

'You're well informed for a man who claims to be traveling to Rhodes for study,' the legate observed when Julius finished.

'I observe carefully,' Julius replied. 'It's a habit that has served me well.'

Vatia studied him for a long moment, then came to a decision.

'The governor has tasked me with addressing the pirate problem in this region. I've been gathering intelligence, planning a larger campaign for next year. Your information is valuable, but a hasty strike could alert them to our broader intentions.'

'Or it could deliver a crippling blow to one of their key bases,' said Julius, 'disrupting their operations and demonstrating Rome's reach. Pharmakonisi is not their main stronghold, but it's significant. Taking it would send a message.'

'And what exactly are you asking of me?' Vatia inquired.

'You

seem to be approaching the Milesians for ships. What role do you envision for Rome in this venture of yours?'

'Legitimacy,' Julius replied. 'Your tacit approval would reassure the Milesians and give my actions the colour of official Roman policy. I'm not asking for troops or ships, merely your acknowledgment that I act with Rome's interests at heart.'

Vatia's lips curved in something between a smile and a grimace.

'You have a politician's gift for asking without seeming to ask,' he observed. 'Very well. I won't oppose your expedition. If the Milesians choose to support you, I'll consider it a local initiative aligned with Roman interests. But understand this,' his expression hardened as he leaned forward. 'If you fail, if you're captured again or killed, Rome will disavow any knowledge of your actions.'

'Understood,' said Julius, 'but if I succeed, you gain valuable intelligence about pirate operations and the elimination of a threat to Roman shipping, yet without risking Roman forces, a favourable arrangement on all sides, it would seem.'

Vatia nodded slowly.

'Then we understand each other.' He rose, signalling the end of the meeting. 'Good hunting, Caesar. If you succeed in this endeavour, Rome will remember.'

'As will I,' Julius replied, the quiet certainty in his voice causing Vatia to look at him with renewed interest before they departed.

Outside, as twilight deepened into night, Quintus finally gave voice to the question that had been building since the harbour master's office.

'How do you do it?' he asked. 'How do you walk into a room with men of power and speak as if you're their equal?'

'Because I am their equal,' said Julius, 'and one day, they will be my inferiors.' There was no boast in the statement, only calm conviction, as if he were describing something as inevitable as the rising of the sun.

They found lodging at a modest inn near the harbour, where the innkeeper, hearing they were Romans recently freed from pirates, provided better rooms than their appearance might have warranted. As they settled in for the night, Quintus made one final attempt to understand his companion's determination.

'Even if the Milesians provide ships, even with Vatia's tacit approval, this is still an enormous risk,' he pointed out. 'You're not a naval commander. You have no official position. If something goes wrong...'

'Nothing will go wrong,' Julius stated with absolute certainty.

'How can you know that?'

Julius was silent for a moment, staring out the small window toward the darkened harbour where, somewhere beyond the city's protective breakwater, the Aegean stretched toward the horizon and the islands where pirates made their home.

'Because I have seen my destiny, Quintus,' he said finally, his voice quieter but no less certain. 'And it does not end on some pirate-infested rock in the Aegean.'

With that, he turned away from the window, effectively ending the conversation. Quintus, recognizing the futility of further argument, retired to his own room, leaving Julius to his plans and the unwavering conviction that shaped them.

The following days passed in a blur of activity. The Milesian defence council, influenced by Anticrates's support and the tacit approval of Rome's representative, agreed to provide four warships, sleek, fast vessels designed for coastal patrol and interception rather than major naval battles. Each carried a complement of archers and marines, mostly Greeks with experience fighting pirates, supplemented by a few Roman veterans who had settled in Miletus after their service.

Julius personally supervised the preparation of the small fleet, inspecting everything from the condition of the rams to the quality of the rations. He spent hours with the ship captains, briefing them on the approach to Pharmakonisi, the signals they would use, the formations they would adopt. Nothing was left to chance; every detail was checked and rechecked with meticulous precision.

To supplement the official resources, Julius secured a personal loan from one of Miletus's wealthiest merchants, a man with extensive shipping interests who had lost several vessels to piracy in recent years. The funds allowed him to hire additional mercenaries to bolster the marine contingents and to purchase specialized equipment for the assault, grappling hooks, boarding planks, and arrows designed to carry fire into the pirates' wooden structures.

Through it all, Julius displayed neither doubt nor hesitation. Each decision was made with the clarity of purpose that came from absolute conviction. The ship captains, initially sceptical of this Roman aristocrat with no naval experience, soon found themselves deferring to his judgment, their reservations overcome by his evident preparation and unwavering confidence.

Two weeks after their release from captivity, the small fleet was ready and as dawn broke over Miletus, Julius stood on the deck of the lead ship, watching as the crew made final preparations for departure. Quintus, who had decided to accompany the expedition despite his misgivings, joined him at the rail.

'Are we're really doing this?' he asked, still sounding faintly disbelieving.

'We are,' Julius confirmed, his gaze fixed on the horizon where Pharmakonisi awaited.

The ship's captain approached, his weathered face betraying a mixture of respect and lingering doubt.

'All is ready,' he reported. 'We can depart with the morning tide.'

Julius nodded. 'Then let us bring Roman justice to those who have mocked it for too long, and as the small fleet pulled away from Miletus, the morning sun at their backs and the open Aegean before them, Julius stood at the prow, his expression set in lines of absolute determination. He had promised the pirates crucifixion, and they had laughed. Soon, they would understand that Gaius Julius Caesar was not a man who made empty threats.

Chapter Thirty-Eight

Pharmakonisi

The night was moonless, the stars obscured by a thin veil of cloud that rendered the sea and sky nearly indistinguishable. Four ships glided silently through the darkness, their sails furled, oars dipping into the black water with barely a splash. Julius stood at the prow of the lead vessel, his eyes straining to make out the darker shape of land against the uniform blackness of the horizon.

'There,' he whispered, pointing toward a barely perceptible change in the texture of the darkness ahead. 'Pharmakonisi.'

Theron, the ship's captain nodded grimly.

'The western cove, as you suggested? It's treacherous, rocks just beneath the surface.'

'But unwatched,' Julius replied. 'The pirates guard the main harbour and the eastern approach. They don't expect anyone to risk the western shoals.'

The captain gave a small gesture of acknowledgment, then turned to relay quiet orders to his helmsman. The other ships followed their lead, the small fleet adjusting course toward the island's western edge, where a narrow, rocky beach offered precarious landing but also the precious gift of surprise.

The approach was painfully slow. Theron's navigator stood at the bow with a sounding line, periodically dropping the weighted rope into the water to measure depth, his whispered reports guiding their path through the submarine maze of rocks. Twice they halted entirely as the keel scraped ominously against submerged stone, the sound magnified in the stillness of the night.

But they persisted, and eventually the lead ship's bow grated softly against the shingle of the hidden cove. Julius was the first to leap into the knee-deep water, wading toward shore with a quiet urgency.

Quintus splashed ashore behind him, his face a pale oval in the darkness, his expression tense but determined.

'We made it,' he whispered, joining Julius at the edge of the beach where it gave way to scrubby vegetation.

Julius nodded, his focus already on the path ahead. The main pirate settlement lay on the island's eastern side, overlooking the natural harbour where their ships were moored. Between their landing site and their target stretched nearly two miles of rugged terrain, rocky hills, sparse woods, and the occasional ravine. They would need to cross this distance in darkness, maintain silence, and position themselves for the attack before dawn revealed their presence.

He turned to Theron and the other ship captains who had gathered around him.

'We move in three columns,' he said, his voice barely audible above the soft wash of waves against the shore. 'Central force with me, directly toward the settlement. Theron, take your men around the northern ridge, there's a guard post there that must be silenced before the main attack. Aristides, circle south and secure the path to the harbour. We cannot let them reach their ships.'

The captains nodded, having rehearsed these movements during the voyage from Miletus. They dispersed to their respective commands, and within moments, the beach was empty save for the minimal crews left to guard the ships.

The march across Pharmakonisi was a gruelling test of endurance and discipline. The terrain was even more challenging in darkness than Julius had estimated, with loose scree that shifted underfoot and thornbushes that tore at clothing and flesh. Yet the men maintained their silence, communicating only through hand signals and the occasional whispered command.

Julius led the central column, setting a pace that balanced speed with caution. His mind was utterly clear, focused on the immediate task yet simultaneously calculating the complex choreography of the three-pronged assault. Every step brought them closer to the pirate settlement, closer to the moment when surprise would transform into bloody reality.

As they crested a rocky hill approximately half a mile from their objective, he called a brief halt. The men sank gratefully to the ground, catching their breath while maintaining their disciplined silence. Julius used the moment to confer with his officers, confirming positions and timing.

'We attack just before first light,' he reminded them. 'Not in full darkness, not after dawn. That moment when night begins to fade but the sun has not yet appeared, that's when they'll be at their most vulnerable, guards drowsy from the night watch, most of the camp still asleep.'

The officers nodded, their faces grim with the knowledge of what was to come. These were experienced fighters, men who had faced pirates before, who understood the brutal calculus of surprise attacks and they harboured no illusions about the violence that would erupt when they fell upon the sleeping settlement.

The march resumed, more cautiously now as they drew nearer to their target. Julius could smell woodsmoke on the breeze, the faint scent of cooking fires banked for the night but not fully extinguished. They were close, so close that a careless sound might alert the sentries they had not yet detected.

They halted again at the edge of a small wood that marked the final approach to the settlement. Through gaps in the trees, Julius could make out the dark shapes of buildings silhouetted against the faintly lighter sky to the east. The first hint of dawn was approaching, the stars beginning to fade as night surrendered its hold.

This was the moment of greatest risk. If they were discovered now, the entire plan would unravel. The pirates would rouse, man their defences, and what was meant to be a swift, decisive strike would degenerate into a prolonged, costly battle. Julius scanned the perimeter of the settlement, searching for the telltale movement of sentries, the glow of watchfires.

A soft whistle from the darkness to his right signalled that Theron's flanking force was in position. Moments later, a similar sound from the left confirmed that Aristides had reached his assigned position overlooking the path to the harbour. All pieces were in place. Now they needed only the final cloak of pre-dawn twilight to begin their deadly work.

The waiting was always the hardest part. Julius felt time stretch like a bowstring drawn to its limit, each heartbeat a small eternity. Around him, men checked weapons with hands that moved on instinct, adjusted armour with the practiced economy of veterans preparing for battle. Some murmured quiet prayers to gods that sailed with them from Miletus, others simply stared ahead with the thousand-yard gaze of men who had seen combat before and knew what waited on the other side of fear.

Then, almost imperceptibly, the quality of the darkness changed. The black of true night gave way to the deep blue of approaching dawn. Julius raised his hand, the signal rippling through the assembled men like a current through water. Weapons were drawn, shields readied, bodies tensed for the command to move.

Julius drew his own sword and took a deep breath, feeling the familiar clarity of impending action settle over him like a mantle.

'Now,' he said, and the word unleashed the carefully orchestrated violence they had planned for two weeks.

The three columns converged on the pirate settlement with the coordinated precision of a well-executed military operation. Theron's force eliminated the northern watchtower with brutal efficiency, cutting down the drowsy sentries before they could sound the alarm while Aristides and his men secured the path to the harbour, ensuring no pirates could escape to their ships.

Julius led the main assault directly into the heart of the settlement and the first warning many had was the crash of doors being kicked in, the shouts of attackers already inside their crude houses. Some stumbled from their beds, fumbling for weapons, only to be cut down before they could mount any meaningful defence. Others surrendered immediately, hands raised, eyes wide with the shock of being on the receiving end of the same terror they had so often inflicted.

A few, the veterans, the more disciplined fighters, managed to form small pockets of resistance. In the central square, a group of twenty made a stand, back-to-back, wielding a motley collection of weapons. Julius directed the assault on this position personally, using the superior numbers and discipline of his force to encircle the defenders, tightening the noose until resistance became futile. Within minutes, the last organized resistance collapsed, and the surviving pirates threw down their weapons, hands raised in surrender.

As the first rays of sunlight crested the eastern horizon, Julius stood in the centre of the captured settlement, directing the systematic search of every building, every potential hiding place. The pirates were herded into the central square, bound and under heavy guard. Among them, Julius recognized faces from his captivity, the guard who had commented on his Greek, the training master Syrax, several young pirates who had participated in the drills he had critiqued.

And there, being dragged from a building that was clearly the captain's residence, was Heracleo himself. The pirate leader's face was bloodied, his expression a mixture of rage and disbelief as he was forced to kneel among his captured men.

The final tally of the assault exceeded even Julius's expectations. Over eighty pirates captured alive, another twenty or so killed in the fighting. The entire base had been secured with minimal casualties among the attacking force, three dead, perhaps a dozen wounded, none seriously. Complete surprise had turned what might have been a costly battle into a one-sided rout.

Julius approached Heracleo, stopping a few paces from the kneeling pirate captain. For a long moment, neither man spoke. The sounds of the mopping-up operation continued around them, marines securing buildings, officers shouting orders, the wounded receiving attention from the expedition's medicus.

'You actually did it,' Heracleo said finally, his voice a mixture of pain and grudging respect. 'You came back, just as you said you would.'

'I told you I would crucify every pirate on this island,' Julius replied, his tone matter-of-fact rather than triumphant. 'And unfortunately for you, I am a man of my word.'

Heracleo's eyes widened slightly at the reminder.

'You wouldn't. Even Rome has laws about such things. We deserve a trial, a chance to…'

'To what?' Julius interrupted. 'To explain why you preyed on Roman citizens? To justify the lives you've taken, the ships you've plundered, the ransoms you've extorted?' He shook his head. 'Rome's justice will be served, but possibly not in the way you would prefer.'

He turned away, leaving Heracleo to contemplate his fate, and found Quintus standing nearby, his sword still drawn but the immediate tension of battle fading from his posture.

'An impressive victory,' Quintus observed, gesturing to the rows of bound pirates. 'What happens to them now?'

'We take them to Pergamon,' Julius replied. 'The governor there, Marcus Junius, will oversee their official processing.'

Quintus's brow furrowed.

'But you told Heracleo…'

'I know what I told him,' Julius cut in. 'And I meant every word. But we will observe the proper formalities. Rome is a nation of laws, even when dealing with those who flout them.'

By midday, the pirate base had been thoroughly searched, valuable intelligence about other pirate operations secured, and preparations made to transport the prisoners. Julius had recovered much of the silver paid for his ransom in Heracleo's quarters, deciding to use it to repay his loans from Miletus and fund the next phase of his plan.

The captured pirates were loaded onto two of the four ships, bound securely under heavy guard. Julius would accompany them to Pergamon, while Theron remained on Pharmakonisi with a contingent of marines to secure the island until Roman authorities could decide its ultimate disposition.

As they prepared to depart, Heracleo was brought to the harbour under special guard. The pirate captain's defiance had faded somewhat, replaced by the grim resignation of a man confronting his mortality.

'You won your game, Caesar,' he said as he was led past Julius toward the waiting ship. 'But remember this, fortune is fickle. Today you stand victorious, tomorrow you may be the one in chains.'

Julius regarded him impassively.

'The difference between us, Heracleo, is that I make my own fortune. I don't wait for it to find me.'

The journey to Pergamon took three days, the ships navigating the coastal waters with the confidence of crews who no longer feared pirate interception. Julius used the time to compile a detailed report of the operation, documenting the pirates' strength, their tactics, the extent of their operations based on documents captured in the raid. This information would be valuable to Rome's ongoing efforts to combat piracy in the eastern Mediterranean.

Pergamon, one of the principal cities of Roman Asia, rose from the coastal plain in a series of terraced hills, its acropolis crowned with temples and public buildings that gleamed in the sunlight. The governor's palace stood near the centre of the upper city, a statement of Roman authority in this Greek land.

Governor Marcus Junius received Julius with the cautious courtesy of a provincial administrator confronted with an unexpected situation. A career politician with little military experience, he was clearly unsettled by the arrival of a private citizen commanding a makeshift fleet and delivering dozens of captured pirates for Roman justice.

'This is... most irregular, Caesar,' he said after listening to

Julius's account of the expedition. 'While I commend your initiative in addressing the pirate threat, such actions are normally undertaken by properly constituted Roman forces under official command.'

'Necessity demanded immediate action,' Julius replied smoothly. 'The pirates were preparing to relocate their base following my release and the opportunity to strike would have been lost had I waited for official authorization.'

Junius frowned, clearly uncomfortable with the precedent being set.

'Nevertheless, there are procedures that must be followed. The prisoners will need to be formally charged, evidence presented, a proper legal process observed.'

'Of course,' Julius agreed. 'Rome's commitment to justice is what separates us from the barbarians. I simply request that the process be expedited, given the clear guilt of these men.'

The governor nodded, seemingly relieved by Julius's apparent deference to proper procedure.

'I'll assign a quaestor to begin the documentation immediately. In the meantime, the prisoners will be held in custody. It may take some weeks to sort through individual cases, determine appropriate punishments...'

'The punishment for piracy is clear under Roman law,' Julius interrupted, his tone still respectful but carrying a new edge of steel. 'Crucifixion for those who have committed violence against Roman citizens, slavery for lesser participants.'

Junius shifted uncomfortably in his chair.

'Well, yes, technically. But in practice, many captured pirates are simply sold into slavery regardless of their specific actions. The treasury benefits, and the end result is much the same, they're removed from circulation, no longer a threat.'

Julius's expression hardened almost imperceptibly.

'These men held a Roman citizen, a member of one of Rome's oldest families, for ransom. They have attacked Roman shipping, hindered Roman commerce, defied Roman authority. The law prescribes crucifixion, and I expect the law to be applied.'

The governor's discomfort increased visibly.

'I understand your personal feelings in this matter, Caesar, but I am responsible for administering justice in this province. I must consider all factors, including the practical challenges of conducting mass executions, the potential value of the prisoners as slaves, the precedents set by previous cases...'

Julius listened to the governor's equivocation with growing impatience, recognizing in it the bureaucratic inertia that plagued Rome's provincial administration. Junius was not corrupt or malicious, merely cautious, a man who would always choose the path of least resistance, the solution that created the fewest complications for himself.

'I see,' Julius said when the governor finally ran out of words. 'You've given me much to consider, Excellency. Perhaps I should review the legal precedents myself before we proceed further. I wouldn't want to pressure you into a hasty decision.'

Relieved by this apparent concession, Junius agreed that Julius could have access to the provincial legal archives and offered him accommodations befitting his status during his stay in Pergamon. The meeting concluded on cordial terms, though both men understood that the fundamental disagreement remained unresolved.

That evening, as Julius dined with Quintus in their assigned quarters within the governor's complex, he outlined the next phase of his plan.

'Junius will delay indefinitely,' he said, breaking a piece of bread with precise movements. 'He sees the pirates as assets to be liquidated for provincial revenue, not criminals to be punished according to law.'

'So, what will you do?' Quintus asked, already suspecting the answer.

'What Rome would do if her will were not diluted by men like Junius,' replied Julius. 'I will ensure justice is served, swiftly and definitively.'

Quintus frowned.

'You're going to override the governor's authority, aren't you? That's...'

'Necessary,' Julius finished for him, 'and entirely consistent with Rome's interests, if not her bureaucracy's preferences.'

They were interrupted by a servant bringing fresh wine, and when the man had departed, Julius leaned closer, lowering his voice though they were alone in the room.

'Tomorrow, I'll meet with the captain of the prison guard. He's a former legionary, not one of Junius's provincial appointees. I suspect he'll understand the importance of proper justice for pirates, especially if that understanding is reinforced by a suitable gratuity from our recovered silver.'

'And then?' Quintus asked, his expression caught between concern and admiration for Julius's audacity.

'And then,' Julius said, his eyes reflecting the lamplight with cold determination, 'I fulfil my promise to Heracleo.'

Quintus stared at his friend for a long moment, searching for some sign of doubt or hesitation in his face and finding none. This was a side of Julius he had glimpsed before but never seen so clearly manifested, the implacable will beneath the cultured surface, the absolute certainty that his judgment superseded conventional authority when that authority failed to serve Rome's true interests as he perceived them.

'You're really going to do this,' Quintus said finally. It wasn't a question but a recognition of inevitability.

Julius took a sip of wine, his movements unhurried, his decision already made and settled beyond reconsideration.

'I gave my word,' he said simply. 'And Rome demands no less.'

Chapter Thirty-Nine

Pergamon

The night was moonless, the kind that shrouded deeds best left unseen. Within the stone depths of Pergamon's prison, guards moved through their rounds with the mechanical indifference of men who had long since learned to ignore the sounds of human suffering. The captured pirates from Pharmakonisi occupied several large cells in the lowest level, packed in like livestock awaiting slaughter or sale, depending on Governor Junius's eventual decision.

Ten days had passed since Julius had delivered the pirates to Roman justice. Ten days of bureaucratic delays, of careful cataloguing and endless documentation, of polite evasions whenever Julius inquired about the progress of their cases. The governor had clearly hoped to wear down his unexpected visitor's resolve through the time-honoured Roman tradition of administrative inertia.

He had misjudged his man.

The first sign that something was amiss came just after the midnight watch change. The door to the guard chamber swung open, but instead of the expected relief officer, several armed men entered silently, their weapons already drawn. They wore no uniforms, nothing to identify them, but they moved with the coordinated precision of trained soldiers.

'Don't move,' the leader said quietly to the four guards on duty. 'We're not here for you. Cooperate, and you'll see the morning.'

The senior guard, a veteran called Lucius who had served twenty years in the legions before accepting this quieter post, assessed the situation with a professional's eye. His men were outnumbered, taken by surprise, and the intruders carried themselves like men who knew how to use the short swords pointed at the guards' throats.

'What do you want?' he asked, his voice steady despite the blade hovering inches from his neck.

'The pirates,' the intruder replied. 'All of them.'

Lucius's expression betrayed nothing, but his mind worked quickly. He knew of the dispute between Governor Junius and the young Roman aristocrat who had captured the pirates. The governor's reluctance to execute the prisoners had been a subject of barracks gossip for days. And these men, for all their efforts at anonymity, had the unmistakable bearing of those accustomed to military discipline.

'Caesar sent you,' he said. It wasn't a question.

The leader of the intruders neither confirmed nor denied, but a flicker of acknowledgment passed across his face.

'Step aside,' he said. 'The keys, if you please.'

Lucius hesitated for just a moment. His duty was clear, protect the prisoners, raise the alarm, resist any unauthorized removal. But another, deeper sense of duty tugged at him. He had spent his career upholding Rome's authority, defending her borders, enforcing her will. The pirates imprisoned below had mocked that authority, preyed on Roman citizens, undermined Rome's control of the sea lanes that were her lifeblood. And the governor's reluctance to punish them properly felt like a betrayal of everything Lucius had fought for.

'The main ring,' he said, reaching slowly for the keys at his belt. 'The large iron one opens the corridor gate. The brass ones open the individual cells.'

As he handed over the keys, he looked directly into the eyes of the intruder.

'I never saw your face,' he said quietly. 'None of us did.'

The leader gave a slight nod, understanding the implicit agreement. The guards would not resist, would not raise the alarm, would claim they had been overpowered and bound. In exchange, no blood would be shed here tonight.

'Bind them,' the leader ordered, and turned to one of the men. 'Are the carts ready?'

'Yes, Domine. Six of them, as you specified.'

'Good. Now let's get this done.'

The operation moved with the methodical efficiency that had become Julius's hallmark. Two men remained with the bound guards while the rest descended to the cells. The pirates, roused from uneasy sleep by the unexpected activity, found themselves confronted by armed men who moved with practised efficiency, opening cells and dragging prisoners out before they could fully comprehend what was happening.

Any who resisted were subdued with swift, economical violence, a blow to the stomach, a fist to the temple, a knee driven into the back. No weapons were used, no blood was spilled, but the implicit threat was unmistakable. Resistance meant pain, and these men were clearly prepared to inflict it without hesitation.

The pirates had their hands bound and gags forced between their teeth to prevent any outcry. Rough sacks were pulled over their heads to disorient them before being led from the prison and hurried through the silent corridors and out into the chill night air of Pergamon.

Outside, covered wagons waited in the shadow of the prison wall. The bound pirates were loaded like cargo, packed tightly onto wooden planks covered with a thin layer of straw.

The small convoy wound its way through Pergamon's darkened streets, avoiding the main thoroughfares where night patrols might be encountered. The eastern gate stood unguarded at this hour, its massive doors pulled shut but left unlocked for early-morning traffic. One of Julius's men dismounted to heave the smaller side portal open, and the wagons slipped through, leaving the sleeping city behind as they turned onto the road that wound into the hills.

They travelled for nearly two hours, climbing steadily into the rugged terrain that surrounded Pergamon. The hills here were not the gentle, cultivated slopes of Italy but a harsher landscape, rocky and scrub-covered, inhabited more by wild goats than humans. Eventually, the road dwindled to a rough track, and finally to a barely
perceptible path that only someone with specific knowledge would attempt to follow.

The site Julius had chosen for his purpose was perfect, a broad shelf of flat ground high on a hillside, visible from the main road that approached Pergamon from the east but sufficiently remote to allow the deadly work to proceed undisturbed. More importantly, it had been prepared in advance.

As the wagons pulled onto the plateau, the first hints of dawn were beginning to lighten the eastern sky. The sacks were pulled from the pirates' heads, though their bindings remained in place. Blinking against even the dim pre-dawn light, they struggled to make sense of their surroundings and the grim tableau that awaited them.

Laid out in a long, orderly row across the hillside were crosses, rough wooden structures crafted from local timber, their surfaces still raw and un-weathered. Beside each cross, a pit had been dug, deep enough to hold the base securely once the cross was raised.

As the light strengthened, the full horror of what awaited them dawned on the pirates. This was to be no trial, no opportunity for appeal or mercy. This was the fulfilment of the promise Julius had made during his captivity, a promise they had laughed at as impossible.

Heracleo, separated from the others and held under special guard, met Julius's gaze across the clearing. The pirate captain's face, visible now as a guard removed his gag, was a study in conflicting emotions, fear warring with defiance, desperation with a strange, reluctant respect.

'You cannot do this,' he said, his voice hoarse from the gag. 'This is not justice, this is murder. We have rights under Roman law to a proper trial, to...'

'You forfeited those rights when you chose to prey on Roman citizens,' Julius interrupted, his tone conversational despite the gravity of the moment. 'The law is clear: pirates are *'hostis humani generis'*, enemies of all mankind. And the penalty is equally clear.' He gestured toward the crosses, their rough-hewn forms stark against the lightening sky.

'You knew the price when you chose your profession,' he continued. 'Every ship you took, every merchant you ransomed, every sailor you killed, each was a step toward this moment. Now you face the consequence of those choices.'

Heracleo's defiance crumbled slightly, reality overwhelming bravado.

'At least grant us a quick death,' he said, his voice dropping. 'A blade across the throat. Not... this.' His eyes flickered toward the crosses, genuine terror bleeding through his mask of courage.

Julius considered him for a long moment. There was no personal hatred in his expression, no pleasure in the pirate's fear, only the cool assessment of a man who had set himself a task and would see it completed with appropriate efficiency.

'Prepare them,' he said to his men, neither accepting nor rejecting Heracleo's plea for mercy.

What followed was a scene of methodical horror. The pirates were untied only to be more securely fastened to the waiting crosses, rough rope binding wrists and ankles to the wooden beams. Some struggled, requiring multiple men to subdue them, others went numbly, the fight drained from them by the inevitability of their fate. A few begged, offering information, treasure, anything to avoid the death that awaited them.

None were spared.

One by one, the crosses were raised, each requiring the strength of six men to lift and position in its prepared pit. The impact as they dropped into place sent shudders through the wooden beams, the vibration transferring to the bodies bound upon them in a cruel prelude to the agony to come.

As the sun cleared the eastern hills, its light fell upon a scene from nightmare, eighty-seven crosses standing in grim rows across the hillside, each bearing a living man who would soon envy the dead.

Crucifixion was not merely execution but elaborate torture, a death designed to be both excruciating and humiliating. The victim's weight, suspended from the arms, made breathing increasingly difficult. To relieve the pressure and draw breath, they would have to push up with their legs, causing searing pain from the raw wounds from the ropes around their ankles. Eventually, exhaustion would make this impossible, and they would slowly suffocate, their deaths sometimes taking days rather than hours.

Some Romans considered it a barbaric punishment, unworthy of a civilized people. Others saw it as a necessary deterrent, a public demonstration that certain crimes placed the perpetrator beyond the protection of humanity's shared codes of conduct.

As the last cross was raised, Julius walked along the line, examining the work with the critical eye of a commander inspecting his troops' preparations. When he reached Heracleo's cross, positioned at the centre of the formation where it would be most visible from the road below, he paused.

The pirate captain's initial bravado had evaporated, replaced by the desperate focus of a man already beginning to feel the first waves of agony washing through his suspended body. Sweat beaded on his forehead despite the morning chill, and his breathing came in short, sharp gasps.

'Remember when you laughed?' Julius asked, his voice pitched low enough that only Heracleo could hear him. 'When I told you I would return and crucify every pirate on that island?'

Heracleo's only response was a groan as he shifted, trying to find a position that would allow him to breathe more easily.

'I want you to know something before I leave you,' Julius continued. 'This isn't personal. You were a man doing what men like you have always done, taking what you could because you could take it. I respect that, in its way.' He glanced along the line of crosses, his expression thoughtful. 'But Rome cannot and will not allow it. And I am Rome's instrument in this matter.'

He stepped back, studying the suffering man with the detached interest of a naturalist observing a specimen.

'You wondered if fortune might one day reverse our positions,' he said. 'It won't. Because I don't leave my fate to fortune's whims. I create my own destiny.'

With that, he turned away, leaving Heracleo to the long, agonizing embrace of the cross.

By noon, the hellish panorama was complete. Eighty-seven crosses stood against the sky, a forest of suffering visible for miles around. The sun beat down mercilessly, adding the torment of thirst to the agony of suspension. Some of the pirates had already lapsed into unconsciousness, a temporary mercy that would not last. Others screamed or begged, their voices growing weaker as their strength ebbed. A few maintained a stoic silence, determined to face death with what dignity they could muster.

Julius stood at the edge of the plateau, looking out over his handiwork with the satisfaction of a man who had fulfilled a difficult but necessary obligation. There was no joy in his expression, no sadistic pleasure in the suffering spread before him, only the calm certainty that justice had been served as Rome defined it.

Quintus approached, his face pale, his eyes avoiding the grotesque display behind them.

'It's done,' he said unnecessarily. 'What now?'

Julius turned to him, and for a moment, Quintus saw something in his friend's eyes that he had never witnessed before, a glimpse behind the mask of controlled composure, a flash of the raw will that drove this man who spoke so casually of creating his own destiny.

'Now,' Julius said, his voice betraying none of the intensity Quintus had briefly glimpsed, 'we return to Pergamon, collect our things, and continue to Rhodes. We have studies to complete.'

Quintus stared at him in disbelief.

'Just like that? After... *this?*' He gestured vaguely toward the crosses.

'Just like that,' Julius confirmed. 'This was necessary but not central to our purpose. A diversion, nothing more.'

The casual dismissal of what they had just orchestrated, a mass execution that violated provincial authority and would undoubtedly create political repercussions, left Quintus momentarily speechless. How could Julius treat something so extraordinary as merely an obligation to be discharged before returning to the normal course of his life?

'The governor will be furious,' he said, finally finding his voice. 'There will be consequences.'

'Perhaps,' said Julius. 'But by the time any official response is formulated, we'll be in Rhodes, beyond Junius's immediate reach. And there is the little matter of what story reaches Rome first, his account of administrative irregularities, or mine of bringing pirates to justice when the provincial governor seemed reluctant to do so.'

He smiled slightly, the expression not reaching his eyes.

'Which do you think Rome's citizens would prefer to hear? That a Roman aristocrat took decisive action against pirates, or that a provincial governor was more concerned with procedural niceties than with avenging attacks on Roman commerce and dignity?'

Quintus had no answer. He was beginning to understand the complex calculations that drove his friend, the precise weighing of risk against benefit, the confidence that came from seeing several moves ahead in the great game of power and influence.

As they turned to leave, Julius paused for one final look at the crosses silhouetted against the bright midday sky. The pirate captain had been right about one thing, fortune was indeed fickle. But Julius Caesar had demonstrated, with terrible finality, that he was not a man who left his promises unfulfilled or his reputation to chance.

Before they continued, he had one last order to issue and turned to the commander who had brought the pirates to the hill.

'I want you to go back up,' he said.

'Surely not to release them?' asked the commander, shocked at the potential leniency.

'No,' said Julius, 'I want you to cut their throats. Every last one of them… It's what they would have wanted.'

Epilogue

Rome

Spring had returned to Rome, bathing the city in golden light and the promise of renewal. The gardens of the Julian villa burst with colour, purple clematis climbing the weathered columns, beds of saffron crocuses nodding beneath young olive trees, and the first roses of the season perfuming the air with their delicate fragrance. It was as if the earth itself celebrated Julius Caesar's homecoming.

One year after his departure for Rhodes, as he had promised, Julius had returned to his family and to Rome. His journey over the past few years had taken many unexpected turns, exile, military service, pirate captivity, all detours that had built his reputation in ways no one could have anticipated. The stories had preceded him, whispered in the Forum, debated in the Senate, repeated in the homes of Rome's elite: Julius Caesar, who had crucified the pirates who dared to capture him. Julius Caesar, who had raised a fleet through sheer force of will. Julius Caesar, who had shown that Rome's justice could not be mocked, even in distant seas.

In the atrium of the Julian villa, the celebration continued well into the evening. Old family clients mingled with new admirers drawn by Julius's growing reputation. Senators who had once dismissed the Julian name now lingered in earnest conversation, reassessing the value of this connection. Merchants and equites, ever sensitive to shifting political winds, made certain to pay their respects.

Julius moved through the gathering with easy confidence. He spoke with measured precision, each word carefully chosen, his rhetoric polished by Apollonius Molon's rigorous training. Those who had known him before noticed the change, this was not merely a Roman nobleman returning from his education abroad. This was a man transformed.

As the night deepened and guests began to depart, the household gradually quieted. Servants moved silently through the rooms, extinguishing lamps, collecting emptied cups, restoring order to the space. In the small garden where fragrant night-blooming jasmine scented the air, Julius sat with Cornelia and Aurelia, the three of them alone for the first time since his return.

'It went well,' Aurelia said, her pride evident despite her understated tone. 'Better than I expected. Even Catulus seemed impressed.'

'He has reason to be,' Cornelia added, her hand finding Julius's in the darkness. 'The stories from the East have changed how Rome sees you.'

'Stories grow in the telling,' Julius replied. 'My actions were merely necessary, not extraordinary.'

'Whether necessary or extraordinary, they've opened doors,' Aurelia observed. 'Doors that were closed to us before. The question is, which will you choose to walk through first?'

The moment had arrived, the question that had lingered unspoken beneath the celebrations and reunions. What path would Gaius Julius Caesar choose now that he had returned to Rome?

Julius looked from his mother to his wife, these two women who had maintained his household and his family's position during his absence. They had navigated the treacherous politics of Rome with skill and discretion, preserving what was his while he forged his reputation abroad. They deserved honesty now, deserved to understand the vision that had crystallized during his time away.

'My path remains the same as it was a year ago,' he said simply. 'I will make my name in the courts of Rome.'

'As a defender?'

'As a prosecutor,' Julius replied. 'Rome has no shortage of corrupt officials, governors who have abused their power, magistrates who have betrayed the public trust. I will bring them all to justice, one by one.'

'A dangerous path,' Aurelia cautioned. 'Each man you accuse will have powerful friends, allies who will not forget the slight.'

'Each conviction will also bring supporters, the victims of corruption, those who value justice, Romans who want to see the Republic cleansed of its worst excesses.' Julius's expression remained calm, but his eyes reflected the intensity of his conviction. 'My studies with Apollonius have prepared me for this. My voice is my weapon now, and I intend to wield it precisely.'

'And then?' Aurelia pressed.

'Then the Cursus Honorum,' said Julius. 'The connections I forge through the courts will provide the support needed for election. Quaestor first, perhaps within two years, and from there, Aedile, Praetor, and eventually Consul. Each step calculated, each position used to maximum advantage.'

'You've thought this through carefully,' Cornelia observed, studying her husband's face in the moonlight.

'I've had time,' Julius said. 'Many nights at sea, many hours in contemplation. The path is clear to me now, clearer than it has ever been.'

Aurelia nodded slowly, her shrewd political mind assessing his strategy and finding it sound.

'You'll need funds,' she said. 'The courts bring honour but little immediate profit. Elections require generous expenditure.'

'I'll secure the necessary resources,' Julius replied. 'Loans, if needed and investment in ventures that promise returns. I will also seek alliances with those who see the value in supporting a rising name.'

'And enemies?' Cornelia asked softly. 'You'll make many.'

'That cannot be avoided,' Julius acknowledged. 'Power always creates opposition. But I'll choose my battles carefully, build sufficient support before each confrontation. Rome respects strength, despises weakness but I must never appear vulnerable, never hesitate when decisive action is required.'

The three fell silent for a moment, the weight of the path ahead settling over them. It was Aurelia who finally spoke, rising from
her seat with the dignity that had carried her through decades of Roman politics.

'It's late,' she said. 'Tomorrow will bring new challenges, new opportunities. We should rest.'

She approached her son, placing a hand briefly on his shoulder, a rare gesture of physical affection from a woman who typically maintained the formal distance expected of Roman matrons.

'Your father would be proud,' she said simply, then turned and walked into the house, her straight back betraying neither age nor weariness.

Cornelia remained beside Julius, her presence a quiet comfort in the garden's darkness. After a moment, she too rose, her movements graceful in the moonlight.

'Will you come to bed?' she asked, her voice soft with more than simple inquiry.

'Soon,' Julius promised. 'There's something I must do first.'

She nodded, understanding without further explanation.

'Don't be long,' she said, leaning down to press her lips lightly against his forehead before following Aurelia's path into the villa.

Alone in the garden, Julius sat motionless for several minutes, allowing the sounds of the night to wash over him, distant street noises from beyond the villa walls, the soft rustle of leaves in the gentle breeze, the occasional call of nocturnal birds.

Finally, he stood and walked through the silent house, past the atrium where servants had extinguished the last lamps, past the sleeping chambers where his family now rested. His destination was the small room at the heart of the house that few visitors ever saw, the family shrine, where generations of Julii had honoured their ancestors and sought guidance from those who had gone before.

The shrine was illuminated only by a single oil lamp that burned perpetually before the household gods. In its flickering light, Julius could make out the masks of his ancestors that lined the walls, death masks created at their passing, preserved to remember their features and their legacy. His father's was among them, the lines of his face captured in wax at the moment of his death.

Below the masks stood the small altar where offerings were made to the family's guardian spirits, and beside it, the niche where his father's ashes rested in a simple marble urn. Daily libations were poured here, ensuring that Gaius Julius Caesar the elder remained connected to the household he had once led.

Julius closed the door behind him, shut out the world, and sat with his back against the cool stone wall, facing the assembled witnesses of his lineage. He had come to this room countless times as a boy with an unknown future, now he returned as a man, bearing the weight of the family name and the promise of its future.

For a long while, he said nothing, simply absorbing the presence of history that permeated the small chamber.

'Father,' he said eventually, addressing the marble urn as if the man himself might hear from beyond the grave. 'I have walked many paths these past few years and was tested in ways I could not have anticipated.'

The flame flickered, casting moving shadows across the ancestral masks, their hollow eyes seeming to watch with ancient judgment.

'But these detours have served their purpose. My name is spoken in the Forum now, not merely as the son of Gaius Julius Caesar, but as a man who has earned notice through his own actions. The Corona Civica opens doors that once would have remained closed and the stories from the East lend weight to my words before I even speak them.' He leaned forward, his voice taking on a new intensity. 'When you died, Rome was already changing. Sulla's shadow had begun to stretch across the Republic. You did not live to see how far that shadow would reach, how deeply the Republic would

be wounded by his ambition, but the wounds remain, even now. The Optimates still cling to power they have not earned, the people still suffer under laws that favour the few over the many, and the men who

should protect Rome's interests too often protect only their own.'

Julius's hand clenched into a fist, his passion momentarily breaking through his cultivated control.

'I will change this,' he vowed, 'Not with unnecessary violence, as Sulla did, but with words, with law, and with the careful accumulation of influence and authority. Position by position, office by office, I will climb the Cursus Honorum not as an end in itself, but as a means to reshape Rome into what she should be.'

The silence of the dead received his declaration, neither affirming nor denying the ambition it contained.

'You taught me that our family name carries obligations,' he continued, his voice softening slightly. 'That we are descended from Venus herself, from Aeneas who carried Troy's legacy to Italian shores. That the Julian line is meant for greatness, not merely survival. I understand that obligation now more completely than I ever did when you lived. I feel it in my blood, in my bones, in every breath I take.'

He stood, moving to the altar where a small vessel of wine waited for the morning's libations. Pouring a measure into the offering bowl, he watched as the liquid gleamed darkly in the lamplight.

'This I swear, Father. I will raise our name higher than any Julian before me. I will restore the Republic to its true purpose. I will extend Rome's reach to lands we have not yet imagined. And when I am done, the name Caesar will be remembered not merely as one family among many, but as the very embodiment of Rome herself.'

The oath hung in the stillness of the shrine, witnessed by generations of Julian ancestors. Julius stood motionless for a moment, the weight of his promise settling over him not as a burden but as a mantle of purpose, clear and undeniable.

He looked down at the Corona Civica in his hands. The golden oak leaves caught the lamplight, throwing gleaming reflections against the stone walls. The award, earned through pain, blood and self-sacrifice had served its purpose. It had begun the building of his reputation and opened the first doors on his journey to power.

Julius gently placed the crown over the urn of his father's ashes, a fulfilment of the silent promise he had made years before at his father's funeral. One achievement completed, countless more to come.

'Watch me, Father,' he said softly. 'Watch what your son will become.'

Finally, he turned, straightened his shoulders, and stepped out of the shrine, closing the door quietly behind him. In the darkness of the corridor, his face bore the expression of a man who had glimpsed his destiny and found it greater than others could imagine.

Rome awaited. Tomorrow would bring the first steps on the next stage of his journey. The courts would hear his voice, the corrupt would feel his judgment, and the long climb to power would begin in earnest. The Julian name would rise, and Rome would never be the same again.

THE END

Author's Notes

Timelines

This novel is rooted in the historical events of Julius Caesar's early years, drawing on real figures, places, and conflicts from the late Roman Republic. I have done my best to remain faithful to the spirit of the time, incorporating as much factual detail as possible to bring the world of 81 BC to life.

That said, some dates, sequences of events, and minor details may have been adjusted slightly for the sake of narrative flow. These changes do not alter the course of history in any fundamental way, but rather serve to enhance the storytelling experience, ensuring that events unfold in a manner that is both engaging and accessible to modern readers.

Wherever possible, I have relied on historical sources, but given the gaps and inconsistencies in ancient records, certain characters and conversations have been reimagined to reflect what might plausibly have occurred. My goal has been to remain true to the essence of the period while crafting a compelling and immersive story.

For readers interested in the real history behind the events depicted, I encourage further exploration of the sources that have shaped this novel. Thank you for joining me on this journey into the past!

Birth and Patrician Lineage

Born on July 12 or 13, 100 BCE into the ancient patrician Julian family, Gaius Julius Caesar could trace his ancestry to the goddess Venus through the legendary Trojan hero Aeneas and the early kings of Rome. Despite this illustrious lineage, the family's fortunes had declined somewhat by Caesar's birth. His father, also named Gaius Julius Caesar, served as governor of the province of Asia and died when Caesar was just sixteen. His mother, Aurelia Cotta, came from an influential plebeian noble family and played a significant role in his upbringing and education, instilling in him the discipline and ambition that would later define his career.

Growing Up in Turbulent Times

Caesar's childhood coincided with a period of unprecedented political upheaval in Rome. The Republic was torn between the populist reforms of Marius (who happened to be Caesar's uncle by marriage) and the conservative reaction led by Sulla. Civil war erupted in 88 BCE when Caesar was only twelve years old. The streets of Rome became battlegrounds as political factions fought for control. These formative experiences during his youth exposed Caesar to the brutal reality of Roman politics and shaped his understanding of power, popularity, and the fragility of the Republic's institutions—lessons he would later apply with remarkable effectiveness.

Marriage and Early Political Connections

At the age of seventeen, Caesar was nominated to become the high priest of Jupiter (Flamen Dialis), but this appointment was derailed when Sulla came to power. Instead, Caesar married Cornelia, the daughter of Cinna who was Marius's key ally and a leading opponent of Sulla. This marriage firmly aligned Caesar with the populist faction in Roman politics. When Sulla demanded Caesar divorce Cornelia, the young man refused—a dangerous act of defiance that forced him to flee Rome to escape potential execution. This early stand against tyrannical authority hinted at Caesar's courage and the political principles that would guide his later career.

His Mission to Bithynia

In 81 BCE, Caesar travelled to the court of King Nicomedes IV of Bithynia on a diplomatic mission to secure ships for the Roman fleet. His extended stay at the king's court later became fodder for gossip and political attacks, with enemies suggesting an improper relationship between the young Roman and the Bithynian king. Though Caesar vehemently denied these allegations throughout his life, they persisted as a political liability. Nevertheless, the mission succeeded in its objective and demonstrated Caesar's early diplomatic abilities, providing him valuable experience in foreign affairs and establishing connections across the Mediterranean that would serve him well in later years.

His Service in Mytilene

During his military service under Governor Marcus Minucius Thermus in Asia Minor, Caesar distinguished himself at the siege of Mytilene on the island of Lesbos in 80 BCE. During combat operations, he saved the life of a fellow soldier, earning the Corona Civica (Civic Crown)—one of Rome's highest military decorations awarded for saving a citizen's life. This first taste of military glory instilled in Caesar a confidence in his battlefield abilities and provided him with a prestigious military honour that enhanced his public image upon his return to Rome.

His Journey to Rome

After learning of Sulla's death in 78 BCE, Caesar saw an opportunity to safely return to Rome and resume his political career. He declined Governor Thermus's offer of a more senior military position, instead choosing to sail for Rhodes to study rhetoric under the renowned teacher Apollonius Molon, whose other students included Cicero. This decision reflected Caesar's understanding that oratorical skill was essential for political advancement in Rome.

His Capture by Pirates

In 75 BCE, while sailing to Rhodes, Caesar's ship was captured by Cilician pirates who operated throughout the eastern Mediterranean. When they demanded a ransom of 20 talents, Caesar laughed and insisted they ask for 50 talents, as he was worth more. During his 38 days in captivity, Caesar maintained an extraordinary composure—reading poetry to his captors, joining their exercises, and repeatedly telling them he would crucify them after his release. The pirates took these declarations as jokes, but Caesar was deadly serious. After the ransom was paid and he was freed, Caesar raised a naval force in Miletus, pursued the pirates, captured them, and—true to his word—had them crucified, though he ordered their throats cut first as an act of mercy since they had treated him well.

Optimates

The Optimates were a political faction in the late Roman Republic, representing the conservative and aristocratic interests of the Senate and the traditional ruling elite. They sought to preserve the power of the Senate, limit the influence of popular assemblies, and oppose reforms that threatened the established social hierarchy.

The Optimates viewed themselves as guardians of Roman tradition and the republic's stability, resisting populist measures that redistributed wealth or expanded rights to the lower classes. They frequently clashed with the Populares, their political rivals who advocated for the common people.

Their policies aimed to maintain the privileges of the patrician class while curbing the power of ambitious generals and Tribunes. The Optimates' resistance to reform contributed to the political instability that eventually led to the Republic's collapse and the rise of the Roman Empire.

Populares

The Populares were a political faction in the late Roman Republic that championed the rights and interests of the common people, particularly the plebeians. They sought to use popular assemblies and the power of the Tribunes to pass reforms, often bypassing the Senate, which was dominated by the aristocratic Optimates.

The Populares advocated for land redistribution, grain subsidies, debt relief, and other policies aimed at addressing social and economic inequality.

While they claimed to represent the masses, some Populares used their populist policies to gain personal power and influence. Their reforms and methods, though often controversial, highlighted the growing divide between Rome's elite and its lower classes. The tension between the Populares and Optimates contributed to the political instability and eventual fall of the Roman Republic.

Equites

The *equites* were Rome's influential middle elite, positioned between the senatorial aristocracy and the common people. Originally cavalrymen in the early Republic, they evolved into a powerful class of wealthy businessmen, tax collectors (*publicani*), and provincial administrators. Unlike senators, who were barred from direct commercial activity, *equites* could freely engage in trade, finance, and state contracts, making them crucial to Rome's expanding economy.

By the late Republic, their influence had grown significantly, particularly as they played key roles in governing Rome's provinces and handling its financial affairs.

Cursus Honourum – The Roman Political Ladder

Quaestor (Age: 30) – Entry-Level Office

- Managed finances in Rome or the provinces.
- Served under governors or in the treasury.
- This was the first step into the Senate.

Aedile (Age: 36) – Public Works & Popularity

- Organized games, festivals, and maintained public buildings.
- A chance to win public favour (Julius spent lavishly on games).
- Not a required step but useful for advancing in politics.

Praetor (Age: 39) – Judge & Military Role

- Acted as a top judge in Rome.
- Had the power to command armies if needed.
- Often governed a province after the term (like Julius's father in Asia).

Consul (Age: 42) – The Highest Annual Office

- The chief magistrates of Rome, two were elected each year.
- Controlled the government and commanded armies.
- Could propose laws and lead military campaigns.

Proconsul (Governor) – Commanding Provinces & Armies

- Former consuls were assigned to govern provinces.
- Often led military campaigns and expanded Rome's borders.
- Dictator (Extraordinary Office – Not in the Ladder)
- Appointed in emergencies, given full control of Rome.

This system was meant to keep power balanced, but ambitious leaders (like Julius) manipulated it. He climbed the ladder quickly, using alliances, military success, and public support to rise above rivals.

Next Book

Caesar's story continues in Rise of the Eagle, the second book in the Seeds of Empire series.

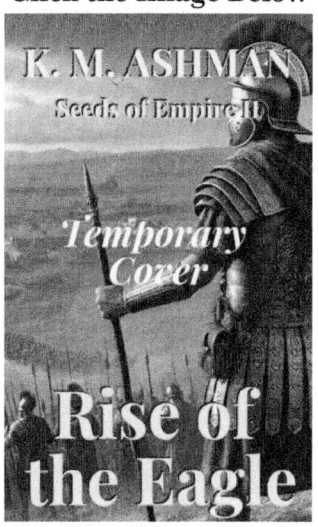

Click the Image Below

From Grief comes Ambition. From Ambition comes Power. From Power... *Destiny.*

Shattered by tragedy, Gaius Julius Caesar transforms grief into unstoppable ambition. As Rome spirals into chaos, he sees his moment.

With silver-tongued oratory, he captivates the masses. Through ruthless political manoeuvring, he ascends Rome's cursus honorum and when conspiracy threatens to devour the Republic, Caesar stands defiant, revealing the principled soul beneath his calculating exterior.

In blood-soaked Hispania, he trades political games for the brutal clarity of battle, his military genius awakening among the savage Lusitanian tribes. Victory there propels him toward an audacious secret pact with Rome's two most powerful men, a triumvirate that will shake the foundations of the Republic.

But as Caesar's star rises, so too do the whispers of his enemies. Scandal shadows his triumph. Envy follows his success. And at each calculated step toward the consulship—Rome's highest office—he must decide how much of his honour he is willing to sacrifice in his relentless climb to power.

In this spellbinding second instalment of the *Seeds of Empire* series, witness the transformation of a brilliant young politician into the military and political force who will forever alter the destiny of Rome.

Subscribe Now to be Informed of New Releases

Click Here

KMAshman.com

Also by K. M. Ashman

Seeds of Empire
Seeds of Empire
Rise of the Eagle

The Exploratores
Dark Eagle
The Hidden
Veteranus
Scarab
The Wraith

The Brotherhood
Templar Steel
Templar Stone
Templar Blood
Templar Fury
Templar Glory
Templar Legacy
Templar Loyalty

The India Summers Mysteries
The Vestal Conspiracies
The Treasures of Suleiman
The Mummies of the Reich
The Tomb Builders

The Roman Chronicles
The Fall of Britannia
The Rise of Caratacus
The Wrath of Boudicca

The Medieval Sagas
Blood of the Cross
In Shadows of Kings
Sword of Liberty
Ring of Steel

The Blood of Kings
A Land Divided
A Wounded Realm
Rebellion's Forge
The Warrior Princess
The Blade Bearer

The Road to Hastings
The Challenges of a King
The Promises of a King
The Fate of a King

The Otherworld Series
The Legacy Protocol
The Seventh God
The Last Citadel
Savage Eden
Vampire

Printed in Great Britain
by Amazon